30106023927774
AF750881

# Migrants, Borders and Global Capitalism

People from west Africa are risking their lives and surrendering their citizenship rights to enter exploitative labour markets in Europe. This book offers an explanation for this phenomenon that is based on close analysis of the contradictory economic and political agendas that create and constrain labour migration. It shows how global capitalism regulates different stages of the process within an interconnected system of economic dispossession, the construction of an illegal status, border control, labour exploitation and processes of underdevelopment. This is summarised as a regime of 'unfree labour mobility'.

Combined with structural and historical approaches, this book is based on ethnographic research. It incorporates those who are left behind, those who decide to stay, migrants who fail and those who are on the move, alongside clustered migrant communities in Senegal, Mauritania and Spain. The book's panoramic approach shows how west-African 'step-wise' journeys to Europe by land and sea show competing territorial and economic policies regulating an unstable and unpredictable trajectory, creating 'illegal' labour through dual logics of border security and selective labour mobility.

This book demonstrates that the diverse channels through which people migrate in the modern era are mediated by European states and labour markets, which utilise border regimes to control labour and be globally competitive. The themes and patterns that emerge, in their context of inter-generational change, present a challenge to the accepted wisdom about the individual and household dynamics of labour migration. This book will be of interest to students and scholars of migration, transnationalism, politics, security, development, economics and sociology.

**Hannah Cross** is a lecturer in International Political Economy at the University of Manchester and an honorary research fellow in the Centre of West African Studies, University of Birmingham, UK. She is also a member of the Editorial Working Group of the *Review of African Political Economy*.

## Routledge Research on the Global Politics of Migration

**Migrants, Borders and Global Capitalism**
West African labour bobility and EU borders
*Hannah Cross*

# Migrants, Borders and Global Capitalism

## West African labour mobility and EU borders

**Hannah Cross**

Routledge
Taylor & Francis Group
LONDON AND NEW YORK

First published 2013
by Routledge
2 Park Square, Milton Park, Abingdon, Oxon, OX14 4RN

Simultaneously published in the USA and Canada
by Routledge
711 Third Avenue, New York, NY 10017

*Routledge is an imprint of the Taylor & Francis Group, an informa business*

© 2013 Hannah Cross

The right of Hannah Cross to be identified as author of this work has been asserted by her in accordance with sections 77 and 78 of the Copyright, Designs and Patents Act 1988.

All rights reserved. No part of this book may be reprinted or reproduced or utilised in any form or by any electronic, mechanical, or other means, now known or hereafter invented, including photocopying and recording, or in any information storage or retrieval system, without permission in writing from the publishers.

*Trademark notice*: Product or corporate names may be trademarks or registered trademarks, and are used only for identification and explanation without intent to infringe.

*British Library Cataloguing in Publication Data*
A catalogue record for this book is available from the British Library

*Library of Congress Cataloging-in-Publication Data*
Cross, Hannah.
Migrants, borders and global capitalism : West African labour mobility and EU borders / Hannah Cross.
pages cm. – (Routledge research on the global politics of migration ; 1)
Includes bibliographical references and index.
1. Foreign workers, African–European Union countries. 2. Labor mobility–Africa, West. 3. Labor mobility–European Union countries. 4. Africa, West–Emigration and immigration–Economic aspects. 5. European Union countries–Emigration and immigration–Economic aspects. I. Title.
HD8378.5.A2C755 2013
331.12'7910966–dc23
2012042255

ISBN13: 978-0-415-62915-7 (hbk)
ISBN13: 978-0-203-10016-5 (ebk)

Typeset in Times
by FiSH Books Ltd, Enfield

MIX
Paper from responsible sources
FSC www.fsc.org FSC® C013604

Printed and bound by CPI Group (UK) Ltd, Croydon, CR0 4YY

# Contents

# Illustrations

## Figures



## Tables

## Boxes

# Acknowledgements

I met many wonderful people over the course of the research for this book. It only felt like a solitary effort during times of writing, but the responsibility for all types of error is mine. Some people pointed me in the right direction at the right time or accompanied me at particular stages, and others offered continuous support. I could not possibly credit all who have contributed, but I will begin with my school and sponsors. Without the initial encouragement of Hugo Radice at Leeds University's School of Politics and International Studies (POLIS) I would not have gained the Economic and Social Research Council studentship, for which I was immensely grateful. I am indebted to Ray Bush and Alice Hills for their consistent guidance and encouragement. I am also grateful to the POLIS staff, especially Caroline Wise and Helen Philpott, for their generous help. This final revision is assisted by detailed and useful comments from Sarah Bracking, and Lionel Cliffe has also contributed much to the concepts.

Jeremy Keenan helped to arrange the initial field visit to Mauritania. Once there, El Hassen Ould Ahmed at the University of Nouakchott connected me with migrants and provided me with study facilities, including tea. I thank Mariam Kane for her research assistance in Nouakchott and Binta Dia for interpreting in Nouadhibou, both of whom endured uncomfortable and long journeys and stopovers, for which I am grateful. I am exceptionally lucky to have met Momoh Joe and Brother Paul, both in Nouakchott, because they knew what I was looking for and took the risk of trusting me. I also thank staff at UNHCR and IOM for their helpful interviews.

Núria Tomàs, at Universitat Autònoma de Barcelona and then UNHCR, offered great friendship and helped me to find my feet in Catalonia, particularly by introducing me to Fadwa and Ana at CEAR, both of whom gave me a good rundown of legal and political matters. I thank staff at CEA, the Red Cross and ACCEM for introducing me to migrant communities. Kheraba Drame presented intellectual challenge and vision as well as telling his own story, as many other respondents did, including Alicia and John. Rashid Awari from CEHDA helped to plan the migration route from Burkina Faso to Senegal.

Returning to Núria, the journey from Ouagadougou to Casamance would not have been realised without the coincidence of her wish to make a documentary in the region, and it became an integral part of the research. Many people supported us along the way, including the Diop family in Bamako, who kindly accommodated us; Egido at ENDA Tiers-Monde in Kayes; Samba Diao, a journalist at Sud Echos, and his friends in Ziguinchor; the fishermen's association in Elinkine; and countless people on the journey who informed, challenged, helped and got us to places safely.

I have numerous scholars to thank in Dakar's formidable research community. Adebayo Olukoshi at CODESRIA was the essential starting point. Also at CODESRIA, I thank Jean-Pierre for his help in the library and Bolaji Olarinmoye for helping to connect me with crucial Francophone literature hours before leaving Senegal. I am indebted to Ndeye Sokhna Gueye at UCAD for her help with contacting people and getting things moving; she was especially kind because she had moved on from migration research. I thank Penda Mbow and Aminata Diaw, also at UCAD. At the West African Research Centre, I thank Ousmane Sene, the staff and the students for their welcome. I am grateful to Mansour Tall at UNDP and to Cheikh Oumar Ba for their advice about fieldwork. I thank Abdou Salam Fall, Pape Demba Fall and Momar-Coumba Diop at IFAN for their guidance. I was fortunate to find Khady Gueye, who was an excellent translator, interpreter and research assistant in Thiaroye-sur-Mer and Rufisque. For this I thank Alioune Diagne at IPDSR. In Thiaroye, I am grateful to Yayi Bayam Diouf for introducing me to the Collective of Women for the Fight Against Clandestine Emigration, and also to Niang and the other association members. I thank Emmanuelle Bouilly for her guidance. In Rufisque, I am very grateful to Khady's family for their hospitality and companionship, particularly from Aminata and Suzanne.

Hannah Cross
Manchester, September 2012

# Abbreviations

| | |
|---|---|
| ACCEM | *Asociación Comisión Católica Española de Migraciónes* – Spanish Catholic Association of Migration |
| AECID | *Agencia Española de Cooperación Internacional para el Desarrollo* – Spanish Agency for International Cooperation for Development |
| AfDB | African Development Bank |
| AFRICOM | United States Africa Command |
| AFSJ | area of freedom, security and justice (EU) |
| AQMI | *Al-Qaïda pour le Maghreb islamique* – Al-Qaeda for the Islamic Maghreb |
| AUC | African Union Commission |
| BBC | British Broadcasting Corporation |
| CARIM | Consortium for Applied Research on International Migration |
| CC OO | *Confederación Sindical de Comisiones Obreras* – Confederation of Workers' Commissions (Spain) |
| CEA | *Centre d'Estudis Africans* – Centre of African Studies (Catalonia) |
| CEAR | *Comisión Española de Ayuda al Refugiado* – Spanish Commission for Refugee Aid |
| CEHDA | Cultural Environmental Human Development Association of Ghana |
| CFA | *Communauté Financière Africaine* – African Financial Community (currency unit in West and Central Africa). Formerly *Colonies Françaises d'Afrique* (French Colonies of Africa) |
| CODESRIA | Council for the Development of Social Research in Africa |
| DfID | Department for International Development (UK) |
| DMA | Developing Markets Associates Ltd. |
| DPS | *Direction de la Prévision de la Statistique* – Office of Statistical Forecasting (Senegal) |
| EC | European Community |
| ECOWAS | Economic Community of West African States |
| EIU | Economist Intelligence Unit |

| | |
|---|---|
| ENDA Tiers-Monde | *Environnement et développement du tiers monde* – Environmental development action in the third world |
| € | Euro: €1.00 = £0.81/$1.31 |
| EU | European Union |
| EUCOM | European Command (United States) |
| EUROSUR | European Border Surveillance System |
| FRONTEX | *Frontiéres extèrieures* – European Agency for the Management of Operational Cooperation at the External Borders of the Member States of the European Union |
| GAMM | Global Approach to Migration and Mobility (EU) |
| GDP | gross domestic product |
| GNI | gross national income |
| GOANA | *Grande Offensive Agricole pour la Nourriture et l'Abondance* – Great Agricultural Offensive for Food Security (Senegal) |
| GSPC | *Groupe Salafiste pour la Prédication et le Combat* – Salafist Group for Preaching and Combat |
| IBM | Integrated Border Management (EU) |
| IFAN | *l'Institut Fondamental d'Afrique Noire* – The Fundamental Institute of Black Africa (formerly the French Institute of Black Africa), UCAD |
| IFI | international financial institution |
| ILO | International Labour Organisation |
| IMF | International Monetary Fund |
| INE | *Instituto Nacional de Estadistica* – National Institute of Statistics (Spain) |
| Interpol | International Criminal Police Organisation |
| IOM | International Organisation for Migration |
| IPDSR | *Institut de Population, Développement et Santé de la Reproduction* – Institute for Population, Development and Reproductive Health (UCAD) |
| IRIN | Integrated Regional News Networks (UN) |
| JHA | justice and home affairs (EU) |
| MIFERMA | *Société Anonyme des Mines de Fer de Mauritanie* – Society of Iron Ore Mines in Mauritania |
| MIREM | *Migration de retour au Maghreb* – Return Migration to the Maghreb (European University Institute project) |
| NGO | non-government organisation |
| OECD | Organisation for Economic Co-operation and Development |
| ONS | *Office Nationale de la Statistique* – National Statistics Office (Mauritania) |
| OPEC | Organisation of the Petroleum Exporting Countries |
| PDLM | *Programme Développement Local Migration* – Local Migration and Development Programme (Senegal River Valley) |
| PDS | *Parti Démocratique Sénégalais* – Senegalese Democratic Party |
| PP | *Partido Popular* – Popular Party (Spain) |

| | |
|---|---|
| PSI | Pan-Sahel Initiative |
| RABIT | Rapid Border Intervention Team (EU) |
| REVA | *Retour vers l'agriculture* – return to agriculture (Senegal) |
| SCTIP | *Service de coopération technique internationale de police* – international service of technical police cooperation (France) |
| SIS | Schengen information system |
| SIVE | *Sístema integrado de vigilancia exterior* – integrated external surveillance system (Spain) |
| SGBS | Société Générale de Banques au Sénégal – General Society of Banks in Senegal |
| SNIM | *Société Nationale d'Industrie Mauritanienne* – National Society of Mauritanian Industry |
| TSCTI | Trans-Saharan Counter-Terrorism Initiative |
| TSCTP | Trans-Saharan Counter-Terrorism Partnership |
| UCAD | *Université* Cheikh Anta Diop |
| UM | symbol for Mauritanian currency (ouguiya) |
| UN DESA | United Nations Department of Economic and Social Affairs |
| UNDP | United Nations Development Program |
| UNECA | United Nations Economic Commission for Africa |
| UNESCO | United Nations Educational, Social and Cultural Organisation |
| UNHCR | United Nations High Commissioner for Refugees |
| UNPD | United Nations Population Division |
| UNRISD | United National Research Institute for Social Development |
| US | United States (of America) |
| USAID | United States Agency for International Development |

# 1 Introduction

## Conceptualising labour mobility and migration

This book is an analysis of the contradictory economic and political agendas that create and constrain migration. It shows how global capitalism dominates modes of production and livelihoods in particular moments through an interconnected system of economic dispossession, illegalisation, border control, labour exploitation and processes of underdevelopment, which is summarised as a regime of *unfree labour mobility*. Labour migration cannot be understood in isolation from the development of markets for migrant labour. The labour market itself cannot be understood separately from the creation of the legal and political status necessary for labour to be cheap and controllable, nor can we make sense of 'illegal' migrants in global capitalism without seeing which processes lead people to surrender their citizenship rights. The tensions between international agendas of labour mobility and mechanisms of control produce an arbitrary outcome for migrants, and their trajectories are also shaped by particular coping strategies and local forms of resistance, overdetermined and constrained by the migration regime but not predicted by it.

The commodification of labour, associated with European expansion emerging in the late fifteenth century, was supposed to free labourers from feudalism. However, this book will revisit and elaborate on the argument that unfree migrant labour, rather than appearing in historical 'aberrations' such as the Atlantic slave trade, colonial labour regimes or the South African apartheid system, is persistently incorporated as part of the capitalist mode of production. In this respect, reference to 'free' or 'unfree' labour refers to the circulation of labour and says little about the autonomy of the labourer, which is argued to be restricted also as 'free labour' (Marx 1867/1970; Miles 1987; Cohen 1987). Consequentially, in combination with the historical and structural dimensions that underpin a materialist political economy approach, this book is also based on ethnographic research among discrete clusters of sending households and migrants in west Africa and Spain. Migrants are not passive recipients of migration regimes, but continuously shape and challenge them, as the EU's Rapid Border Intervention Team (RABIT) would testify (Commission 2007a). However, if migrants place 'urgent and exceptional pressure' at the EU borders and the RABIT is summoned, this confrontation is the culmination of various processes of displacement and restricted mobility, requiring a detailed analysis of migrants' histories.

Through this broadened perspective, it is hoped that this book will resonate with those who are interested in the relationships between migration and, respectively, inequality, poverty and 'globalisation'. The northward flows of labour migrants from west Africa are principally concentrated between sending households that are dispossessed of the means of production and subsistence, and areas of transit or recruitment found in the ports and market districts in Mauritania or the farms in Spain, among other places of convergence in the Maghreb and southern Europe. The channels of migrants are narrower than would be expected if inequality of income, poverty or the pursuit of wealth were the *principal* driving forces: it is more the case that 'the geographical mobility of capital permits it to dominate a global labour force whose own geographical mobility is constrained' (Harvey 2005: 168–9). Because labour-power is a commodity, it is subjected by global capitalism to patterns of trade that resemble other commodities, thus geographically concentrated and unequal (Cooper 2008: 182). Just as capital is 'globe-hopping, not globe-covering' (Ferguson 2006: 38), the movement of labour is also characterised by hops from one key place to another.

The first three chapters of this book establish a framework for understanding the contemporary migration regime. This begins with an outline of the contradictions found in migration management. It is followed by an explanation of the fieldwork and a discussion of the use of ethnographic research methods in a political economy framework. Different approaches to international migration are examined and the rationale is established for locating it in the trajectory of global capitalism. With this said, the historical and geographical contexts are presented in an overview of contemporary global migration patterns and the concepts that may be applied for understanding their regulation (Chapter 2). This is followed by the regional background to west African labour mobility (Chapter 3). The regional focus is not an attempt to aggregate migration flows, but instead aims to establish common patterns of movement in comparison to the historical labour systems that are particular to west Africa. At the same time, because many processes in the migration regime are managed by global and international institutions, it may also draw comparison with other regions of Africa and the world. The subsequent chapters focus conceptually and empirically on different instances of the migration regime, in turn examining processes of dispossession and displacement in sending communities (Chapter 4), the EU's approach to migration (Chapter 5), the projection of EU boundaries into Africa (Chapter 6), the labour market for illegalised migrants (Chapter 7) and, finally, the management of remittances (Chapter 8).

## What shapes the migration regime?

The Organisation for Economic Cooperation and Development (OECD) and the International Monetary Fund (IMF) encourage receiving countries to maintain competitive and low production costs, while this has been achieved by receiving a regular supply of 'irregular' migrant workers. Notwithstanding border restrictions, the World Bank promotes the creation of 'portable human capital' in sub-Saharan Africa (World Bank 2009c: 282). Paul Cammack (2008) has linked this policy to a 'universal convergence on competitiveness'. He hypothesises that the OECD, the World Bank and national development agencies are committed to global labour mobility in support of competitiveness and this produces a 'global proletariat' (Cammack 2008). This challenges human capital theory, which conceptualises labour markets as commodity markets that will grant upward mobility to those with more education, training and experience. In another set of policy measures that promote labour migration, development institutions and migration research institutes converge in promoting the use of remittances as a poverty-alleviation strategy, concentrating on their volume (Addy *et al.* 2003; Ratha 2007). This largely informal process has created an expanding market for the finance industry.

However, the more apparent form of migration management is restrictive. The political and cultural significance of Africans' ostensibly unwelcome reception in Europe is considerable. European and US policy-makers and security agencies lead a governance network in favour of reducing the 'threat' of cross-border movement and this is more so since the 11 September 2001 attacks on the US (Huysmans 2000; AFRICOM n.d.; Bigo 2005b). The EU, since 2005, has emphasised an integrated and holistic approach to migration management, also developing so-called mobility partnerships with African states. They are intergovernmental and integrate politico-legal and military means of keeping unwanted migrants out of Europe, whilst encouraging the mobility of handpicked workers who can relieve member states' labour shortages for as long as is necessary (Commission 2006, 2007, 2011). Deterrents to migration from Senegal include stimulation of employment, anti-migration education, and co-development in the agricultural sector. Beyond Europe's territorial borders, security forces co-ordinated by FRONTEX (*Frontières Extérieures*) patrol the Atlantic and the Mediterranean, attempting to intercept and identify 'illegal' migrants. The 'people in the middle' informing this book, who slip through the nets of labour and asylum policy, are furthermore banned from leaving Africa's shores (Bigo and Guild 2005). Even the intention to depart from the Mauritanian coast can result in detention or expulsion; but, moreover, the transit country receives expelled migrants from Europe. The overlapping security framework of the EU migration regime and the US Africa Command (AFRICOM) support the rentier economy and migrant labour system that have underpinned Mauritania's development. This means that, in contrast with Senegal, narrow security measures are used to manage migration.

This book explores what emerges from the contradiction between labour mobility and borders, wherever and however these latter are delineated. King *et al.* (1997) argued that in southern Europe, 'To view international migrants as "desperate" or "illegal" groups, who would be better off in their countries of origin, is to miss the essential economic rationale that has brought them to the region in the first place' (p. 23). Moreover, between restricting migrants because they are a 'threat' and enabling them because they serve the labour markets of destination countries, neither option is appealing to west African workers and sending communities. This book examines the manifestations of a global trade in people that underpins the global management of resources and production. It also examines the impact of strengthened border security and restrictions on migration to Europe. These opposing economic and territorial regimes are interdependent (Ashman and Callinicos 2006) and should not be viewed in isolation. The labour/security/development regimes' combined impact on migrant labourers produces a labour reserve with restricted mobility, which is essential to the capital accumulation process. The regime creates dichotomies of order and chaos, or over-exploitation and abjection. This book identifies migrants' struggles against such constraints.

## The ethnography of migration

From diverse households, west African migrants converge in transit and in areas of recruitment that favour sub-Saharan Africans. Their journey is unorganised in the sense that travel, settlement, employment and return plans are mostly unknown at the outset. By exploring what happens before, during and after migration, this book seeks a holistic understanding of the forces that determine cross-border movement and shape its impact among migrants and communities. While it examines the process of migration and labour mobility in three countries, it is not primarily a study of transnationalism, nor is it comparative. It examines the causes and consequences of multifarious trajectories, including staying and returning. Migrants' confrontations with the state political economies and global security, or labour regimes that they enter, are in focus, rather than the mechanisms of a particular network or stream approached as a single socio-cultural entity.[1]

The fieldwork commenced with a three-month stay in Mauritania in the spring of 2007. In spring/summer 2008, Dakar became the main base for research in migrant-sending Lebu communities. There were short visits to Catalonia surrounding the Dakar stay and into the next year, and a return visit from Senegal to Mauritania in spring 2008. This time period is therefore the main focus, a moment when economic crisis began to overshadow global political discourse, yet this was an overly familiar concept and reality among migrants. Since 2008, the repressive components of the migration regime, the instability of migration and the boundaries of migrants' agency have all expanded. The *status quo* is being fought for and challenged, and these changes will be considered at different levels of labour mobility, although the available data is limited.

Migration features prominently on the political-economic landscapes of Senegal, Mauritania and Spain in their role as sender, transit zone and destination respectively. Official estimates based on the difference between overall population growth and natural increase in 2008 indicated that Senegal had maintained a negative migration rate of 20,000 people per year since 1990. Spain had a positive net balance of 350,000 people annually. Mauritania was gaining around 2,000 migrants per year (UN DESA 2009c). This means that, by quantity, Mauritania is a receiving country. However, its politics of migration are concerned with its role as a 'buffer zone' between Africa and Europe and, more recently, a restricted area that holds some of the US's regional interests (Baldwin-Edwards 2005a; Amin and El-Kenz 2005). Table 1.1 summarises the main focus of research in these countries. Additionally, journeys along land routes in Mauritania, Senegal, Mali and Burkina Faso informed the development of questionnaires and interview processes, all of which are explained in more detail in the Appendix.

*Table 1.1* Fieldwork locations and focus

| *Country* | *Location* | *Context* | *Focus of fieldwork* |
|---|---|---|---|
| Senegal | Thiaroye-sur-Mer<br>Rufisque | Sending country | Sending and non-sending households: changes in labour and migration over time; economic and social resources; occupations and use of remittances; decision-making; destinations; legal and illegal channels; perceptions of labour migration to Europe and expectations. |
| Mauritania | Nouakchott<br>Nouadhibou | Transit country | West African migrants: family and individual labour and migration history; economic and social resources of sending household and current lodging; past and present occupation; decision-making; sending of remittances; experiences with controls; perceptions of labour migration to Europe, aims and expectations. |
| Spain | Barcelona<br>Salt<br>Lleida | Destination country | West African migrants: family and individual labour and migration history; economic and social resources of sending household and current lodging; past and present occupation; decision-making; sending of remittances; experiences of journey and arrival, aims and expectations. |

The fieldwork was located among clusters of respondents in places of convergence and along west African roads that link with the journey to Europe. The intention was to incorporate the potential migrants who are left behind as well as those who are mobile. The reason for this choice is based both on scholarship and on observations during the scoping visit to Mauritania in 2007. Contemporary migration is multifarious, turbulent and unpredictable, appearing to be chaotic (Papastergiadis 2000: 6). The initial three-month visit to Mauritania substantiated this understanding. Kin, compatriots and other associates may inform departure strategies and can be sought at the crossroads, but they act more as itinerant signposts than as known links in any sort of chain. Oscillating between tediousness and volatility, combinations of travel, settlement, detention, diversion and deportation feature in the land and sea journeys when migrants survive.

Migration research originating in Dakar is extensive and helps to address the gap between qualitative analysis and existing macro research. The fieldwork in Senegal was informed by the academic community in Université Cheikh Anta Diop and CODESRIA (Council for the Development of Social Research in Africa). This group was forthcoming in what the research over that timeframe could and could not achieve. The study of remittances and their impact on the household and village could supplement existing, long-running research projects including those led by Abdou Salam Fall and Pape Demba Fall at l'Institut Fondamental d'Afrique Noire (IFAN).

Life histories were combined with semi-structured interviews and participant observation. The empirical research for this book coincided with the height of Atlantic boat journeys to the Canary Islands and was considered by some observers to be topical. Yet this book is about the sustained phenomenon of the movement of cheap, undocumented labour from countries that are economically and politically marginalised to those with greater power. The means of emigration are here viewed as a vehicle, carrying people, with a history and social dynamics, in the journey from one place to another. As interesting and revealing as the vehicle is, the people and the outcomes of the journey hold the greater fascination. Thus the passengers' histories shape the debates set out in this book, yet it is equally important for migrants' motivations, expectations, plans and experiences to be understood in their time and place.

Ethnographic methods can be rooted in quite different methodological frameworks (Brewer 2000: 56). My methodology represents a 'modern Marxist' approach, signifying, epistemologically, that there is an external world that is independent of our knowledge of it, but the discursive construction of this external world has a crucial affect on political outcomes; and the nature of this external world constrains and/or facilitates the actions of agents who, importantly, can deconstruct and reconstruct structures (Marsh 2002: 160). This framework therefore asserts that a purely structuralist approach will inevitably fail the research question because migrants are in a dynamic relationship with the structure(s); but so will a postmodern ethnographic approach. Ethnography, crucially, represents the field not as it 'is' but as it is 'seen' by the ethnographer (Wolcott 1999), and the ethnographer will self-consciously 'impose perspectives on reality' (Brewer 2000: 76). Multi-sited 'global' ethnography has been critiqued because it 'takes places for granted and leaves no room for accounting for the production and transformation of sites... history remains an afterthought' (Gille and Ó Riain 2002: 287–8). This signifies that it is conducted through the lens of an uninterrogated, unsubjective, depoliticised globalism, which 'pretends not to be an ideology but just scholarship or description of the world as it is' (Marcuse 2004: 811; cf Said 1978). To some extent, 'the world that ethnography confronts has changed', and 'national boundaries and identities blur' (Denzin 1997: xii). This book, however, contests an approach that 'sees the process of globalisation as new, as the dominant feature of our time, a structural process independent of specific acts of choice, inevitable in its really existing form, and ultimately beneficial to all' (Marcuse 2004: 810).

For this reason, in this methodological framework, modern technologies and modes of interconnectedness and their sometimes empowering, sometimes oppressive, repercussions are supplementary to an investigation of the continued domination of global capitalism in a physically and otherwise bordered world. The approach is multi-scalar, with an attempt to explain the overall outcome of contradictory national, regional and global migration regimes and to show the boundaries that these place on migrants; and, concurrently, to examine the localised meanings and struggles for migrants and sending communities in dialectic enquiry.

While I have highlighted that ethnographic research supports different methodological approaches, the method of ethnography more consistently establishes 'procedural rules' for the study of people in naturally occurring settings or 'fields', by means that capture their social meanings and ordinary activities. The research develops in a process of co-ordinated and planned actions, which, however, are flexible (Brewer 2000: 56). The research design was stepwise, beginning with the development of major topics for investigation, to be researched in stages during return visits to locations (Wolcott 1999: 217). These methods are qualitative, and in Barcelona, when migrants contributed to a documentary and to public seminars, they also entered the sphere of participatory research (Mayoux 2006: 117; Cross and Tomàs 2009b).

## Debating migration

This book is mainly concerned with 'stepwise' migration *inter alia* and highlights its growing importance. Migrants from the global south began to move away from colonial labour patterns and to map their own routes in the latter part of the twentieth century. Breaking from labour mobility between colonies and the colonisers, African migrants would seek opportunities in a greater range of countries in geographically 'stepwise' patterns. Thus migration patterns adopted a voluntary quality in light of previous labour regimes of slavery, colonial labour and postwar labour contracts in Europe. However, this era of migration is also linked with economic collapse and subsequent structural adjustment programmes in the 1980s and 1990s. Migration became a way for households to diversify in difficult economic circumstances. As former labour regimes dissolved, migrant workers were increasingly distanced from employers. It is comparable to processes of development and contraction in peasantries, defined as producers who combine commodity and subsistence production to varying degrees. 'Disappearing peasantries' (Bryceson 2000), as well as disappearing labour reserves, also gave rise to new labour reserves that were distinct from those developed in colonial economies. This reflects the dual characteristic of labour. Producers needed to sell their labour-power as a result of the collapse of commodities; and the 'commodity' of labour-power from underdeveloped communities also faced political and economic change (Albert 2008).

To place this in context, Amin (1972a) defined the west African macro-region, south of the Sahara, as 'Africa of the colonial economy' or *l'economie de traite*. This describes the dialectic that emerged between colonial policy and the existing social formations during the colonisation period that started in the late nineteenth century (Amin 1972a: 115; Chapter 3). This regional political economy led the coastal areas to be served by labour in the interior. The 'development' occurred on the coast, where in Senegal the Mouride brotherhood and French colonial administrators expanded the groundnut economy with the use of low-paid peasant labour. This would adopt a forced characteristic and was maintained until World War II, after which the mobility was directed towards France. In the contemporary era, Senegalese labourers in Mauritania are likely to come from the Senegal River Valley areas, and to have family histories of migration to Europe with an established role for remittances in household income. The Senegalese coastal cases, on the other hand, will show that the crisis of fishing is an important factor in attempts to seek work overseas. Therefore it is a newer phenomenon. On this basis, migration towards Europe is understood in the context of west African migration in general. The distinction between international migration within Africa and outwards to Europe, in terms of the underlying causes and the profile of the migrant, is in many instances negligible and is not defined simply by social class.

Peasantries, and also labour migrants, can be characterised by differentiation in class, gender, age and locality. Furthermore, they have 'an enigmatic dual character as both partially autonomous and highly vulnerable producers' (Bryceson 2000: 300). Similarly, stepwise migration in this context is characterised by a contradictory mixture of coercion, compulsion and repression combined with choice, opportunity and mobility. This is reflected in the accounts of migrants. For example, Pascal[2] is a Nigerian migrant who is living in Barcelona (interview no. 27, Barcelona, 28 February 2008). He felt compelled to leave because his ageing parents' farm was not sustaining the family; in his own words; 'they are making little; if I give them more support they will be fed fine' (ibid.). So he left alone and after failing to find paid work in Ghana, Ivory Coast or Senegal, he settled among some fishermen in Sierra Leone, who told him that there was no money to make here. However, he was accepted on a fishing boat that was heading to the Canary Islands and did not pay for the journey. The fact that he was detained for 40 days in Tenerife and was presently homeless in Barcelona did not overpower the luck of embarking on and surviving a 25-day sea voyage and then living in a situation in which cash might eventually be sent home. Pascal's story is typical in that he left alone and without plans; he did not inform others of his departure, and he followed a unique trajectory to his destination. This is a characteristic 'stepwise' story that raises questions about mobility and choice.

Stepwise migration was connected with intergenerational social mobility and patterns of movement from the rural, traditional setting to urban, modern life (Conway 1980). For the 'suicide crossing' by land and sea from Africa to Europe, the migration could, however, be described as 'stepwise' solely in terms of human mobility. This means that the journey begins by road with a small amount of money and requires stopping the journey and working for cash on the w Europe (Manuh, cited in Albert 2008: 14). To provide a broad numerical esti of this type of migration, excluding direct Atlantic journeys from the coast, it was estimated in 2008 that between 65,000 and 120,000 sub-Saharans entered the Maghreb annually, of which between 20 and 38 per cent proceeded to Europe (de Haas 2008b: 9). However, pioneering migrants like Pascal still prevail and the turbulence of their migration is detached from patterns of chain migration and social mobility. How has it evolved in this way, and what is particularly new about it?

Migration is considered, in the book, to be motivated by economic constraint and opportunity in various combinations. Analysis begins rather than ends here. Interpretations vary between glamorous city lights attracting young men who are seeking prestige, or families that risk all to send someone overseas in order to avoid 'staying here to die'. Narratives of greed and grievance divide opinion within migration research and also between west African households, given the risks involved and the complicated trade-offs between being present in the family and sending remittances from abroad. Even these basic characterisations have complex underlying factors. To consider these factors, analysis can aim to 'historicise economic dispositions which, like the economic field, have a social genesis' (Bourdieu 2000: 18). The convergence between migration from the south and the voluntary nature of migration in the north has commonly been denaturalised by an ahistorical approach, which 'obscures both the colonial genealogies of development and the historical continuities in the theory and practice of development' (Kothari 2005: 50). Similarly, contemporary labour issues are 'regularly formed as a distinctively modern problem, in which processes associated with globalisation play decisive roles', yet these problems have historical roots (Quirk 2006: 566).

Transformations of land, labour and economy in west Africa led workers to seek wage labour across borders. Showing the importance of context, Riddell argued that the underlying force of population movement could not be determined by extrapolating causes from empirical patterns; instead, the implications of processes that lead to the pattern must be analysed. It is important then to consider the impact of changes in mobility that were enforced and then directed by colonial administration, particularly because migration was 'manipulated' as a separate but related process to the restructuring of the economy (Riddell 1981: 372–3). The causes of migration cannot be separated from their consequences, 'for migration is not just the consequence of unequal development' but is 'also an element in unequal development, reproducing the same conditions and contributing in this manner to their aggravation' (Amin 1974: 9).

The examination of historical development diverges from the current orthodoxy, in which migration processes are sometimes documented in near isolation from their historical and situational context in dedicated centres of migration study. This partly results from varied and complicated routes and is also due to pragmatic efforts to explain these routes and subsequently offer policy goals. A member of an important migration research team commented in a typical conversation that because contemporary migration is so complicated, it would be impossible for the team to analyse the causes and consequences – simply to say what people are doing would be achievement enough and would be useful for policy. This began, at the start of the PhD project, my perception that migration research has a tendency to be atomistic; not for lack of effort or available funding, but more to establish some sense and order from a very chaotic phenomenon. Hence the vehicle of migration is popularly, the focus, while the passengers and loads are glossed over and generalised, independent of their context (Collinson 2009: 2–3). This book will show, however, that if migrants are suspended in time or isolated from their space, a very different conception of their situation emerges, which misses their subordinated position within the labour force.

West African migration research shows that migrants' eventual return home is expected once obligations have been met. Migrants' efforts are made on behalf of their villages, not as a 'traditional' or 'customary' practice but as a reflection of economic considerations such as previous investments in the migrant and the preservation of the community through times of struggle (Potts 2011: 39; Cooper 2008). Didier Bigo has pointed out, however, the 'Europe narrative' in which outside this regional historical context, 'globalisation and unequal distribution of wealth in the world push the poor to immigrate to prosperous countries and to remain there' (2005b: 69). The conceit that migrants wish to remain in Europe runs through different policy areas, despite overwhelming evidence to the contrary in west Africa.

This regional model of mobility would be missed in the neoclassical approach to migration, which places the individual migrant at the centre of analysis. The 'push–pull' framework supports the centrality of migrants' choices. It is assumed in this framework that rural population growth and higher wages lead people to move from one place to another. However, this excludes explanation of people deciding not to migrate and also is prone to the 'push' and 'pull' factors of migration mirroring each other, so that workers' low wages 'push' them to areas that have the 'pull' of higher wages (de Haas 2008a: 8–11). An important dialogue then emerges in the perception of 'economic' migrants, which relates to their relative wealth or deprivation. The latter informs the view that migration is a possible 'escape' from political, economic, social and overpopulation problems (Zohry 2005). It is more frequently contested that migrants are relatively wealthy. Arjan de Haan argued:

> The poorest have most need to improve their income, but at the same time are less able to migrate. Migration needs investment, for transport, for food during the journey, bribes for employment officers or officials implementing immigration and settlement policies, and it needs contacts – assets that the poor are less likely to possess.
>
> (2000: 7)

Especially in a rural setting, it is expected that 'poor Africans never think about international migration' (Hahn 2008: 3). Similarly, it is argued that migrants to southern Europe are not 'escaping to survive'. Rather, they 'possess the material and cultural resources to face the costs and hardships presented by emigration' (Reyneri 2003: 119–20). This argument was supported by empirical evidence to show that migration to Italy in the 1990s was dominated by elite youths who aimed for a higher social position or to avoid downward mobility. They were motivated by expectations that were raised by the 'globalisation of the everyday Western life model' (Reyneri 2003: 119) and by optimism and 'modern values' (Van Dalen *et al.* 2004). Thus it is expected that migrants are 'connected', ambitious and concerned about status. Azam and Gubert (2006) similarly argued that social status drives families to send migrants from selected villages in the Senegal River Valley. They claimed that the status of the clan would be seriously tarnished if the consumption of those remaining in the village were to fall drastically in the wake of a failed harvest; furthermore, 'it is less an aversion to consumption fluctuations which is at stake than the shame that would affect the whole clan were the family to be visibly weakened after an exogenous shock' (Azam and Gubert 2006: 435–6). This study shows patterns that have derived from empirical research, which omit the processes that normalise labour migration. In the Senegal River Valley these processes relate to its establishment as a labour reserve and to the decline of peasantries.

This book will show that in 'stepwise' migration to Europe migrants do not always make the initial 'investment' but, instead, may leave home with very little and work for wages along the way, with few contacts. One migrant who had gained residency in Barcelona explained that at the time of his stepwise journey from Ghana, the pattern had been for migrants with cash to go to Mauritania and pay for a boat passage to Spain, while those without the means would go to Libya and try to earn the funds to go to Italy (interview no. 79, Barcelona, 26 July 2009). The fear of deportation is critical for migrants in north-African 'transit' countries because months may be spent in border towns attempting to gain the funds for re-entry. The relative wealth of migrants, and often their households by extension, is therefore diverse, and this signifies that, although important, it is not a guiding factor in determining who migrates and who stays. This book connects the migration instead with dispossession, as seen in regional history and in the historical accounts of individuals and families that reveal loss of land, livelihoods and security (see Box 1.1). This is why capturing the dynamics is important, not only questioning why people migrate but also what enables/encourages them to do so.

Linked with considerations of the relative wealth and deprivation of migrants are questions pertaining to agency. Contemporary international migration is often characterised by 'transnational social spaces', which contain multidimensional economic, political, cultural and demographic processes in which 'movers', 'stayers' and 'returnees' frequently cross borders (Faist 2000: 9). The transnational networks produce forms of 'cosmopolitanism', here signifying an openness to difference, 'from below' (Kothari 2008: 501). Thus the 'de-nationalisation' of social science is promoted and has been integrated in contemporary understandings of migration (Beck 2004). Having said that, Ralph Grillo (2007) raised his objection to decontextualising and conflating personal positions, whilst overlooking the

**Box 1.1** Migrants' stories of accumulation by dispossession

Note that there is a combination of personal experiences and grander narratives that are usually a response (unprompted) to questions about reasons for migration or changes in family livelihoods.

Our family developed this district; it's why we have influence over the youth against emigration. We train them in fishing although we don't have many means. From here to Gorée costs 8,000 francs CFA [€12.20][a] in oil [see Map 4.2]. Principal activities before were fishing and agriculture. People go clandestinely because of the fishing crisis . . . there are family members everywhere. Sometimes the father sells his land or the family contribute by selling the jewels. I have two brothers who have left and they send [remittances] to their immediate family. Their wives or mothers receive it. It's to feed the family. Up to now, they haven't yet built their houses, they just send it for food. It's hard because they have to work for ten hours, they're a little exploited. They say they have 800,000 francs [€1219.60] in Europe but the cost of living there is difficult.

(returned migrant, interview no. 40, Thiaroye-sur-Mer, 3 June 2008)

I'll no longer fish. You will have seen the fish jumping near the beach but because of fishing agreements that Senegal has signed with other countries, it has become very difficult, and that's without counting the raised price of oil.

(repatriated migrant, interview no. 47, Thiaroye-sur-Mer, 7 June 2008)

[My son's] father gave him the expenses for the journey by selling the plot of land that his father had left him. I asked [my son] to send money to his brother here. The latter couldn't even pay for breakfast while he has a wife and child.

(mother of migrant in Spain, interview no. 42, Thiaroye-sur-Mer, 6 June 2008)

Their father sold one of his houses to help our children to leave for Italy. My son sends 60,000 francs per month [€91.47] to meet our basic consumption needs. He does the same activity there as he was doing here – building. He told me that it is difficult and if he's not working, he is asleep.

(mother of migrant in Spain, interview no. 43, Thiaroye-sur-Mer, 6 June 2008)

I dropped fishing for building because it isn't profitable anymore, because of fishing agreements signed by our state. I am often unemployed. There are buildings in this district constructed by our grandparents. How to build now when we don't have the means to do it?

(unsuccessful attempt to go to Spain, interview no. 51, Rufisque, 18 June 2008)

The youth are not interested in fishing – maybe it interests those who practised it before but now it's not profitable here. A big heap of fish only gets 100 francs [€0.15].

(brother of two clandestine migrants, interview no. 59, Rufisque, 24 June 2008)

All the factories that were built here are closed, Bata [shoes] and ICOTAF [textiles]. There are not many offers of work here. When travelling to Europe it's firstly to meet the needs of the house. Emigrants must also think of investing to prepare for their retirement. For investment, emigrants will have to do 15 years abroad.

(clandestine migrant who gained legal status in Spain, interview no. 61, Rufisque, 24 June 2008)

[My son] even had his own pirogue and the machinery, but he sold it because of clandestine emigration .

(mother of migrant, interview no. 64, Rufisque, 2 July 2008)

The situation for fishermen was better in the past. It was not good but it was better than today. It's not because of the lack of fish, but it's the price of fish – it's very little. For ten years, people have had to sell the fish to Europe.

(Senegalese migrant, interview no. 11, Nouakchott, 7 May 2007)

Before there weren't many constraints in fishing, but today we are confronted with a lack of materials and the expensiveness of oil.

(Senegalese fisherman, interview no. 14, Saint-Louis, 15 May 2007)

We have some land. It is still farmed by some of my sisters and relatives. Before they could have some profit from it but now the situation of the country has changed. We can't depend on farming. It is the prices – with the money made, you can only spend on family needs. Before we had 80 goats; now we have 16. We don't have tools for farming.

(Cameroonian migrant, interview no. 22, Barcelona, 26 February 2008)

You will see a lot of mismanagement of resources and there is more poverty and more inflation. Twenty years ago, people could survive even with minimum money. But now, even if you have a lot of money, it will still be very difficult for you to survive. I would say that in the last ten years, the middle class is being disintegrated . . . you will find it very difficult to send your children to school. I want to make sure that all of my children have university education because even my parents, with little or nothing they had, were able to train some of us to university level. My father, before giving me his land, made sure that we were committed to it . . . we are not going to dispose of the land under any circumstances.

(Nigerian migrant, interview no. 25, Barcelona, 28 February 2008)

Many companies from America, they come to Ghana and most of the European [companies] there have the machinery, the basic means of production.

(Ghanaian migrant, interview no. 32, Nouadhibou, 17 May 2008)

We have gold, we have many companies, but because of the bad condition of Nigeria, children are dying, people are suffering, getting sick, this is what we are doing here, to see whether we can survive and help our family to eat.

(Nigerian migrant, interview no. 16, Salt, Girona, 23 February 2008)

[European colonisers] have lived in Africa, slaughtered people, enslaved people, turned the remaining Africans under its dominion. For 40 years, people have been saying, 'helping Africa, helping Africa' – they are not helping Africa, they are helping themselves. The resources have been abused by the use of cruel force.

(Senegalese migrant, interview no. 76, Barcelona, 21 February 2009)

a The franc CFA is pegged to the euro: €1.00 = 655.957 francs. As of September 2012, €1.00 = £0.81 / $1.31.

extent to which transnational migrants remain bound to nation and class. Citing Kahn (1995), he argues:

> Displacement is celebrated, and the displaced hailed as archetypal hero(ine)s/victims who, obliged to live betwixt and between, must, metaphorically and usually practically, be multilingual and multicultural . . . Thus transmigration is thought to give rise to subject positionings transcending traditional boundaries.
>
> (Grillo 2007: 212)

This is why an emphasis on the 'structural' factors of migration may appear to undermine the 'agency' of migrants, but there is also the risk of an over-exuberant focus on migrants' 'choices' reifying a limited notion of autonomy. This calls for a careful balance. Furthermore, a focus on the cultural power of migrants can overshadow the more complex discussion of economic inequality. More generally, Africa has been included in accounts of a culturally globalised world but is excluded from discussion of global capital flows (Ferguson 2006: 30–4). The reason for this book to focus on west African migration in the context of capitalism is that it will show the significance of ongoing accumulation in all elements of contemporary labour mobility (Perelman 1983: 6–12, Harvey 2003). Modern economic dispossession and the continual demand for unfree labour are both mediated by the processes and local meanings of capitalist globalisation. It is this demand that leads migrants to disappear into the desert and sea in uncountable numbers, with a small proportion ultimately entering northern labour markets that are none the less essential to the growth of those economies.

## Capitalism, accumulation, underdevelopment and migration

In the Senegalese fishing communities of Thiaroye-sur-Mer and Rufisque, international fishing agreements have undermined the capacity of fishing activity to support livelihoods. The price hikes in imported food and oil combined with the lowered selling price of fish illustrate the inconsistent and uneven character of global capitalism (Chapter 4). We saw in Box 1.1 that because of global and international markets, people are separated from land, boats and tools. In some cases they sell this property to fund a journey to Europe. By then selling their labour in Europe, migrants can sustain households to a greater extent than is possible by staying. Box 1.1 substantiates the argument that migrant communities have been faced with 'progressively more distanced but more sophisticated and insidious power over their labour' (Bryceson 2000: 300). The connections between home circumstances and labour mobility are explained here as processes of 'accumulation by dispossession' (Harvey 2003), beginning with the problem of expanding capital:

> The capitalist system pre-supposes the complete separation of the labourers from all property in the means by which they can realise their labour. As soon as capitalist production is once on its own legs, it not only maintains this separation, but reproduces it on a continually extending scale. The process, therefore, that clears the way for the capitalist system, can be none other than the process which takes away from the labourer the possession of the means of production; a process that transforms, on the one hand, the social means of subsistence and of production into capital, on the other, the immediate producers into wage labourers. The so-called primitive accumulation, therefore, is nothing else than the historical process of divorcing the producer from the means of production. It appears as primitive, because it forms the pre-historic stage of capital and of the mode of production corresponding with it.
>
> (Marx 1867/1970: 714–15)

'Primitive accumulation' is a translation from German that referred to previous accumulation of stock. Adam Smith claimed that previous accumulation must precede the division of labour. Because the origins of capitalist accumulation were 'an anecdote of the past', Marx likened this notion to 'original sin': 'Adam bit the apple, and thereupon sin fell upon the human race'. But in the economic original sin it is not essential for everyone 'to eat his bread in the sweat of his brow'; instead 'it came to pass' that there were those who accumulate wealth and the others who sell their labour-power. Marx described primitive accumulation as a process based on expropriation rather than as a legend of the past, and he also alluded to its ongoing nature (Marx 1867/1970: 713; Perelman 1983: 6–10).

That capitalist production reproduces the separation of labourers from the means by which they can realise their labour, on a continually extending scale, evinces a conundrum: capitalist production is underpinned by labourers who have been separated from the means of production. However, labourers sometimes gain access to the means of production when they have sold their labour-power. A reserve of labour is the inevitable outcome of incorporating wage labourers into production. However, it can be expected that 'in any society beyond the most primitive there will be saving of produce to form means of production for the future, whether it be in the form of hunting weapons, corn seed, animal stock or other implements' (Fine and Saad-Filho 2004: 75).

Therefore, what is the process by which 'two very different kinds of commodity-possessors must come face to face and into contact', being the owners of money, who buy people's labour-power to increase the sum of the value they possess; and the 'free labourers' who are sellers of labour-power? They are free labourers in the double sense that:

> neither they themselves form part and parcel of the means of production, as in the case of slaves, bondsmen etc., nor do the means of production belong to them, as in the case of peasant-proprietors; they are, therefore, free from, unencumbered by, any means of production of their own.
>
> (Marx 1867/1970: 714)

Labour is 'freed' as a result of primitive accumulation. It becomes available when masses are 'torn from their means of subsistence, and hurled as free and 'unattached' proletarians on the labour-market' (Marx 1867/1970: 716). Therefore it is linked with exploitation in which 'the threat of starvation and the lack of alternatives compelled the "free" labourers "voluntarily" to sign up to the labour contract and "spontaneously" turn up to work even under the most appalling conditions' (Fine and Saad-Filho 2004: 81).

Primitive accumulation is supposedly linked with the historical expansion of capitalism as a global system of production. This occurred during the mercantilist period from 1600 to 1800, when feudal relationships declined and the poles of wealth accumulation and proletarianisation developed. North America was peripheral to western Europe's wealth, and slave labour was supplied by Africa. West Africa, lacking the natural resources of the centre or the settler colonies of the south, was organised as a trade monopoly that would force peasants to pay taxes by producing export crops. Samir Amin argued that it retained 'traditional' appearances but was 'completed as a dependent society, a peripheral one', in global capitalism (1972a: 115). However, this book will show that dependence is never complete.

The context for this book is the character of global capitalism and the persistence of capital accumulation, which binds the causes and consequences of migration with the process of working across borders. The geographical expansion of capitalism is linked with accessing cheaper inputs such as land, raw materials and labour-power. The logic is that territories should be continually opened up, rather than held back from capitalist development (Harvey 2003: 139). The book will show that this is a key underlying factor in contemporary west African migration. The fishing agreements that restrict access to markets for peasant fishermen and the labour-power that is freed as a result reveals the particular character of capital accumulation and the persistence of its primitive form. It arises in migrants' personal histories to include: the suppression of alternative (indigenous) forms of production and consumption; neo-colonial and imperial processes of appropriation of assets (including natural resources); the monetisation of exchange and taxation; national debt; and the credit system (Harvey 2003: 145). We will see in the case of the Senegalese coastal communities that the latter form of capital accumulation has led young workers to sell fishing boats and abandon fishing activities. Thus primitive accumulation becomes accumulation by dispossession, which has a key historical difference. This is because the former opened up the path to expanded reproduction, yet the latter disrupts and destroys a path that is already opened up (Harvey 2003: 164). In other words, people are thrown out of the global economy – discarded and sometimes reincorporated.

There are labour reserves that are incorporated in capitalist development, and then there are 'wasted lives' that have been left behind by modernisation (Bauman 2004). Labour reserves signify established labour regimes within Africa and those that were abruptly halted in Europe, such as mobility from the Senegal River Valley to France. The key to having geographical separation, and therefore migration, can be explained as a separation of the means of renewal (new recruits to fill vacancies) from those of maintenance (workers' day-to-day subsistence). The cost of renewal is largely covered by the state economy of the migrant and, furthermore, the employer is not accountable to the external political and economic systems. This separation is not natural but it is enforced through political and legal mechanisms that determine that the migrant is without citizenship rights. This system reproduces itself as a result of 'mechanisms that enforce the circulation of labour, restrict its upward mobility, and establish the migrant's powerlessness' (Burawoy 1980: 149).

This characterises migrant labour from the north of Senegal to Mauritania, or from the south of Mauritania to Nouakchott. Women who seek paid housekeeping work may be imprisoned for claiming unpaid wages, but along with male migrants they continue to cross the border or to migrate from the south because their households depend on remittances (interviews nos 2, 4, 5, 7, 9, 11, Nouakchott, 7 May 2007). It is part of a process that is also known as 'straddling', by which different family members move back and forth between local agriculture, urban wage labour and overseas jobs, contributing to village social resources. This does not reflect:

> an outdated culture that values collectivity over individual achievement, but rather strategies to preserve social ties vital to communities whose historical experiences include the slave trade, colonial depressions and the ups and downs of government programmes and export markets.
>
> (Cooper 2008: 188)

The stepwise labourers who are 'left behind' by globalisation are also built into patterns of accumulation that are distinguished from established labour regimes by their high volatility. This book suggests that west African labour mobility to Europe and transit migration in the region is in persistent flux as a result of expanded reproduction. Migrants' high-risk venture aims to put an end to the danger, criminalisation and destitution that precedes sending remittances. The system of migrant labour is, however, reproduced because new territory is continually opened up by similar measures to those in Thiaroye-sur-Mer and Rufisque. The case of Spain will show the importance of African migrants in agriculture and industry, with significant numbers entering by land and sea rather than by air (Chapter 7). This is a system of unfree labour, which, like other unfree labour regimes, has great human and economic cost.

Unfree wage labour is linked to political and legal constraints, which proscribe free circulation in the labour market, for example by indentured labour or by legal constraints that prevent labourers' entry to particular sectors. Unfreedom in this context does not refer to forms of political restriction, such as withdrawal of rights of political participation or trade union activity. Rather, political-legal restrictions are:

> .specifically intended to restrict the circulation of certain categories of labour-power within the labour market. Such restrictions may be overdetermined by related political constraints (e.g. the absence of the right to vote) but the latter do not by themselves constitute the defining feature of unfree labour.
>
> (Miles 1987: 33)

This differentiates it from the Senegal–Mauritanian migration described above in which political restriction prevents labourers from being paid, but it does not prevent circulation in the labour market. Transit migrants are subjected to imprisonment, extortion and expulsion, but if they maintain freedom of movement, they are free to circulate in different sectors of employment because Mauritania's economy is largely informal. There must be extra-economic restrictions on the circulation of labour, as implemented and regulated by the state, for it to be unfree. Migrant labour is unfree in Spain because it is subject to legal restriction, for example by the issuance of expulsion orders that limit migrants to the sectors that are willing to hire 'illegal' workers (Martínez-Veiga 1999; CEAR 2007). Although migrants have 'chosen' to seek wage labour, these restrictions locate them as an unfree source of labour (Miles 1987: 159; Cohen 1987: 26). Legal contracts also restrict circulation. The state has the central role in this, keeping the territorial and capitalistic logics of power 'always intertwined though not necessarily concordant' (Harvey 2003: 145). The EU in this case determines the political status of migrants by constructing them as a threat and co-ordinating FRONTEX, which plays a key role in determining that entry to Europe is clandestine and undocumented. The state, however, will determine the legal status that guides migrants to particular sectors.

Forms of unfree labour are both 'anomalous' and 'necessary' to ca (Miles 1987). They are anomalous because free wage labour tends to d but they are necessary because historical conditions obstruct the convergence of wage relations. Receiving countries are under pressure to keep labour costs down and they do this by incorporating migrant labour. This is important because it implies the persistence of poverty and underdevelopment in sending regions if migration is encouraged while facing legal and political restriction. Therefore, migration and processes of remitting are rejoined and problematised in this book, leading to exploration not only of migrants' resistance to social and political exclusion in host countries but also to the process of migration itself.

Placed within the historical context, the interaction of individual circumstances with macro structures provides a useful framework for understanding the causes and consequences of migration (Kothari 2002: 10). Although historical accounts are often Eurocentric, generalisations can still be reached about particular regions of Africa and broad historical patterns can be determined (Coquéry-Vidrovitch 1991; Austin 2007). The book attempts to do this, although there is inevitably a disjuncture between specific current situations and general historical trends. This is partially addressed by migrants' accounts of events, which are often located within structural causes, including macroeconomic policy and political exclusion. The point here is not that the book offers a historical account but instead it aims to establish how states and livelihoods have developed over time as they are, and to analyse the role of these developments in the contemporary picture of migration.

## Notes

1 A research note appeared in the LUCAS Bulletin soon after the completion of fieldwork (Cross 2009).

2 All names are pseudonyms.

# 2 Capitalism, the state and labour migration

The previous chapter presented a holistic approach to labour migration, in which there is equal focus firstly on migrants' various trajectories in their geopolitical–economic context, and secondly on historical and consequential processes in migrant communities. This chapter and the next will construct the lens for this panoramic view of migration by examining the dynamics in which labour is displaced from sending to receiving economies. It will develop the theoretical and historical basis for capturing labour migration in motion in the subsequent chapters of this book.

In attempting to quantify, identify and analyse global migration patterns, this chapter shows that, in aggregate terms, human mobility is astonishingly low for the 'global' era. At the same time, it will be argued that migrant labour remains integral to the development of capitalist economies. This is because, beyond international migration signifying an imbalance between regions, the state and the global economy it enters are in a dialectical relationship, which mediates between sending communities and capitalist employers, thus concentrating migrant flows. It is important, in this light, to understand how labour is displaced from one place to another and migrants' trajectories, both historical and geographical, are key to explaining this displacement. The next chapter examines west Africa's labour history through this lens. The transformation of land, labour and economy in favour of commodity export, and the interactions between these transformations and population movements, are of particular relevance to labour mobility in this region (Amin 1972a). There continue to be regional regimes of labour that compel workers to seek wages across borders, even at the cost of freedom and stability. The contemporary era of migration also presents some interesting discontinuities with past movements of labour, which will frame the debates in later chapters.

## Migration in the global era

Contemporary migration is complex, to the extent that its nature is considered to have essentially changed in the global era (Papastergiadis 2000). This section offers an overview of current transnational mobility, which is complicated by the multidirectional impact of neo-liberal globalisation and 'the sheer messiness of real world politics' (Bernstein 2005: 124). An important question to consider here is the extent to which this apparent disorder represents discontinuity with the forced labour of the past; or is the chaos of migration instead a new way of extracting cheap labour from overseas? The situation of migrants is subject to sudden change. An increase in undocumented migration, in the absence of legal channels, presents difficulties in gaining statistics, as well as varied lengths of stay for migrants and, in some cases, a lack of accurate reporting. In north Africa, for example, it is claimed that migrant numbers have been misreported in important transit towns such as Tamanrasset in Algeria, partly as a result of authorities' embroilment in the 'War on Terror' and associated obligations and gains (Keenan 2004). Although this book favours the disaggregation of migrations and the use of qualitative data, some key general patterns can be discerned from global statistics, which will contribute to later considerations of the relationship between globalisation and migration.

To summarise global figures, the *Financial Times* reported a doubling of people living in countries not of their birth between 1965 and 2000, from 75 million to 150 million (Fidler 2002) and this figure reached 214 million by 2012 (IOM 2012). In relation to population growth, however, the increase in migrant stock has been less impressive, rising from 2.2 per cent of the world population in 1970 to 3.1 per cent by 2012 (UNDP 2009: 146; UN DESA 2009b; IOM 2012). When considering the advances in global interconnectedness that consolidated in the latter part of the twentieth century, this increase in migrant stock is staggeringly low. Furthermore, this figure includes 27 million people who had formerly lived in the Soviet Union and were recorded as international migrants at independence. The international migrant percentage of world population in 2005, excluding the former Soviet Union and Czechoslovakia, was therefore lower than the recorded 3.1 percentage, instead amounting to 2.7 per cent (UNDP 2009: 146). Table 2.1 shows that the distribution of migrants is uneven and corresponds with regional inequalities.

*Table 2.1* Migrant stock and migration rates in regions, 1960–2010

| | *Annual rate of growth (%)* | *International migrants as % of total population* | | | *Emigration rate (%)* | *Average annual net migration (1000s)* | *Average annual net migration rate per 1000 of population* |
|---|---|---|---|---|---|---|---|
| | *1960–2005* | *1960* | *1990* | *2010* | *2000–2002* | *2005–2010* | *2005–2010* |
| Africa | 1.7 | 3.2 | 2.5 | 1.9 | 2.9 | –532.0 | –0.5 |
| Europe | 2.9 | 3.0 | 6.9 | 9.5 | 7.3 | 1,340.6 | 1.8 |
| Asia | 0.7 | 1.7 | 1.6 | 1.5 | 1.7 | –1,075.7 | –1.1 |
| Latin America and Caribbean | 0.2 | 2.8 | 1.6 | 1.3 | 5.0 | –1,049.1 | –1.8 |
| Northern America | 2.8 | 6.7 | 9.8 | 14.2 | 1.1 | 1,219.9 | 3.6 |
| Oceania | 1.7 | 13.5 | 16.2 | 16.8 | 4.9 | 96.4 | 2.8 |

Source: UNDP 2009, 143-7; UN DESA 2009a, 2009b; IOM 2005: 396

Europe and northern America have each gained over a million migrants per year, while Africa, Asia and Latin America are sending continents. Over a fifth of the world's migrants now live in the US, giving it the largest number of international migrant stock, with 42.8 million people, followed by the Russian Federation with 12.3 million. Germany, Saudi Arabia, Canada, France, the United Kingdom, Spain, India and the Ukraine follow (UN DESA 2009a). Mexico sends the largest number of migrants, with an average of 486,000 emigrants per year, followed by China with 342,000 annual emigrants. The five countries that receive the highest percentage of international migrants relative to their populations are all in western Asia: these are Qatar, United Arab Emirates, Kuwait, Jordan and Occupied Palestinian Territory. However, as China, Pakistan and India follow Mexico in sending the largest numbers of migrants, Asia is still a net sending region. The prominence of migration in the oil-producing countries of western Asia reveals labour movement that does not follow south–north patterns of movement; nor does Chinese migration serve the interests of industrial capitalism in Europe and the US. Over two thirds of Chinese migration remains in Asia (UNDP 2009: 148).

However, the south–north migration pattern persists, as Mexico and the US have the clear lead as sending and receiving countries. Note in Table 2.1 that Europe and Latin America have the highest emigration rates at 7.3 per cent and 5 per cent respectively. Table 2.2 shows that these flows are towards the countries of very high development. European migration is primarily intra-continental, while most migrants from Latin America and the Caribbean go to northern America. Yet in Africa, while the largest share of emigrants go to the high-development countries, just over half of migrant destinations are within the continent. All southern African countries except for Lesotho are listed as medium-development and form the only African region to make net gains in migrants (UNDP 2009: 150; UN DESA 2009a).

*Table 2.2* Human development category of emigrants' country of residence, 2000–2002 (% of total emigrant stocks)

| | *Very high* | *High* | *Medium* | *Low* |
|---|---|---|---|---|
| Africa | 35.9 | 8.3 | 25.7 | 30.0 |
| Europe | 52.6 | 28.1 | 18.1 | 1.2 |
| Asia | 41.7 | 23.2 | 34.5 | 0.6 |
| Latin America and Caribbean | 81.7 | 12.1 | 5.6 | 0.5 |
| Northern America | 62.8 | 23.5 | 12.6 | 1.1 |
| Oceania | 84.3 | 2.8 | 12.3 | 0.6 |

Source: UNDP 2009: 150

Labour migration, both legal and illegal, is linked with inequality both within states and in the state system (Graham 2000: 188). The Africa Trade Forum (2011), composed of the UN Economic Commission for Africa (UNECA), the African Development Bank (AfDB) and the African Union Commission (AUC), reported that Africa's share of world trade was in decline despite an exponential increase globally. It listed Africa's dependency on the export of primary products, which have declined in price, as a factor of trade distortion. It also noted the negative impact of domestic support and export subsidies provided by 'developed' countries to their producers (Africa Trade Policy Centre 2011: 2).

This type of macroeconomic inequality undermines employment opportunities in sending regions if economic development is lagging. Samir Amin and Ali El Kenz noted worsening inequality between Europe and Africa:

> We should remember that, at the gates of the European Union, to the south of the Mediterranean, there are countries with fast population growth which provided Europe, during the 'Thirty Glorious Years' (mid-1940s to mid-1970s), with the workers it needed. New job opportunities for them are closing up in Europe, while in their own countries, Structural Adjustment Programmes have already produced their quota of unemployment, under-employment and pauperisation.
>
> (2005: 81)

This double strain of lack of opportunity at home and restrictions across the border has led to volumes of 'uncontrollable' migration, which, according to Amin and El Kenz, have reinforced unequal development (2005: 81). At the same time, economic inequality between countries does not produce the direct link between their populations or sufficiently explain why particular cohorts of workers would cross continents at particular times. Migration is often viewed as the 'mere displacement of a labour force', with a surplus labour force on one hand, and no questions asked as to the reasons for this surplus; and then jobs that are available on the other hand, with no questions asked about the reasons for this availability (Sayad 2004: 3). The 0.5 per cent increase in international migrant stock between 1970 and 2005 shows that, in global terms, migration is not 'phenomenal' and has not expanded in line with the supposed ease of travel. Instead, it continues in constrained forms, which develop as processes of dispossession expand the mass of wage labourers or 'labouring poor' (Marx 1867/1970: 615).

## Capitalism and migrant labour

Migrations connected with the growing dominance of capitalism are widely described in three phases. Firstly, in colonial regimes from the sixteenth to the nineteenth centuries, large numbers of Europeans brought lasting and divisive social orders and means of resource management to the colonies, accompanied and fuelled by the slave trade. Secondly, European settlement in the New World, from the early nineteenth to the mid-twentieth centuries, satisfied the labour needs of industrial expansion with the aid of wealth generated by as many as 30 million indentured workers. Finally, labour movements from the colonies to Europe took place after World War II, in a reversal of the first phase (Papastergiadis 2000: 22–7). The previous chapter also discussed a broadened range of destinations for migrants from former colonies, which dates from the 1970s and constitutes a sub-phase. Before returning to contemporary patterns, this section situates south–north migrant labour within debates about forms of labour mobility in capitalist development, including some discussion of its commodification.

European colonisation included movements from Europe to Africa, Asia and then the Americas and Oceania, laying the roots of dispossession. These conquests were tied with the Atlantic slave trade, which continued fully fledged for more than 400 years after its introduction in the mid-fifteenth century (Chapter 3) and the intersecting slave trade in the Indian Ocean region, connecting east Africa to the Middle East, Ottoman Empire and European colonies. From the late seventeenth century to mid-nineteenth century, chattel slavery formed the basis of commodity production (including sugar, tobacco, coffee, cotton and gold) in New World plantations and mines; especially important to the political and economic power of Britain and France. By 1870, slaves were producing a third of the total value of European commerce in the 'triangular trade', in which ships would leave European ports with manufactured goods, exchange those goods with chiefs for slaves in west Africa or otherwise forcibly abduct them, and then transport the slaves to the Americas and the Caribbean, selling the slaves for cash. This cash would be used to purchase products from the plantations to bring back and sell in Europe (Castles and Miller 2003: 52–3). There were over 12 million African slaves transported during this period, who would cultivate rice, sugar, tobacco and indigo in north America, and would work in pearl-diving or mining in the Caribbean and Latin America. Slavery continued after official interdictions from England and America in 1807–8, so that 36,120 so-called post-emancipation Africans, seized from slave ships and often taken to Sierra Leone and St Helena in west Africa, were then re-exported to the British-held Caribbean between 1839 and 1867 (Gomez 2006: 5–9).

Industrialisation in Europe was accompanied by increased European labour mobility. More reliable and less costly transport drove this expansion, and, moreover, there was a surplus of agrarian workers in Europe as it industrialised. Total estimates of settler movement towards north America, south America, South Africa, Australia and New Zealand vary from 46 million international migrants between 1821 and 1914, to 50 million people between 1850 and 1914 (Held *et al.* 1999: 291). Indentured workers replaced slaves as the main source of plantation labour: large groups of workers were recruited, sometimes by force, and transported to an area for work. They were bound by strict labour contracts for a period of several years. British companies recruited workers from the Indian subcontinent for work in Caribbean countries (Miles 1987: 90), in addition to the Indian and Chinese 'coolies' in Malaya working for the British colony; while Dutch colonial authorities employed Chinese labour in the Dutch East Indies. Indentured workers were used in 40 countries by the major colonial powers between 1834 and abolishment in 1941 (Castles and Miller 2003: 55; Bush 2007: 55).

From the mid-1940s to the mid-1970s, northern Europe drew on its 'labour reservoir' north and south of the Mediterranean to complete its postwar reconstruction. Named the 'Golden Age' or 'Glorious Years', this period saw European countries gain relatively cheap labour, while it is claimed that the Mediterranean countries also benefited from a less pressured labour market and the large external resources gained by emigrant earnings (Amin and El Kenz 2005: 107). Certainly, the risks of migrating were comparatively low and workers were directly recruited. In 1970, Italy had 820,000 workers in northern Europe, Turkey sent 770,000 workers, and Yugoslavia sent 540,000. Germany's foreign workforce grew from 461,000 in 1960 to 2.5 million in 1973, while France's workforce grew from 1.3 million to 1.99 million in the same period (Sassen 1988: 102). The groups of migrants to South Africa, northern Europe and the US in this period could be described as 'historical descendants' of earlier generations of unfree workers, similarly prevented from becoming citizens and settlers (Cohen 1987: 29).

The use of labour as an economic resource echoes throughout capitalist history, so that migrant labour is, in the eyes of the World Bank, an *import* (2004: 37). Labour-power is, however, different to the buying and selling of other commodities due to its twofold character. It produces value as other commodities do; but also it creates and forms the value of commodities (Marx 1867/1970: 46). Slave labour transforms the labourer 'forcefully into an item of exchange' (Miles 1987: 31), but the 'free' labourer disposes of her or his labour-power in a market. The distinction between them may be based on appearance rather than substantively on the experiences of the labourer. By means of dispossession, commodity producers are incorporated in labour reserves, and their labour commodified. Hannah Arendt described the rise of a capitalist economy as a process of expropriation, in which 'the deprivation for certain groups of their place in the world and their naked exposure to the exigencies of life, created both the original accumulation of wealth and the possibility of transforming this wealth into capital through labour' (Arendt 1958/1998: 254–5).

Wage labour was directed by the historical process of primitive, or original, accumulation, which signifies the commodification and privatisation of land, labour-power and assets, including natural resources. This occurred in the form of the slave trade, colonisation and neo-colonialism. The persistence of accumulation 'based upon predation, fraud and violence' after this 'original' stage led to Harvey's substitution of 'primitive accumulation' with 'accumulation by dispossession' (Harvey 2003: 144; Chapter 1). This provides the context for understanding postcolonial processes of migration.

There were a number of attempts to explain post-1945 migration to Western Europe. The trend sought to explain these movements as a consequence of capital accumulation that led to the incorporation of people as wage labourers who were previously outside those relations of production (Miles 1987: 4). Robert

Miles has captured the burning questions running through the study of labour migration as follows:

> because not all migrations are determined by demand for wage labour, and because not all migrations result from individual choice under structural constraint, the connection between capitalism and migration should not be conceived as a necessarily direct one but may be, at the very least, a mediated connection. Moreover, the positions to which migrants are recruited, characterised as they are by various forms of physical and legal compulsion, suggest again that we need to establish the nature of the relationship between capitalism and unfree labour.
>
> (Miles 1987: 6)

Questions are raised here about the agency of migrants and their structural constraints. This consideration extends to the necessity of migrant labour as a conduit of capitalism, an issue which divides Marxist analysts. It is argued that there is nothing necessary about the system of migrant labour: rather it is a 'functional substitute for other modes of organising labour' under capitalism (Burawoy 1980: 143). Other modes include extending the work time of the national population, moving capital to less-developed regions, or inducing large-scale unemployment to push wage rates down (Harvey 2003: 141). Miles argued, however, that the presence of migrant workers is central to the reproduction of the capitalist mode of production (1987: 155). The low cost of reproduction of labour-power is key to the importance of migrant labour as a national strategy for development.

Capitalist interests seek to pay the labour force at the lowest possible cost, and this can be done by externalising the cost of labour renewal to sending economies (Burawoy 1980). Imperialism established 'organic relations' between capitalist and 'domestic', or non-capitalist, economies: subsistence agriculture would continue outside the sphere of capitalist *production*, but by supplying workers it would belong to capitalism's sphere of *circulation* (Meillassoux 1975: 95). This gives rise to an 'improved' form of primitive accumulation in which temporary and rotating labour migration simultaneously preserves and exploits the domestic subsistence economy. The entire community bears the costs for the exploitation of an individual worker as long as she/he still belongs to it (Meillassoux 1975: 109 – 111). It reproduces, nourishes, houses, trains and habituates workers without extra cost to the receiving state (Cohen 1987). This can also be achieved with a supply of workers who have remained in national boundaries. It was crucial to colonial development in west Africa, for example as Halpulaar workers migrated to the Senegalese groundnut plantations that were managed by Wolof aristocrats. It is more commonly associated with international workers by virtue of the state's ability to limit the autonomy of cross-border workers (see below). A paradox emerges in which the 'domestic' sector needs to be preserved in order to keep supplying low-cost workers, but also its destruction has enabled such exploitation to occur. Development finance institutions authoritatively promote migrants' remittances as a development opportunity (Chapter 8), but in some cases remittances merely return some of the value produced by labour, and this will pay for renewal in the community. Thus at least one member must continue to earn wages in the capitalist sphere if the community is to avoid destruction.

Migrant labour has been considered to be so important to industrial development that the 1970s recession has been linked with the high price of stabilising second-generation labour, after primitive accumulation had systematised the role of unpaid workers in capitalist economies (Meillassoux 1975). The historical geography of capitalism is shaped by the dual problem of expanded reproduction and the violence associated with accumulation by dispossession. The latter intensified in the mid-1970s to overcome the problems of overaccumulation arising in the former (Harvey 2003: 156–7). In other words, if it is particularly problematic to accumulate raw materials and labour from outside the capitalist sphere, the 'other' might be created by means of dispossession. This manifests in people's experiences of struggles against the extremes of abjection and over-exploitation, which reflect the exclusion and inclusion created by this logic.

Driving these changes, the international financial system, largely led by the US and implemented by the IMF and World Bank, galvanised the neo-liberal economic doctrine of global economic integration (Bernstein 2005: 115–16). Africa was advised to 'export its way out of poverty' by actively participating in global trade; the success of this based unrealistically on the growth of world trade, the stability of commodity prices and the absence of protectionist barriers in western powers (Cheru 2002: 13).

The balance of job opportunities in the north and available workers in the south was altered in this context. Neoliberalism represented a radical shift from the 'embedded' liberalism that favoured a commitment to full employment and social welfare. It would persistently undermine the Keynesian framework of the welfare state around the globe. Zygmunt Bauman has described the production of 'superfluous' and 'wasted' lives produced by modernisation, people whose 'labour cannot be usefully deployed' since goods can meet demand more 'swiftly, profitably and "economically" without keeping them in jobs' (2004: 39). He argued that the 'overpopulation' connected with poor countries is, in fact, a 'code name' for their populations, pointing out that Africa has 55 inhabitants per square mile compared to an average 261 people per square mile in Europe (including Russia), or 1,100 in the Netherlands (2004: 43). Furthermore, the tendency of industrialisation has been 'to replace human skill by the skill of machines', 'human labour by mechanical forces', and therefore to throw people out of work (Hobsbawm 1994: 413). However, in analysing the changes in work and labour caused by industrialisation, Hannah Arendt argued that the division of labour, rather than increased mechanisation, replaced the specialisation formerly required for all workmanship (1998: 124–5). A combination of division of labour, as described by Arendt, and mechanisation led employers in 1970s Britain to 'undercut the bargaining power of the craftsmen' through the introduction of bulk casting, largely produced by migrant labourers (Cohen 1987: 129).

As for the labourers, the previous chapter raised the importance of considering the basis of economic motivations to seek paid work overseas. Bourdieu's postcolonial study of Algeria in this light describes migrants' transformation to *homo economicus*, characterised by gaining a *métier* (profession) and demanding wage labour (2000: 18). Eric Hobsbawm, similarly, quoted Abdul Rahim, for whom discussion of cash loans in his village in 1973 led to villagers being 'increasingly calculating in their approach to money matters' (1994: 344). Capitalist transformation of land into a commodity 'gave a "voluntary" quality to the resulting migrations', in contrast to the forced population transfers of earlier times. The disintegration of autonomous modes of subsistence resulted in the emergence of labour reserves in which people were 'willing' to enter the mobile labour market (Sassen 1988: 33). To what extent was postcolonial south-to-north movement, therefore, still the product of Schumpeter's 'creative destruction' (Bauman 2004: 36), creating a living for displaced migrants and labour-power to the receiving economy, or simply destruction?

It is important to note that in the use of the term 'labour migration', the distinction between labour migrants from the south and forced migrants is uneasy. For example, the case of Haitians in the 1980s (and after) showed that, 'it is impossible to separate brutal political repression from sheer grinding poverty' in their desperate attempts to leave for the US or Canada (Cohen 1987: 31). More recently, 'economic violence' is understood as a political function of warlords aimed at 'bringing threat on human life and dignity' (Le Billon 2000: 13). 'Labour migration' is likely to become more contested as the option of asylum closes: it has been argued that in world historical terms, asylum was a short period, beginning in the 1980s and ending in the early twenty-first century (Van Hear 2007). This closure of refugee admittance inevitably results in an increase in both 'labour' and 'illegal' migration (Kyle and Koslowski 2001; Crisp 1999).

## The state and the labour market

We have explored the circumstances by which international migrants leave their communities to enter countries with higher levels of economic development. We now turn to examining the states that they enter. States play a 'central and directing role' in the 'legitimation of an involuntary labour regime through legal and ideological means, in defining the relationship between free and unfree workers' and in the policing of the frontiers (Cohen 1987:26). These borders add another dimension of cheapness to the separation of renewal from maintenance. By assigning criminal status to a segment of the working class, border enforcement reinforces the international division of labour. We will see in the case of west African migrants that it is 'illegal' not only to breach Europe's geographical borders, but that criminalisation also pervades migrants' experiences from conception of the journey through to settlement. West African workers can face detention or expulsion in Mauritania for the intention to go to Europe (Chapter 6); this also occurs in Europe when unrealistic terms of work and residence lapse. The distinct legal category for contract migrant workers affects participation rights in civil society and their ability to sell their labour-power freely. Political 'unfreedom' within the democratic process is over-determined by the state's power 'to deprive the migrant worker of permission to remain a resident of the social formation wherein labour-power is commodified' (Miles 1987: 165; Sassen 1988: 36). This leads to a disincentive for activism and what Papastergiadis has termed a 'police state' for the migrants entering on an illegal basis or for temporary periods (2000: 8; Chapter 5).

This occurs because migrants are distinguished from indigenous workers by ethnicity. We have seen that colonial transformation developed labour reserves in the global south by compelling workers to seek wages from capitalist employers. Labour reserves can also be determined by state regimes that subordinate specific communities (Lemarchand 1992: 184). The Mauritanian state has systematically excluded black citizens in the south from political participation. It thus gains a reserve of Halpulaar and Soninké workers, whom European states have also called upon to meet demand for migrant labour. The 'immigrant' is clearly defined as an outsider, sometimes meeting fierce opposition in society as well as dehumanisation sanctioned by the state. During economic crisis, struggles over employment and state resources can link to racist attacks on foreign workers. The climate of Islamophobia in Europe, post-9/11, has also stigmatised migrants and has moved migration further towards a security discourse (Bush 2007: 52–3). Various political and economic approaches to international migration have aimed to counter populist anti-immigrant rhetoric in countries of the north by proving northern dependence on cheap (illegal and exploitative) labour, particularly in North America and Europe with their 'labour reserves' in Latin America and Africa respectively (see Stalker 2000; Hayter 2000; Andreas 2001).

It is argued, however, that the relationship between states and xenophobic groups is not, in fact, an awkward one, but, instead, is essential for the persistence of unfree labour in economic development (Meillassoux 1975). The different conditions of life for migrants and citizens form a double labour market that produces two categories of workers: those who are integrated and reproduce wholly within the capitalist sphere; and migrants who only partially reproduce themselves within the capitalist sphere. Returning to the earlier discussion about the renewal of migrant labour, migrants are excluded from receiving 'indirect wages' in the form of family allowance, pensions, unemployment benefits and sickness cover; thus sending communities cover these costs. Racism, xenophobia and other ideologies of discrimination are essential to the operation of a double labour market. The discrimination serves dual purposes: firstly, to create an atmosphere of racism, propagated by the far right, which enables the over-exploitation of 'underdeveloped' peoples; and secondly, to keep migrants in a state of fear and crush demands for improved conditions. This also divides immigrants and indigenous workers, thus diminishing the scope for resistance (Meillassoux 1975: 120–2).

Meillassoux's vintage argument has intensified. Migration policies in receiving countries have 'hidden agendas', which are rhetorically against immigration but, in reality, encourage it or can do both simultaneously, talking to different audiences at one time (Castles 2003: 214; Scott 1998). The power of nationalism and racism in immigration countries makes it preferable for politicians, social movements and the media to propagate public opinion against immigration.[1] An understanding of the functions of discrimination provides a more thorough and fulfilling response to xenophobia than attempts to justify immigrants' existence because they are mostly useful. Although the discrimination dynamic may have been 'efficient' in postwar France, however, it is not so clearly the case that controls on immigrant workers 'make it easier to fix their length of stay in accordance with the needs of economy', say in Spain (Meillassoux 1975: 122).

We will see in the case of Spain that the pressures of unmanageable borders and shipwrecks at the gateway add to its limited ability to control increasingly resourceful foreigners in its labour market (Chapter 7). Furthermore, the post-9/11 'securitisation' of migrants is pursuing its own particular logic as well as serving the interests of state accumulation. However, the double, or dual, labour market is integrated in its development. Miles (1987) argues that production relations are inseparable from political and ideological relations, and specifically from the process of racialisation, where racism is a dominant ideological element. This is because the expansion of capitalism established social relations, which would be abstracted to 'race relations', and these relations would develop their role as unfree labour in commodity production (Miles 1987: 9). This illuminates the dialectical relationship between the political and the economic. State managers and capitalists promote their respective territorial and economic logics of power, but enter into interdependent partnership with each other in the regulation of migrant workers.

## Conclusion

Capitalist production balances on the value produced by unfree migrant labour. Receiving countries and the global economy mediate this movement. The preference for migrant labour over other types of cheap labour arises in the twofold benefits, firstly of sending the bill for renewal of workers to sending communities, and secondly in determining that by foregoing citizenship rights and protection by the state, workers must accept the most basic remuneration possible for their labour. The state is central both to preventing unwanted immigration and to determining that the migrants who enter are exploited more than citizens. This understanding of territorial power *vis-à-vis* the flow and circulation of capital enables a richer analysis of 'contradictory' migration regimes than a framework of 'realist' international relations or Marxism alone (Harvey 2003; Ashman and Callinicos 2006: 111–16).

Global migration figures show the continuing significance of migration from less-developed regions to those with higher levels of economic development, which is not statistically representative either of innovations in human mobility or the inequalities that have persisted. More precisely, these patterns of movement reflect displacements that are the outcome of waves of dispossession in sending communities. The problem of capitalism operating on a continually extending scale predetermines the incorporation of labour that is external to this system.

This generates complex patterns of mobility that reflect and also contest the inherent failures of predatory modes of trade and production in successive international orders. Migrants continue to be coerced away from their homes but viable destinations are few and far between, leaving people in the desert, the sea or moving between European agricultural centres in search of dwindling work opportunities. This will be considered in west Africa's economic historical context.

## Note

1 A British example emerges in the failed campaign of the Conservative Party towards the 2005 general election. 'It's time to put a limit on immigration' was scrawled across billboards and underneath: 'ARE YOU THINKING WHAT WE'RE THINKING?' The billboards' strategic location in districts where conflict emerged between workers and migrants (including Armley in Leeds) and the suggestiveness of the message exposed the campaign as an attempt at 'dog-whistle' politics. This signifies a message with a pitch that can be heard at the fringes without openly opposing the centre (see Parris 2003).

# 3 Primitive accumulation and labour mobility

## West African migration in historical perspective

This chapter explores changes in the nature of labour and the various trajectories of labourers. It considers the dynamic relationships between African producers and administrators over time, speaking to the overall question of coercive labour mobility (Austin 2009). Following this, it examines the links between colonisation and the era of international development. This provides the context for the analysis of contemporary migrations. I consider a genealogy of labour migration and the possibility of bridging the epochal divides between pre-colonial, colonial and postcolonial labour migration. An in-depth analysis of the historical 'individuals, institutions and ideas' (Kothari 2005) that influenced the development of production and labour regimes in west Africa is beyond the scope of this book but the broad periodisation that follows highlights many of the historical connections and issues of continuity and change in both the institutions of development and among the managers of large temporary or seasonal labour forces. It presents a 'radical' approach in that migration-related literature about west Africa tends to give more weight to the cultural and social elements of migration, as Deborah Potts recently summarised (2011: 42). This chapter instead argues that economic history can illuminate some of the contemporary migratory processes, taking some of its conceptualisation from labour scholarship based on southern Africa (Cross and Cliffe 2012).

Capitalist transformation in west African societies was imposed, and in many respects remains superficial: a significant part of labour migration since the start of the nineteenth century has occurred in response to coercion from one place and towards another. Accompanying more palpable methods of coercion during colonisation, land was transformed to meet the requirements of European import–export markets and local authorities, leaving an environmental, economic and political structure that confines contemporary labour movements to similar patterns. This was noted in a report from sociologists in l'Institut Fondamental d'Afrique Noire, Dakar (Fall and Cissé 2007: 11). This claimed that contemporary migration flows follow the historical contours of the circulation of products in a regional landscape that has seen little change. Pape Demba Fall, on the other hand, argues that current migratory movements no longer correspond with patterns of rural exodus and movement from landlocked regions to the coast. This is not necessarily a contradiction as the flows of migrants have historically pursued numerous channels, with some eluding the Atlantic focus (L'Hum... 2008; McDougall 2007: 19).

## Transformations in mobility caused by the Atlantic slave trade

Prior to European mercantilism, gold mines in Upper Senegal and Asante supplied the Mediterranean, European and Arab regions. A network of trade routes in west Africa (except for the densely forested coasts to the south) was linked with caravan routes across the Sahara by the fifteenth century. The network was operated by Diola traders of western Sudan (modern Mali). They were active along the river Niger, up to northern Nigeria and towards the southern part of the Sahara. Long-distance canoe trade along the river Niger depended on donkeys or human porters for carriage of stock, and therefore was centred on commodities that were high in value and small in size, including salt, gold dust, expensive textiles, small copper and brass objects, and beads. The Hausa led the development of an equivalent trading network in the eastern half of west Africa (Fage 1989: 103–5). From the eighth century, commercial expansion stimulated the growth of urban centres in the Sahel region, including Tombouctou, Gao, Koumbi Saleh and Oualata. It is estimated that Tombouctou, Gao and Djenne, all in modern Mali, had populations ranging from 15,000 to 80,000 people in the fifteenth and sixteenth centuries. Around half of the population of Hausaland lived in towns in the period before 1900 and Yoruba was also highly urbanised (Hopkins 1973: 19). Hausa and Mandinka groups established an economic presence throughout west Africa, as did the Soninké, who engaged in trans-Saharan trade including the exchange of slaves (Swindell 1995: 196; Findley *et al.* 1995: 470; Jonsson 2007: 2).

Societies in feudal Europe and in the Sahara-Sahel region of Africa developed along similar autonomous lines as a result of the long-distance trade. When European mercantile capitalism shifted the emphasis from the Mediterranean to the Atlantic, the development trajectory of the Arab world and the Sahara-Sahel region began to diverge from Europe's, and these former regions became a source of accumulation for the western European centre (Amin 1972b: 511). The significance of weakening existing trade structures, oriented inland, was that coastal states, previously peripheral, embedded themselves in European trade and preserved their power with military assistance. From the fifteenth century, the Atlantic trade strengthened the port towns of Abidjan, Saint-Louis, Dakar, Banjul and Bissau, diminishing the importance of the Sahel towns. The port towns were later connected by rail with major rivers or colonial outposts, the latter becoming the locations of new cities including Bamako, Bobo-Diolasso, Kayes, Thies, Ouagadougou, Niamey and Maradi (Findley *et al.* 1995: 471).

The transatlantic slave trade caused great turbulence and displacement as well as massive loss of population on the sea and beyond: this wave of mercantilism led to wars, anarchy and flight to safe areas (Amin 1972b: 513). In Asante, warfare to procure slaves was profitable while there was European demand for the captives in exchange for guns (McCaskie 1995: 26; see Wilks 1975). In

Senegambia, European companies in the coastal forts bought slaves from Berber, Fouta and Waalo traders. In the Waalo kingdom, French colonialists used force to cut off trans-Saharan links (L'Humanité 2008; Amin 1972a: 512). Islam was adopted as a popular resistance movement at this time in the 'War of the marabouts' from 1673 to 1676, organised by the Mauritanian Nasr al Din (L'Humanité 2008). The movement prevented the Compagnie du Sénégal, a French company with a trade monopoly, from finding more slaves, leading it to offer military support to other raiding groups. Droughts in Senegambia were aggravated by warfare, slave raiding and pillage by the emirates of Trarza and Brakna, which were also in conflict. Famine and food shortages were connected with these changes and forced Gambians to sell each other for survival (Barry 1998: 111).

Slaves became 'commodities in the world economy' as west Africa became a labour reserve for New World plantations. Almost 60 per cent of all slaves across the Atlantic were west African, and all but roughly a quarter of a million were taken during the seventeenth, eighteenth and nineteenth centuries (Fage 1989: 102). While slavery was already existent in west Africa, the 'slave' was not commodified and could be a synonym for a 'commoner', as was the case with the King of Casanga on the Casamance river, whose subjects were described as slaves (Rodney 1966: 432). The slaves of emperors in Mali and the Askia (rulers) of Gao had freedom of movement: a slave of Askia Daoud made the costly pilgrimage to Mecca and was freed upon return (Diop 1960: 115–16). Slaves in the Waalo kingdom were tenants bound to the household, owing either two thirds of the labour day or a heavy tribute payment to their master, along with half of what they produced from weaving (Searing 1988: 475–8). The development of slave labour corresponded with the Atlantic trade as slaves and peasants were sold off. Producers then became the 'main product brought to market' and a predatory economy developed, which stalled economic development in Senegambia (Barry 1998: 121). In the Gold Coast, the work of slaves transformed from mine work to agricultural labour as a result of capitalist transformation. Their role thus altered from producers of gold to one of export commodity in exchange for gold from Brazil (Kea 1982). Key differences between existing slaves and those shipped to the Americas lay in their treatment and the latter's centrality to accumulation and market expansion (Hopkins 1973). Reflective of the problems associated with accumulation in commodified unfree labour regimes, Boubacar Barry noted:

> Given the disastrous economic, political and social impact of the slave trade, Europeans were caught in a bind in their attempts to achieve two major commercial objectives. Their first objective was to buy the largest possible number of slaves. Their second was to provide regular food supplies for slave factories and slaving vessels. The first objective they achieved by multiplying wars, pillaging expeditions, and local conflicts. But the second required peaceful security in the source countries.
>
> (Barry 1998: 112)

The proclaimed ending of the slave trade from 1833 led to repatriations from the Americas or release from slave ships. By 1860, 100,000 manumitted Africans were in Freetown and their rising numbers led to their movement to other locations including the Gambia (Swindell 1995: 197). The move from slavery to colonisation has been linked with the aftermath of the American Civil War, which redirected cotton production to the north and led to a 'cotton famine'. Areas of cultivation needed to be increased, and this would be done by keeping African labourers at home rather than exporting them to the New World. This change was led by the British Cotton Growers Association. The 'cotton, Christianity and civilisation' that Livingstone claimed would rejuvenate Africa would signify the defeat of nineteenth-century slave-based conquest states (Mamdani 1996: 37–9).

## Primitive accumulation and labour mobility in the colonial era

Cotton did not, however, gain ground in west Africa. In northern Ghana, the colonial office opposed it because cocoa and palm oil were considered to be more lucrative. Furthermore, it was considered that cotton growers would be challenged in the colony by labour competition with the mines (Plange 1979: 9). This shows that the availability of labour in particular locations constituted a pillar of the colonial regime. More than an epiphenomenon of shifting patterns in production, labour reserves were integrated in colonial trade. Thus it was expected that northern Ghana could provide a 'valuable recruiting ground' to meet European demand for labourers (ibid.: 12). Compared to the establishment of labour reserves in South Africa, manipulation of migration in west Africa was less distinct as an economic policy from geographical patterns of commodity production (Riddell 1981). It should still be considered as a channelled movement that was, however, shaped by resistance and complex social forces as well as the economic rationale of forced labour.

Colonial trade signifies, at its simplest description, 'the exchange of agricultural products against imported manufactured goods', in which a peripheral society provides the agricultural commodities against products imported or produced on the spot by European industries (Amin 1972b: 521). In its fuller description, it was characterised by: the existence of a dominant trade monopoly; the taxation of peasants to force them to produce what monopolists offer to buy; political support to the strata and classes who may appropriate lands and organise migration from the regions that are left in poverty; political alliance with brotherhoods; and recourse to forced labour when these policies are ineffective (Amin 1972a: 115; Arthur 1991: 70). Imperialist policy aimed to turn individual countries into specialist producers of one particular type of raw material. From the 1830s, European merchant capital developed the export of agricultural commodities including palm produce, groundnuts, cocoa, coffee, cotton and rubber, accompanied by a lasting redistribution of populations. Commercial crop zones were established near to the coasts, exploiting the moister climate and proximity to rivers. Large numbers of seasonal workers migrated to the Gold Coast, Ivory Coast and south-west Nigeria. In the Sahel region, interior countries of

Dahomey (modern Benin), Sudan (modern Mali), Niger and Chad provided a labour reserve for colonial enterprises in Ivory Coast, Senegal and Cameroon (Crowder 1968: 337). Agricultural products could be exported on attractive terms to buyers because labour required little return.

The head tax system drove men to migrate to the colonial plantations, coastal cities and, later, mines, altering previous patterns of family migration to new lands. The change was not only geographical but also affected the fundamental nature of migration. This is because there was a shift from migrations of *people*, which leads to the setting up of organised societies, to migrations of *labour*, which take their place in an organised and structured host society (Amin 1995: 29). Residents of Matam in the Senegal River Valley were forced to sell their livestock and harvest in order to pay the taxes. In Senegal, although forced labour was less intense than in Guinea or Sudan, violent methods of mobilisation were used in a class alliance between the administration and indigenous authorities (Findley *et al.* 1995: 476). Similarly, British imposition of poll and hut taxes in Ghana, Nigeria, Sierra Leone and the Gambia pushed people away from the rural economy and towards the poles of industry and manufacturing. Therefore, in addition to the limitations on farming set by merchant capital and export-oriented crops, disincentives for the continuation of pre-colonial livelihoods were also personalised and institutionalised by the colonial authorities. The regime of indirect rule led by Lord Lugard accordingly required the colonisers to:

> endeavour to find a man of influence as chief, and to group him under as many villages or districts as possible, to teach him to delegate powers, and to take an interest in his 'Native Treasury', to support his authority, and to inculcate a sense of responsibility.
>
> (cited in Mamdani 1996: 53)

The chief would have the power to make bylaws in his locality, assess the amount of tax payable, enforce penalty if tax was not paid, and oversee prison sentences and forced labour. He would be 'the petty legislator, administrator, judge, and policeman all in one', in a system which encouraged demands of fees and fines from the peasantry, which then would be directed towards government authorities (ibid.: 54).

Migrant labour was essential in the cocoa plantations established in the Gold Coast and workers crossed the boundaries of British and French territories. The introduction of cocoa seeds at the end of the nineteenth century led to a decrease in other exports: between 1910 and 1919, while exports of copra rose by 27 per cent, from 775 to 984 tons, palm oil over the same period fell by 54 per cent, from 2,044,868 gallons to 938,595 gallons, palm kernels fell by almost a third and rubber fell by 60 per cent (Nzula *et al.* 1979: 45). The rise of cocoa from 22,631 tons to over 77,278 tons in 1915 and 133,195 tons in 1921 was aided by government customs policy in which cocoa export was duty-free. The African and Eastern Trade Corporation, which enjoyed a virtual monopoly on agricultural exports, raised the buying price of cocoa and lowered the price of other agricultural products, leading to their decline (ibid.). At the turn of the century, British concerns about the abolition of domestic slavery led the released slaves to sell their labour, constituting a second wave of migrant workers. The Gold Coast, between 1900 and the mid-1930s, amassed: 150,000 cocoa farms covering 1,400 square miles of land; the port of Takoradi; a network of carriage roads; and gold and diamond mines that provided employment for over 25,000 workers (*International Labour Review* 1936: 508). After the substantial flow of migration connected with colonial consolidation, movement remained fairly slow, except in the cocoa belt where the labour force increased until the 1960s (Amin 1974: 69).

Groundnuts constituted another migrant labour system in west Africa from the 1850s onwards. Returning to the earlier comment about marabouts' changing role in Senegal's experience of primitive accumulation, French colonialists adopted a *laissez-faire* policy towards Wolof Mourides' migrations (N'Doye 1974: 376–9). The brotherhood expanded its influence in central Senegal among peasant communities that had been expropriated by colonial military campaigns and raiding. Although Mourides had resisted the Atlantic slave trade, they had an important role in commercialising peasants' tributes after 1859, when the Waalo kingdom was defeated by the French General Louis Faidherbe (Amin 1972b: 520). Large population movements developed as a result of the French taxation system and labour policies.

Groundnut agriculture and trade developed that could support forms of autonomy and avoid assimilation. The French administration also, however, restricted Mourides' development, and the latter adopted the hierarchy and structures of colonial command:

> Murids thus first incorporated themselves into the colonial agricultural economy, and, at the same time, they preserved, in a displaced manner, Wolof values that had been renegotiated and reinvested in the authoritarian architecture of the colonial administration of management and labour.
>
> (Diouf 2000: 683)

Seasonal workers from the neighbouring French colonies of Sudan and Guinea worked on the Senegalese plantations. These workers, known as *navétanes*, were engaged in share contracts, which required them to work for two or three days on the host's farm in return for land on which to grow groundnuts. Rather than constituting a class, the *navétanes* represented a transitory stage in the life of a young unmarried man, who would engage in this monotonous seasonal work in order to return and marry. Drought in Baol and Cayor would lead workers towards the humid regions of Sine-Saloum, English Gambia and the Casamance in order to return to their village and marry, while others would remain in Dakar as wage labourers (Diop 1960: 114–15).

Although the *navétanes* were better off than city labourers, specialist skills for the latter could be obtained on worksites that were relatively well developed in Dakar, Saint-Louis and Rufisque. This salaried workforce met the demands of entrepreneurs and could supply labour to other French colonies. Illustrative of the

LEEDS UNIVERSITY LIBRARY

colonial drive to control labour mobility, this led to early measures to protect Senegal from loss of skilled labour from 1895 (Fall and Mbodj 1989: 257). By the 1870s, the volume of migrants into Senegal reached 70,000 annually, spurred by the imposition of taxes, construction of a transportation infrastructure and price manipulation (Swindell 1995: 198; Fall and Mbodj 1989: 256). Experiments in mechanising groundnut production, led by Marseilles' Companie Française de l'Afrique Occidentale (French West African Company) were undertaken at Lat-Mingué between 1921 and 1925. These attempts, aimed at beating rivals in Bordeaux, failed and led to more requisitioned labour (Fall and Mbodj 1989: 265).

Henri Labouret, sent to investigate 'native labour' by the French Colonies-Science Association, described the migrant labour situation as follows:

> Migrant workers are sure to find good lodgings in the villages, where they do odd jobs for the women folk such as fetching wood and water and pounding millets and yams. Small jobs of this kind help them to live until they reach Kumasi. On arrival in that town they go to the market-place, where a kind of unofficial labour exchange is held, and there learn from their compatriots where there is work to be had... before the depression the daily wage for unskilled workers varied from 1s. 6d. to 2s. 6d. a day [£2.85–£4.74 today].
>
> (*International Labour Review* 1936: 508)

It was observed that migrants 'have a lively sense of the value of wages', causing Ivory Coast to suffer a labour shortage as a result of higher wages in Senegal, Kumasi or Tarquah, which workers could then remit in their towns and villages. This signifies a combination of free and unfree labour, both however originating in primitive accumulation. The Secretary-General of the Upper Volta reported migrant remittances of over 15 million francs in 1930. Migrant labourers would return to their districts with large quantities of goods bought with their savings, for which they paid heavy customs duties (ibid.). Given Labouret's stated intention not to consult migrant workers but only colonial and indigenous authorities, this microeconomic insight is likely to be a generous appraisal of working conditions for migrants. This description of transit migration, informal labour exchange and remittances, however, could easily apply to migrants' trajectories today, which involve varied periods of transit and arrival at urban zones to seek work.

Senegal's colonial reputation for free labour was based on the classification of types of labour into public and private. In French west Africa, the General Decree of 25 November 1912 stated that every healthy adult male in the indigenous population should be subjected to the system of *corvée* labour, which demanded tax payment in kind in addition to cash. This payment in kind would consist of a number of days' labour in local public works, in 1926 averaging eight days a year in Senegal, ten days a year in Guinea and 12 days a year in Sudan and Mauritania. Because this was not plantation work and the labourers would work within five kilometres of their village, the colonial authorities distinguished *corvée* labour from forced labour, which was becoming unpopular in French public opinion.

The Geneva Conference in 1930 on forced and obligatory labour, however, defined this system as forced labour and the French government subsequently reduced the number of working days and stipulated that taxes were payable in cash or in kind. The distinction from forced labour made by the French government 'unilaterally drains forced labour of its essence, namely the application of an extra-economic constraint, whether administrative or political, in order to force an individual to work' (Fall and Mbodj 1989: 257–9).

From 1900 to 1928, pre-existing roads and tracks were expanded with *corvée* labour, connecting urban areas and economic zones. Over 65,000 Burkinabe labourers entered into the construction of the Dakar–Niger railroad between 1920 and 1924 by coercion, a route that continues to transport migrant labourers in the present day (Swindell 1995: 197; Fall and Cissé 2007: 8). From the beginning of the 1920s, the road network became increasingly important in the distribution of grain, and by the end of 1926 the network reached a total length of 11,155 km. Between 1928 and 1940, the roads were reinforced for trucks transporting groundnuts and to link the neighbouring French colonies of Sudan, Mauritania and Guinea. The administration also supplied labour to private enterprises, transporting workers from Sudan and Upper Volta to work in the Kaolack salt mines for La Société des Salins du Sine-Saloum (the Sine-Saloum Salt Company), and for the Compagnie des Cultures Tropicales en Afrique (the Tropical Crop Company) in Tambacounda province. The unpleasant nature of working for these enterprises led the authorities to operate a policy of 'domestication' and to transport labourers as members of the *deuxième portion militaire*, which was a military labour service (Fall and Mbodj 1989: 264). The level of coercion involved in *corvée* labour was sufficient to drive part of the Senegalese population into Mauritania and the Gambia. This included large-scale desertion by Senegalese Pulaar (ibid.: 266). There were also migrations from Ivory Coast, Upper Volta, Portuguese Guinea, from the Yoruba areas of Nigeria, and from Liberia, which resisted the colonial imposition of forced labour and conscription (Riddell 1981: 380).

As World War II ended and the strike movement in Dakar emerged, French officials began to consider reform, initially with application to the *évolué*s, or 'educated Africans', who lived in the colonial 'communes', including Rufisque (Chapter 4). Their vision was that *évolués* would adopt a modest role in legislative assemblies and that forced labour, excessive taxation of rural populations and extrajudicial punishment would gradually be abandoned; although little was planned for wage workers (Cooper 2005: 206).

In 1945, the CFA (Colonies Françaises d'Afrique, later Communauté Financière Africain) franc was established with its value fixed at approximately twice the metropolitan franc, thereby entering the French west African territories into a single unit (Mabogunje 1972: 118). The franc zone was created as 'simply an institutional reconstruction of the colonial relationship', advancing a zone of preferential relations between France and its colonies *vis-à-vis* the international economy (Coussy 1995: 160). Growth would be fostered through French public financing and the establishment of French firms and industries whose right to the free transfer of profits and capital within the zone was assured. All of the states except Mauritania retained the CFA currency, with Guinea and Mali leaving in 1960 and 1962, respectively, and then rejoining. Mauritania's disengagement is connected with its iron and copper resources and links with Arab states, allowing a 'sense of adventure', which included monetary independence (Constantin 1995: 187). The British territories followed Ghana's lead in opting out of the west African currency board, West African Airways and the West African Research Organisation. National economies, already strongly linked to those of colonial powers through investment in export crops, opted for industrialisation policies and neglected subsistence agriculture, which had already been sidelined by plantations (Findley *et al.* 1995: 473).

French colonial administrators introduced postwar changes that aimed at encouraging labour to stay within French west Africa. These included the abolition of forced labour; salary increases on plantations; and organisation of labour migrations, so that Ivory Coast became the principal receiving country (ibid.: 477). At this time, too, Ghanaian labour conditions were being debated and negotiated between employers and migrants as the latter became free labourers and gained a share of the land rents (Austin 2005: 442–3). Frederick Cooper's account of colonial history focuses on African agency and the failings of colonial power against African resistance. He argues that the vast expansion of cocoa production in the Gold Coast, Nigeria and Ivory Coast from the start of the twentieth century to the 1940s was the work of smallholders, and that this cash cropping was 'neither a colonial imposition nor an unmediated African response to price incentives': it gave rise to accumulation without creating a *bourgoisie* (1994: 1529–30). Polly Hill's study of migrant cocoa farmers in southern Ghana also rebuts the absolute agency ascribed to Europeans. She illustrates that the farmers were capitalists, accumulating capital (land) without European influence, albeit 'old-fashioned' capitalists who kept consumption to a minimum (1963: 178–81). Ghanaian producers owned land as individual operators or members of a family network, but their Senegalese counterparts, in contrast, were often landless farmers, exploited by landowning marabouts and other entrepreneurs (Davidson 1992: 212).

Challenged by these struggles and forms of resistance, colonisation altered patterns of labour and migration as a result of primitive accumulation. The transformation of land and labour for the purpose of capital accumulation forged the way for multinational corporations and agribusiness. Samir Amin highlights this connection between the colonial and present eras as follows:

> Groundnut-based agriculture is . . . imposed on Senegal by foreign capital against all economic rationality from the point of view of the country's real development. Foreign 'aid' continues to play a role in the orientation of African countries similar to that which was directly imposed on them earlier by colonial administrations (here we are concerned with the decisive role played by the state under the guise of a laissez-faire ideology).
>
> (Amin 1972b: 87)

West African land was moulded, both with 'illusory' borders and physical land conversion, in favour of external interests, from colonial authorities to global markets, irrational for west Africans' livelihoods and patterns of movement. Transnational migration in colonised African countries took different forms as white settlers moved freely between countries and could gain full citizenship, while the black population gained only partial citizenship and movement was heavily regulated to enable export production. While a lack of transport and communication also hindered inter-regional movement during the colonial era, long-developed west African trade between localities and regions continued during this period, with the stronger economies of Nigeria, Ivory Coast and Ghana drawing migrants from the region while Saharan migrations continued (Mafukidze 2006).

Alongside the changes in migration patterns brought about by the establishment of plantations, ports and mines, restrictions on mobility affected nomadic Tuareg people in the northern Sahel and created tensions with sedentary groups. Additionally, as land was confiscated for forest reserves, the amount available for cultivation and livestock diminished. Pressures on land from a growing population led to the intensification of land use and decline in soil fertility, worsened by drought (Findley *et al.* 1995: 474). Historical research shows that sub-Saharan Africa had been, for much of its history, land-abundant and short of labour and capital (Austin 2007: 15; Hopkins 1973: 15).

## Labour and migration in the postcolonial era

By the period of independence, starting with Ghana in 1957, France had nine territories in west Africa, Britain had four and Portugal one. Liberia was independent. Ghana at this time was the world's leading cocoa producer and continued to attract migrant labour, on a monthly or annual basis, from Nigeria, Togo, Sierra Leone, Benin and Upper Volta, towards the Ashanti and Brong-Ahafo areas (see Figure 3.1).

Labourers also moved towards Accra-Tema, Volta and western Ghana for industrial, construction, agricultural and domestic work. The Akosombo Dam project attracted labour in the Volta Basin; and gold and bauxite deposits at Obuasi and Konongo, in the Ashanti region, drew migrant labour from Liberia, Nigeria and Mali (Arthur 1991: 71). Rene Lemarchand notes that after the removal of European presence:

> What was left was a highly fragmented social prism through which the state entered the consciousness of Africans in different ways, reflecting in part the patterns of access and exclusion built into the newly emergent state structures, and the manner in which these came to be perceived by specific social categories or communities.
>
> (1992: 182–3)

Postcolonial African states were broadly understood to be disastrous. The 'nation-statism' that appeared as a liberation did not proceed in this way. It reflected

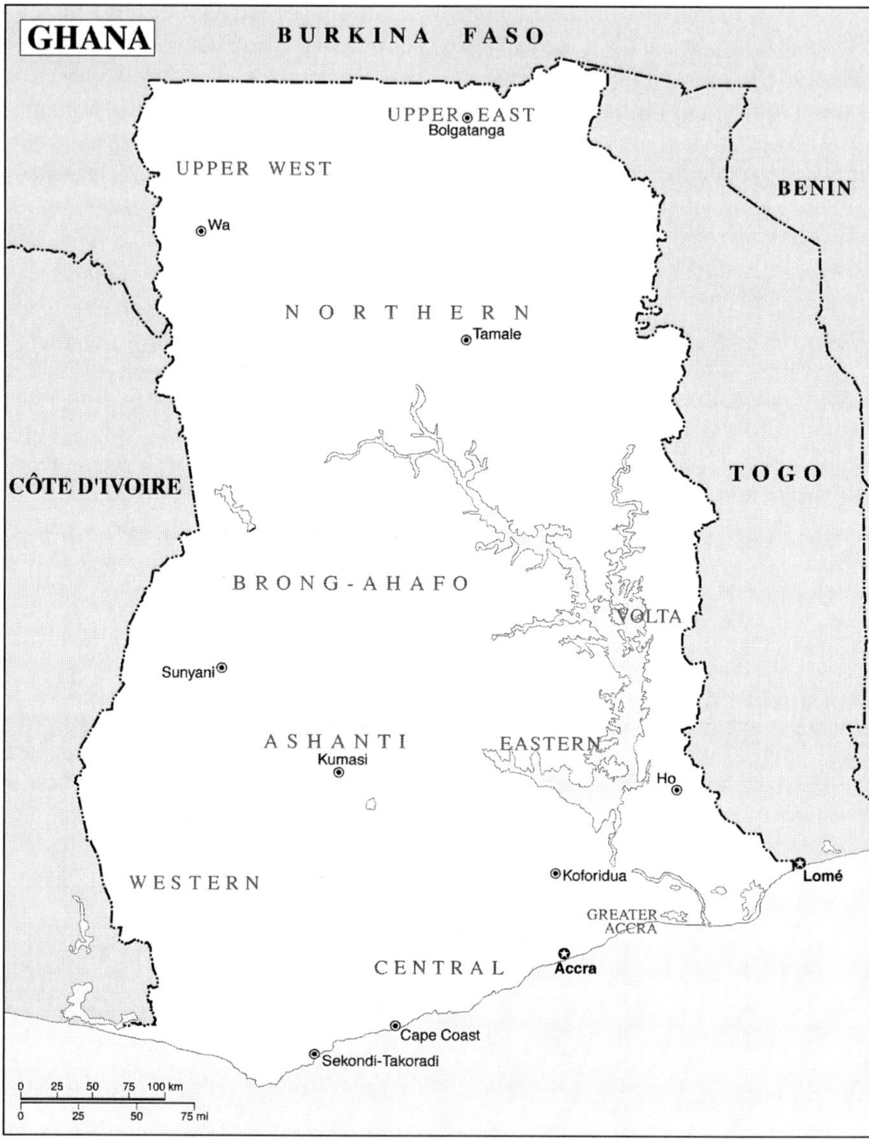


*Figure 3.1* Ghana and neighbouring countries
Illustrator: Alex van Zomerplaag

British and French models rather than the 'restoration of Africa' (Davidson 1992: 10). Chinua Achebe's literature in the case of Nigeria attributed this failure not to corruption, subservience to foreign manipulation, or 'second-class, hand-me-down capitalism' but to the 'failure of our rulers to re-establish vital inner links with the poor and dispossessed of this country' – the latter was the cause, and the former were the effects (Davidson 1992: 290). The previous section showed that as well as the sheer destruction caused by the Atlantic slave trade and colonial development, changes to structures of governance are a key factor in the continuing accumulation of resources and labour. This is reflected in migrants' histories (see Box 1.1). Development was regressive in the 1970s, which witnessed the OPEC petroleum price hikes, drought and the application of a cash-crop industrialisation model. In Ghana, plummeting cocoa prices led to labour shortage, while Ivory Coast became west Africa's leading coffee and cocoa producer. Nigeria was experiencing political turmoil and civil war, leading to a flow of Nigerian labour to Ghana (Arthur 1991: 71–2).

### *The ECOWAS Protocol*

On 28 May 1975, 16 west African states signed a treaty in Lagos, establishing the Economic Community of West African States (ECOWAS) . The treaty aimed to strengthen regional economic integration through increasingly freer movement of goods, capital and people, and to consolidate states' efforts towards peace, stability and security. In May 1979, the Protocol relating to Free Movement of Persons, Residence and Establishment stipulated the right of Community citizens to enter, reside in and establish economic activities in other members' territories. There was a three-phase approach, in which Phase I would consolidate right of entry and abolition of visas within five years; Phase II would extend residency within the next five years, including the right to gain employment, to Community citizens; and in the final five years for Phase III, Community citizens would have access to, carry out and manage economic activities (Robert 2004).

Nigeria emerged as a world petroleum producer, accompanied by two to three million migrants between 1975 and 1983. Over one million people entered from Ghana, half a million from Niger, 150,000 Chadians, 120,000 Cameroonians, 5000 Togolese and 5000 Beninoise (Swindell 1995: 198). The period of national conciliation led to daily recruitment in Accra and Kumasi for work in oil fields and construction. Migrant flows were high despite a downturn of the economy in the early 1980s. As oil prices fell from 1979 and interest rates rose, industry contracted and in turn, unemployment increased. The flow of skilled and unskilled labour induced political tension, culminating in the Nigerian expulsion of around a million Ghanaians and a million other west Africans in 1983, with two weeks' notice (Arthur 1991: 74).

Agriculture was in crisis in Senegal, when low prices received for peasants' products left them barely able to pay their debts, which had been incurred with loans for productive inputs. This issue was intensified by drought and bad harvests, with famine taking hold in the countryside. Resisting impoverishment, peasants refused to pay debts or to market crops, and boycotted the purchase of fertiliser and equipment offered under the state's agricultural programme. Basil Davidson noted a struggle between producers and the state economy that persists:

> In short, the groundnut producers upon whom the health of the nation-state economy depended turned to producing food for their own needs, or else grew groundnuts for sale on what now became known as the 'parallel economy.'
>
> Smuggling of produce within frontiers and across frontiers became an almost universal rural response to the antirural discriminations of the official and city-based economy.
>
> (Davidson 1992: 213)

Elsewhere in west Africa, conflict led to massive displacement. In 1990, the overthrow of the Doe regime in Liberia created 500,000 international refugees and a million displaced in Liberia with division into warring factions. The conflict spilled over into Sierra Leone, displacing 200,000 in the eastern region (Swindell 1995: 199). This regional decline halted progress on Phases II and III of the ECOWAS Protocol. Whether Phase I has been implemented in full is questionable, as its inclusion of visa-free entry for up to 90 days in member states has been at times jeopardised by unofficial payments at border posts. These payments are the most evident in Mauritania, which left ECOWAS in 2000, possibly in opposition to the common regional currency (BBC 1999). An ILO report claimed that there was 'poor linkage between migration and development processes, inadequate administrative and institutional capacity' for effective migration policies and management, 'lack of protection for migrant workers, poor quality of migration statistics', and 'loss of human capital through emigration of highly skilled workers' (Robert 2004: 20).

Article 4 of the Protocol permits refusal of admission under domestic laws. The domestic refusal laws that are still in place are less stringent and absolute than those of the EU, but they include Gambia's prohibition of persons without viable means of support or undesirable persons; Ghana's prohibition of destitute people or those not conducive to the public good, and Burkina Faso's law in which the health minister may prevent travellers of all nationalities and origins (Adepoju *et al.* 2007: 8–9). Residence permits are charged at differential rates, from less than US$10 in Burkina Faso and Guinea, to almost $400 in Cape Verde. Differential rates are applied in Nigeria: Togolose citizens pay 25,000 naira (£104.19), Ivorians pay 6,580 naira (£27.42) and other ECOWAS citizens pay 5,500 naira (£22.92) (ibid.: 7).

The postcolonial era in west Africa was punctuated by major expulsions rather than free movement (Table 3.2). In sum, these included, in 1982, Ghana's closure of borders with Togo and Sierra Leone's expulsion of Fula community members; in 1983, expulsions from Nigeria, Liberia and Ghana; and in 1985, a further 700,000 citizens of Ghana, Niger and other member states (ibid.: 14). In 1989, conflict between Mauritania and Senegal led to the expulsion of Mauritanian residents from Senegalese towns and then southern Mauritanians were pushed into Senegal. By July 1990, 27,000 Mauritanian Pulaar had been moved into the Senegalese district of Matam, while 20,000 Mauritanian-owned shops in Dakar were destroyed (Chapter 4). Swindell notes that this conflict could have been a revival of the historical push southwards by Arab-Berbers of

*Table 3.1* Net migration (per year) in west African countries, in thousands, 1950–2010

| | *1950–55* | *1955–60* | *1960–65* | *1965–70* | *1970–75* | *1975–80* | *1980–85* | *1985–90* | *1990–95* | *1995–2000* | *2000–05* | *2005–10* |
|---|---|---|---|---|---|---|---|---|---|---|---|---|
| Benin | –5 | –5 | –5 | –5 | –5 | –4 | –2 | –2 | 21 | –6 | 20 | 10 |
| Burkina Faso | –20 | –20 | –29 | –29 | –34 | –43 | –43 | –26 | –26 | –24 | –20 | –13 |
| Cape Verde | 0 | –1 | –1 | 0 | –5 | –3 | –3 | –3 | –2 | –2 | –3 | –3 |
| Gambia | 0 | 2 | 3 | 3 | 5 | 4 | 5 | 9 | 9 | 9 | 6 | 3 |
| Ghana | 30 | 28 | 0 | –72 | –33 | –113 | 41 | –6 | 8 | –10 | 2 | –10 |
| Guinea | 0 | –2 | –3 | –4 | –55 | 7 | –8 | 14 | 70 | –45 | –85 | –60 |
| Guinea–Bissau | –2 | –2 | –8 | –5 | 0 | 13 | 0 | 0 | 4 | –2 | 0 | –2 |
| Ivory Coast | 14 | 20 | 40 | 50 | 70 | 84 | 86 | 65 | 75 | 35 | –68 | –29 |
| Liberia | 0 | 2 | 2 | 2 | 2 | 2 | 0 | –74 | –105 | 105 | 12 | 50 |
| Mali | –7 | –10 | –14 | –20 | –19 | –35 | –44 | –48 | –52 | –57 | –27 | –40 |
| Mauritania | 0 | 0 | 0 | –1 | –1 | –2 | –3 | –6 | –3 | 2 | 6 | 2 |
| Niger | 1 | –5 | –2 | –2 | –3 | –4 | –19 | –18 | –1 | 5 | –6 | –6 |
| Nigeria | 1 | 1 | 0 | –9 | –8 | 171 | –134 | –18 | –19 | –19 | –34 | –60 |
| Senegal | 7 | 9 | 10 | 17 | 13 | –8 | –8 | –8 | –20 | –20 | –20 | –20 |
| Sierra Leone | 0 | 0 | 0 | 0 | 0 | 0 | 0 | 13 | –90 | –30 | 67 | 12 |
| Togo | –9 | –11 | –16 | 28 | –10 | –20 | 10 | 0 | –24 | 26 | –1 | –1 |

Source: UN DESA 2009c

the Maghreb, which had been suspended during the colonial period (1995: 200). See Table 3.1 for an indication of annual migration rates in west Africa from 1950 to 2010. More recently, at least 200,000 people fled the Ivory Coast following its election crisis in November 2010, with the majority fleeing into Liberia, and more than 250,000 Malians fled to neighbouring Sahel countries, mainly Mauritania, Niger and Burkina Faso, after its *coup d'état* in March 2012 and displacements continued as the conflict escalated (UNHCR 2012a; UN News Service 2012).

West African migrants cut across the refugee, labour and clandestine movements that characterise African migrations. However, it must be noted that the three categories of movement are increasingly conjoined in the west African context: women often choose economic migration over asylum in crisis situations, as the option of movement through a trusted network is more attractive than stepping into the unknown and hazardous refugee and asylum system (interview, UNHCR 2007a). Aderanti Adepoju (2006: 27) has argued that a large proportion of emigrants from west Africa, particularly from Senegal and Mali, are moving to new destinations with which they have no colonial, cultural or linguistic ties.

*Table 3.2* Key population movements in west Africa, 1957–1990

| *Year* | *Migration from:* | *Migration to:* | *Linked with:* |
|---|---|---|---|
| From 1957 (independence) | Nigeria, Togo, Benin, Sierra Leone, Burkina Faso | Ghana: Ashanti, Brong Ahafo | Cocoa production |
| | | Ashanti, Brong, Accra-Tema, western Ghana | Industrial, construction, agricultural and domestic work |
| | | Obuasi, Konongo (Ashanti) | Gold and Bauxite |
| | | Volta Basin | Akosombo Dam project |
| 1960s–2002 | Primarily from Mali, Burkina Faso, Niger, Guinea: est. 500,000 per year in 1960s | Ivory Coast | Coffee and cocoa production (overtaking Ghana) |
| 1970s | Nigeria | Ghana | Political turmoil and civil war |
| 1975–83 | One million from Ghana and one million from other west African states | Nigeria | Petroleum |
| 1982 | Ghana: expulsion of Togolese | Togo | Closure of borders |
| 1982 | Sierra Leone | | Expulsion of Fula community members |
| 1983–5 | Nigeria: expulsion of around one million Ghanaians and one million other west Africans; also expulsions from Liberia and Ghana | | Oil price hikes and political tension |
| 1989–90 | Mauritania/Senegal | | Expulsion of black Africans from Mauritania and of Bidan from Senegal |
| 1990 | Liberia | | Conflict (500,000 refugees) |
| 1990 | Sierra Leone | | Conflict |

Source: Adepoju *et al.* 2007; Arthur 1991; Mafukidze 2006; Swindell 1995

## Conclusion

The violent and socially divisive appropriation of slaves as a commodity heralded Europe's primitive accumulation in Africa. This was followed by coercing people in newly peripheral societies to join the colonial economy as wage labourers. The coercion lay in the underdevelopment of communities, where production was hampered by trade monopolies and subsistence had to be paid for with wages, leading dispossessed producers to enter the labour reserve. It is widely accepted that colonial labour lacked freedom of circulation. It revolved around agricultural production and development of the urban infrastructure required for Europe's global trade. There were, however, different forms of colonial labour, some of them 'free', reflecting the complexity of interactions between workers, local authorities and government regimes. During the better days of colonial labour mobility, the trajectory of a migrant would include moments of choice and opportunity as well as constraint. In Senegal, early patterns similar to 'stepwise' migration provided the choice of a few destinations and opportunities for marriage and social mobility, but this mobility was necessitated by a stringent taxation policy. Producers also, however, persistently sought alternatives against powerful attempts to disrupt development and to ensure that communities would continue to provide labour for the poles of production. An informal economy developed that could thwart attempts to integrate unfree workers in export production. Furthermore, producers were not torn from their land when Ghana successfully developed the cocoa industry after independence. Consideration of the dynamics of labour mobility in west Africa reveals the partial weakness of foreign capitalism in colonial and postcolonial societies. However, the struggles continue as subsequent waves of migration continue to be linked with capital accumulation.

# 4 Accumulation, dispossession and labour mobility

## The political economy of migration in Senegal and Mauritania

Chapter 3 showed that land and labour were commodified and privatised in west Africa during the colonial period in processes of 'primitive' accumulation. More precisely, this chapter shows that these processes continue in the modern era, focusing on the political economy of migration and labour mobility in Senegal and Mauritania. It incorporates case studies from the Dakar region, where clandestine migration erupted in the mid-2000s, and from Mauritania, where diverse migrants circulate in historical and more contemporary patterns.

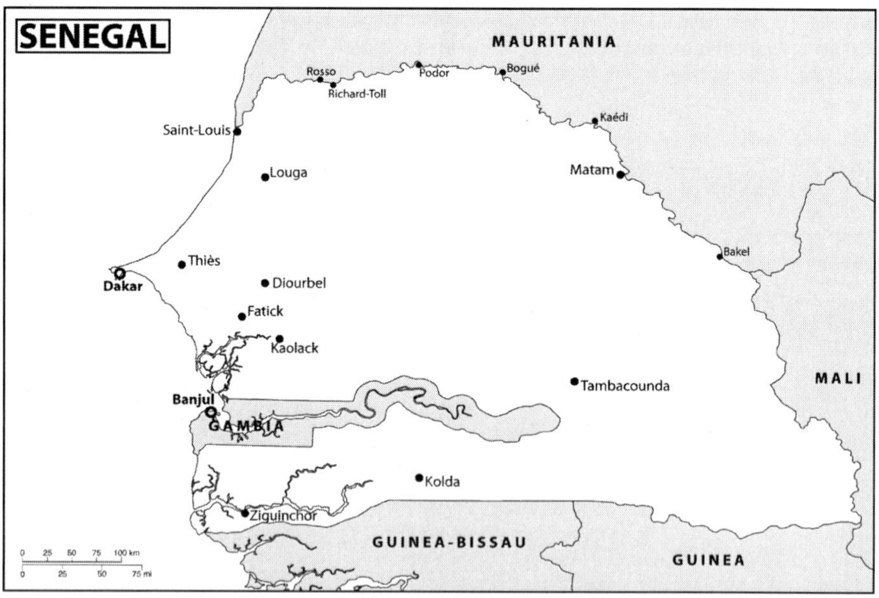


*Figure 4.1* Senegal
Illustrator: Alex van Zomerplaag

In Senegal, the colonial economy was centred on groundnuts, which led to the concentration of populations in the *bassin arachidier* (groundnut basin) and seasonal migrations to this region. This area encompasses the western areas from the north of Gambia up to Louga and eastwards beyond Kaolack (see Figure 4.1). Seasonal *navétane* labour towards groundnut production laid the foundations for temporary migration as a survival strategy. It also contributed to a strong migration culture, which generated continuous pressures to emigrate as a rite of passage that was said to offer the migrant suitable distance from the family to gain autonomy and social status (Willem 2008: 282; Mbodji 2008). Cheikh Anta Diop's description of colonial plantation workers claimed that they did not constitute a class, but 'represented a transitory stage in the life of a young unmarried man, who would engage in this monotonous seasonal work in order to return and marry' (1960: 114–5). This echoes in contemporary analyses of Senegalese migrants, in which the description of the journey as *l'aventure* (Ba and Choplin 2005) implies a rite of passage under social pressures and is still overwhelmingly dominated by young men. This economic 'disposition' originates, however, in the displacement that is part and parcel of capital accumulation. In some regions, such as the Senegal River Valley, there remains a reliance upon cross-border movement to meet subsistence needs.

Rural zones are the most vulnerable in Sahelian countries, where non-agricultural revenues have become essential to the survival of households. This reliance is well-developed along the Senegal River. While Dakar extracted foreign labour for groundnut plantations in the valley, Soninké people living in Senegal, Mali and Mauritania began labour migration to France during the 1950s (Swindell 1995: 198). All Senegalese citizens could enter with an identity card or passport, vaccination certificates and a 1,500-franc guarantee of return. From 1954 to 1969, this flow expanded fast, and then diminished in 1970/71 as a result of French government restrictions (Dussauze-Ingrand 1974: 243; Tall 2008). Total annual savings of migrants at this time were estimated to be around 480 million francs CFA/ €1.3 million, including goods and commodities, accruing to a population of slightly over 25,000 inhabitants. The remittances were targeted at taxes, food, housing and household commodities, clothing and jewellery, and cattle as safe capital (Dussauze-Ingrand 1974: 245–6). Women and children would replace the agricultural manpower, followed by wage-earning seasonal migrants from Mali in the millet fields and Halpulaar cattle herders (Dussauze-Ingrand 1974: 249). Soninké villagers constituted 85 per cent of sub-Saharan immigrations in France in 1968. By 1981, almost 55,000 emigrants from Mali, Mauritania and Senegal were in France (Findley *et al.* 1995: 477; Jonsson 2007). Long-established transnational trade networks facilitated this travel and the transfer of remittances.

Severe famine in the early 1970s accompanied repeated droughts in the Sahel zone. Governments and donors then developed agriculture by subsidising fertiliser and seed programmes. Despite increasing yields, however, the oil price crises undermined farmers' ability to export and market their produce (Bryceson 2000: 304). Rural production was aggravated by the collapse of global prices of certain speculations including groundnuts, which were the main drivers of the economy. The real income of Senegalese peasants declined when the groundnut sector stagnated, thus emphasising the role of peasant communities in supplying labour to the capitalist sector of Senegal and to Europe (de Jonge 1979: 105–6). Senegal altered at this time from a country of immigration to one of emigration. In the first half of the 1970s, it gained 13,000 migrants annually, and then after 1975, the net migration rate was a negative balance of 8,000 people per year (UN DESA 2009c).

Also in the 1970s and 1980s there was a strong increase in Senegal's urban population. The population of Dakar increased from 940,920 in 1976 to 1,488,941 in 1988 and rising, with the biggest concentrations of people in Pikine and the outskirts of the Cap Vert peninsula (Sow 1999: 147). Demographic factors have been important to patterns of migration. By the late 1970s, around half of Sahelian populations were between the ages of 15 and 59; around 20 per cent were aged 15–24 (Findley *et al.* 1995: 473–4). By 2004, 65 per cent of the Senegalese population was under 35 (DPS 2004).

From the start of the 1980s, the industrial sector was in crisis in towns and this was connected with capital flight. The labour market collapsed as public services froze recruitment in order to pay debtors under structural adjustment programmes, allowing complex networks of brotherhoods, relatives, neighbours and colleagues to flourish within the informal economy (Fall 2002: 8; Mbow and Tamba 2007). The middle classes experienced a sharp decline in standards of living as the public sector was squeezed. Migrants from Senegalese villages who sought work in Dakar began turning to the informal sector and increasingly going abroad.

As borders closed, more than 10,000 Senegalese emigrated to France with family regroupment visas over the next 20 years, or became overstayers if they were already working there. Entry visas were enforced in France in 1985 and in Italy in 1990. Southern Europe and the USA became the new destinations. Italy drew the largest numbers from rural zones of Louga and Diorbel, and from urban centres of the west and central-west, aided by the Mouride brotherhood. Traders from the Sandaga market in Dakar began seasonal migrations to the Fulton Street Market in Brooklyn, New York (Tall 2008: 43).

The devaluation of the CFA (Communauté Financière Africain) franc in 1994 led to slow growth rates attributed to the high price of petrol and the collapse of agriculture, fishing and industry sectors. Remittances gained particular significance in Senegal at this time. A process of formalisation began as modes of transfer diversified. Banks were adapted to collect emigrants' earnings with Western Union and MoneyGram acting as intermediaries. Senegalese banks including SGBS (General Society of Banks in Senegal) introduced external accounts to mobilise emigrants' savings. Informal financial transfers, via relatives or brotherhoods, continued to be significant, and included the transfer of goods such as vehicles or containers of products for sale. In 2001, more than half of emigrant transfers to Dakar escaped banks and postal circuits (Fall 2002: 17).

Around 70 per cent of the working labour force in Senegal is employed in the agricultural sector, which, along with the fishing sector, is in economic and environmental crisis. Industry has also suffered, notably Industries Chimiques du

Sénégal (Chemical Industries of Senegal), a phosphate company that has declined in connection with resource depletion (Mbow and Tamba 2007: 6). Labour reserves in the Senegalese case can be examined on similar terms to 'disappearing peasantries' (Bryceson 2000). Combining commodity and subsistence production, peasantries have emerged under European colonialism, have consolidated during decolonisation and have dissolved within global trade networks. Peasantries engage in continual negotiations over the following: firstly, access to productive resources, i.e. land, labour and capital; secondly, external extractive claims on their labour product; thirdly, terms and conditions of production, notably the level of externally provisioned social and productive service infrastructure; and fourthly, the amount of risk that production carries (Bryceson 2000: 299). They are not proletarians, as the producer retains some control over the organisation of production. The conditions of peasant production are, however, reproduced because the household must allocate a certain proportion of its labour and land resources to commodity production (Bernstein 1977: 63). Most importantly, peasantries are not homogenous so there is variation in negotiating power within the four elements of production described above.

Similarly, underdeveloped communities that did not produce commodities for export became habituated to sending migrants to work in centres of production, living on the remittances and with subsistence agriculture. Their commodity was labour, and this commodity collapsed in the neo-liberal era. It has not disappeared because labour continuously underpins production as commodities do, but it is disappearing because modernisation is accompanied by a 'thinning out' of the labour market, leaving populations 'superfluous, unnecessary, unneeded and unwanted' (Bauman 2004: 40). It is not a naive optimism that drives many Senegalese to the European 'El Dorado' but a lack of alternatives combined with the common knowledge that it is possible to earn over €600 per month in Europe, a wage that is practically unreachable in Senegal's traditional communities and has a greater capacity to preserve the household.

## Senegalese migration flows

By the last census in 2002, 44,355 international migrants were residing in Senegal, mostly from neighbouring states (Di Bartolomeo *et al.* 2010: 1). Almost a quarter of the foreign resident population in Senegal is Guinean, followed by Malians and Mauritanians. The Mauritanians in Senegal represent both traders and refugees, mostly Halpulaar, who were expelled from the south following a land dispute in 1989. Moroccans, Lebanese and French nationals comprise around 15 per cent of Senegal's immigrant population, and there is a growing number of Chinese immigrants (Willems 2008: 279). Although Senegal may feature in land journeys from the south when migrants are heading towards Europe, it does not offer the opportunities for informal labour that can be found in Mauritania and the other Maghreb countries. Most migrants, therefore, are likely cross the country in a day and then find work in Mauritania, especially if they have travelled from further afield than Guinea or Mali.

Emigration from Senegal amounted to 648,600 people living abroad in 2003/4, equalling 12 per cent of the resident population (Di Bartolomeo *et al.* 2010: 1). This meant that almost 70 per cent of households in 2001 had a member who had migrated (IOM 2009: 130). See Table 4.1 for an indication of Senegalese migrants' origins and destinations according to census data from 2002 – but note that there have been some subsequent changes in migration patterns, as this chapter will explain. The purpose of including this table is to indicate the difference in the destinations of urban and rural Senegalese migrants as well as men and women. It presents a convincing case for the disaggregation of migrations, even on the national scale.

*Table 4.1* Stock of Senegalese emigrants (who migrated in the period 1997 to 2001) by sex and previous place of residence, 2002

| | *Urban* | | *Rural* | | |
|---|---|---|---|---|---|
| *Destination* | *Male* | *Female* | *Male* | *Female* | *Total* |
| Burkina Faso | 177 | 60 | 257 | 26 | 520 |
| Cameroon | 450 | 44 | 1,480 | 34 | 1,940 |
| Canada | 296 | 197 | 70 | 12 | 575 |
| Congo | 835 | 66 | 2,558 | 102 | 3,561 |
| France | 11,578 | 6,030 | 9,593 | 1,384 | 28,585 |
| Gabon | 2,016 | 251 | 5,525 | 190 | 7,982 |
| Gambia | 3,303 | 1,239 | 12,605 | 5,278 | 22,425 |
| Germany | 687 | 196 | 245 | 33 | 1,161 |
| Guinea-Bissau | 600 | 287 | 1,147 | 491 | 2,525 |
| Guinea | 948 | 554 | 920 | 562 | 2,984 |
| Italy | 16,028 | 2,051 | 15,244 | 418 | 33,741 |
| Ivory Coast | 2,911 | 533 | 7,033 | 464 | 10,941 |
| Libya | 164 | 14 | 451 | 13 | 642 |
| Mali | 1,281 | 386 | 1,959 | 261 | 3,887 |
| Mauritania | 4,047 | 1,822 | 5,687 | 2,228 | 13,964 |
| Morocco | 451 | 214 | 451 | 31 | 1,147 |
| Portugal | 556 | 112 | 328 | 18 | 1,014 |
| Spain | 4,916 | 848 | 6,578 | 385 | 12,727 |
| Switzerland | 438 | 160 | 98 | 18 | 714 |
| USA | 5,570 | 2,344 | 2,759 | 214 | 10,887 |
| Total | 61,932 | 18,800 | 79,560 | 12,680 | 177,338 |

Source: CARIM 2010

A general pattern can be seen in which African countries have greater numbers of migrants from rural areas of Senegal, while urban migrants compose most of the Senegalese population outside of Africa. A closer look, however, shows that in France, just over 60 per cent of Senegalese workers were from the urban setting; in Italy around 53 per cent; and in Spain there were more workers from the rural setting by just under 5 per cent. In the US, however, over 70 per cent of migrants were from urban areas. Migrants to the USA, usually mourides, are concentrated in Dakar and Thiès, the hometown of former President Wade. Over half of the emigrants from Dakar, Diourbel, Louga and Tambacounda are in Europe. The majority of Senegalese migrants in Italy are Wolof. Soninké and Halpulaar groups have led emigration to France and Italy (Fall 2008: 199). Geographical proximity is also significant in regional migration. Migrants from Saint-Louis in the north are mainly concentrated in neighbouring Mauritania. In the southern Casamance region, close to Guinea-Bissau, emigrants from Ziguinchor and Kolda mainly stay within Africa. Lebu in Dakar and Rufisque are more recently the principal migrants to Spain, often gaining free passage through ownership of *pirogues* or work in the fishing industry. The coast of Casamance is also a significant departure point. Therefore the origins of Senegalese migrants abroad are based on a range of factors that include ease of travel to the destination (by proximity or access to transport), colonial links with particular regions, established trade networks and labour markets in the destination.

Like other west African states, Senegal has experienced an altered geography of migration that outdates the known origins and destinations. Table 4.1 does not capture seasonal migrations but includes census data from migrants who have been abroad for more than a year. Thus Ghana and Nigeria are excluded, listed with 74 and 285 Senegalese migrants, respectively, although numbers of seasonal migrants will be higher than this. It is reckoned, in contrast with these figures, that around 40 per cent of emigrants are women, strongly represented in commerce with neighbouring states such as Mauritania and Mali. The range of destinations is likely to broaden as labour migration becomes less certain in host countries (Fall 2002: 5). Principal destinations remain within Africa compared with Europe, but only by a slim margin of a few per cent (Daffé 2008: 110; de Haas 2008b). Migration in west and central Africa continues to be unstable. While migration within west Africa is significant, there is less opportunity for labour migrants than there had been in Ghana, Nigeria and Ivory Coast in the 1960s and 1970s. Ivory Coast had the largest stock of migrants in sub-Saharan Africa, still with over two million people in 2005, yet collapse of the state in 2002 led to a large exodus and there were further displacements in 2010 (IOM 2008: 407). Additionally, the reduced availability of legal routes to Europe has led migrants to the Atlantic coast instead, departing from the peninsulas of Nouadhibou, Dakar and Bissau. Migrants are displaced from their livelihoods and in many cases have nowhere to go (Bauman 2004). Illustrating this instability, in February 2009, Senegalese migrants were included in a group in Burkina Faso that had been expelled from Equatorial Guinea via Benin (IRIN 2009).

## Dispossession in Thiaroye-sur-Mer and Rufisque

The Lebu fishing communities in Thiaroye-sur-Mer and the Diokoul district of Rufisque are roughly nine kilometres apart on the Route Nationale 1 (see Figure 4.2). Their proximity to the capital lends the youth Dakaroise levels of education,

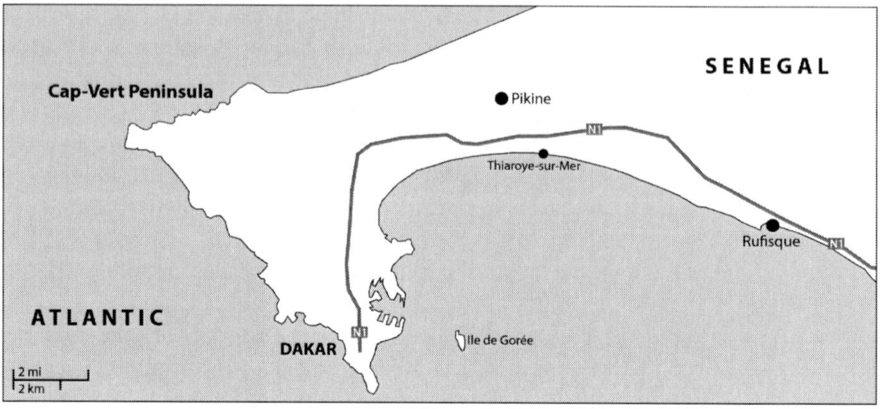


*Figure 4.2* Thiaroye-sur-Mer and Rufisque
Illustrator: Alex van Zomerplaag

training and aspiration. Moreover, Rufisque, located outside the Cap Vert peninsula, is one of the four original 'communes' of French west Africa, along with Dakar, Ile de Gorée and Saint-Louis. Therefore, *evolués* here were politically incorporated in Senegal's independence. It is now considered to be a suburb of Dakar, although the small number of cars and the use of horses and carriages in the narrow streets of the Diokoul district contrasts sharply with the capital. Thiaroye-sur-Mer is located on the outskirts of Dakar in an area of heavy industry and high population density. According to Samir Amin's (1972a/b) categorisation, this part of Senegal would be one of wealth and in-migration from the famished inland areas, yet, on the contrary, it is known for the '*pirogue* phenomenon' wherein successful journeys from here to the Canary Islands at the start of the 2000s led to further attempts to navigate the Atlantic on a larger and sometimes disastrous scale. In March 2006, 162 youths were lost at sea in two *pirogues* (small wooden boats) leaving from the beach (Bouilly 2008a). These and other losses did not in themselves internationalise the issue in Thiaroye; it was, instead, the mobilisation by bereaved mothers and relatives into the Collective of Women for the Fight against Clandestine Emigration (Chapter 8).

This recent wave of accumulation finds young adults barely able to maintain the houses that their parents and grandparents constructed. According to Boubacar (interview no. 40, Thiaroye-sur-Mer, 3 June 2008), emigration from Thiaroye-sur-Mer was uncommon before the latter part of the twentieth century. During the fieldwork period in 2008, the primary cited reason for clandestine emigration was that fishing is in crisis, intersecting with Harvey's criteria for accumulation by dispossession by way of the suppression of domestic modes of production and consumption and imperial processes of appropriating assets, including natural resources (Harvey 2003: 145). This crisis is the outcome of fishing agreements that have been signed between the Senegalese state and European companies, affecting 15 per cent of the active population in Senegal (Sall and Morand 2008: 34). There was an increase in the number of foreign ships from Europe and east Asia that keep their fleets in the Senegalese waters, undermining artisanal fishing (Mbow and Tamba 2007: 5–6). According to local fishermen, the ensuing loss of access to pelagic resources is exacerbated by the expensiveness of materials and fuel for ever-longer fishing expeditions.

This combines with the lowered selling price of fish. A heap of it gains less than 15 pence, and it is the contradiction between these earnings and price hikes in purchased food that resonate with the colonial economy (Amin 1972a). Prices of food and oil increased steeply following the devaluation of the franc CFA in 1994, at which point remittances from Europe gained particular importance in many Senegalese communities. Food prices increased sharply again before the global economic downturn towards the end of 2008. In the year leading up to July 2008, the purchase price of rice in Dakar increased by 113 per cent of the average 2002–07 price (Cohen and Garrett 2009: 13). A food crisis of this scale is not attributable to poor weather, low grain reserves, high oil prices and increased global consumption, but instead these fluctuations expose a precarious food system, constructed on corporate power (Bush 2010: 120–1). This unbalanced system might be exacerbated by a further currency devaluation if France looks south for higher profits to alleviate the Eurozone crisis (Thiaw 2012). Intersecting with another of Harvey's (2003) criteria, a returned migrant argued:

> The issue is the financial system. You go to the bank for a loan, but for the guarantee they ask to mortgage your possessions, your house . . . when you're abroad, you will be able to save while in Senegal, you'll save nothing.
>
> (interview no. 61, Rufisque, 24 June 2008)

These forms of modern economic dispossession are created because capital accumulation persists in its primitive form, continuing with the 'historical process of divorcing the producer from the means of production' (Marx 1867/1970: 715). Box 1.1 showed that community members among other migrants connected emigration to a lack of productive means, which people have sometimes abandoned or sold in order to migrate. Box 4.1, similarly, shows that in addition to finding safer ways to migrate, access to the means of production would prevent clandestine emigration.

Labourers continue to be separated from the means by which they can realise their labour, and this continues on an expanding scale (Fine and Saad-Filho 2004: 75). The separation is reproduced and expansive because it ultimately incorporates people into the capitalist economy, whereas its growth depends on the accumulation of raw materials and labour from beyond its own boundaries. Where this is not possible, owners of capital instead find ways to create the 'other' by means of dispossession. This was evident when, at the start of the 1980s, land organised around family networks was commodified and the Lebu progressively lost their land. The rise in land value is a result both of changes in customary law and the buying power of returning migrants,

**Box 4.1** What should be done to prevent clandestine emigration?

Young people should have the materials and the means to do their trade .
(interview no. 41, Thiaroye-sur-Mer, 6 June 2008)

We need to encourage the creation of enterprises and massively promote youth recruitment.
(interview no. 48, Rufisque, 18 June 2008)

We need to help workers in their domain. For example, for the fishermen we could find them the means to sell their products outside this district .
(interview no. 49, Rufisque, 18 June 2008)

I have sought contracts from the state for emigration to Spain.
(interview no. 50, Rufisque, 18 June 2008)

All I suggest is to help young people in their domain of development and if not, they will continue to take boats to Spain.
(interview no. 51, Rufisque, 18 June 2008)

The GOANA [Great Agricultural Offensive for Food Security] project conceived by President Wade is a good strategy for reducing the rate of unemployment because the agricultural sector will constitute the first stage of a process of development.
(interview no. 56, Rufisque, 24 June 2008)

What's difficult here is that we work to the death. Sometimes, I joke with my friends about GOANA and tell them that they must reclaim the land if they want to cultivate the land. And they joke that Wade should get his son to cultivate his land!
(interview no. 59, Rufisque, 24 June 2008)

Just offer work to the youth. To do this, there must be appropriate tools and materials for people in the fishing sector and the same for other sectors because if they have good work here, they won't try clandestine emigration.
(interview no. 64, Rufisque, 2 July 2008)

Just do campaigns to inform people of a good route because emigration is a necessary evil. We held a press conference covered by Radio Dioko FM and have called on a journalist from a bigger radio station who lives in our district. We have even applied to our mayor for visas for 2,000 young people, knowing that we can't have that many beneficiaries. We descended on the street but it hasn't worked.
(interview no. 66, Rufisque, 2 July 2008)

The mayor who lives in our district promised finance to help young people and a meeting was held with a view to creating a cybercafé. Sometime after, they organised demonstrations and raised 500,000 francs CFA (€762.25), but unfortunately it didn't come off. It was political issue, giving money here and there, organising meetings. The objective had been to support youth in all sectors – fishing, carpentry, building, to prevent them from trying clandestine emigration.

(interview no. 75, Rufisque, 8 July 2008)

If we could have a profession we can count on, there would be no problem. But it's hard here, it's why young people try the journey, to earn a living like the other emigrants do.

(interview no. 67, Rufisque, 2 July 2008)

The youth waited for the government to realise many projects in their favour. But it's not the case and all the millions that were invested in our country for the fight against clandestine emigration haven't reached their destinations, it's why they take the pirogues and risk their lives to reach Spain.

(interview no. 75, Rufisque, 8 July 2008)

I think we should do what Yayi Bayam* does. If there was in every locality three or four women who did this, we wouldn't hear more talk about clandestine emigration.

(interview no. 44, Thiaroye-sur-Mer, 6 June 2008)

We organised a lutte [wrestling match] to raise awareness so they forget the illegal voyage.

(interview no. 46, Thiaroye-sur-Mer, 7 June 2008)

* Founder of the Collective of Women for the Fight Against Clandestine Emigration (Chapter 8).

which leads to a 'negotiated expulsion' of the poorest to areas away from the centre (Tall 2008: 52–7). To view returned migrants as the new accumulators, however, would obscure the dispossession and unfree labour that precedes, and importantly succeeds, this role as migrants crossing the Atlantic and the Sahara recount their experiences of selling up what their parents have gained. Ame attempted clandestine emigration five times, and explained, 'I do everything and I haven't managed to save. Even the bedroom I stay in with my family was constructed by my father' (interview no. 49, Rufisque, 18 June 2008). Amadou explained:

> Since our father is retired, every member of the family should contribute at the end of the month... Thirty years ago, they practised agriculture but the position has quite changed now. There is no estate here, because people are building all around and there are no fields here. We have no houses. Apart from fishing, there are no other activities.
>
> (interview no. 74, Rufisque, 2 July 2008)

In Diokoul, young people have turned to carpentry, welding and building. The daily wage for a carpenter is 1,500–2,000 francs CFA (€2.29–€3.05), and there were frequent claims that wages are not paid. Furthermore, work was rarely available, reflecting the disruption of local industry. Over 40 per cent of Senegalese of working age are unemployed and this figure reached 80 per cent in Thiaroye-sur-Mer by the peak of its wave of emigration (Bouilly 2008; Chauzy 2006). In addition, the population is young: the average age is 21.8 for men and 22.6 for women (DPS 2004). The migration is economically driven, but not based simply on the 'pull factors' of Europe. On the contrary, migrants did not consider staying where they were to be an option:

> Here, if youth leave clandestinely for Spain it's because there's no work here and people who lead us don't take responsibility, otherwise young people wouldn't try *l'aventure*. No *clandestin* wishes to leave in these conditions. But the situation obliges it, to take a wife, to start a family and to meet the need of our relatives... nothing is more beautiful than leaving the house in the morning and going to work.
>
> (interview no. 62, Rufisque, 24 June 2008)

> The individual can only bloom in his country of origin. And if we travel to Europe it's because we don't have a choice, because emigrating is not an easy thing... we are obliged to leave in order to have a good future.
>
> (interview no. 63, Rufisque, 24 June 2008)

Pape, when asked if his brother contributed to the household before leaving for Spain clandestinely, jokes about his country: 'yes, but *Sénégalaisement quoi*, it didn't always work' (interview no. 59, Rufisque, 24 June 2008). Although urban dwellers can usually manage and are trained in professions, their source of income is unreliable. Mamadou claimed: 'If you stay here for a few hours you'll see the house filled up like a national [football] team. We spend the whole day here drinking tea' (interview no. 68, Rufisque, 2 July 2008).

An emigrant working in a meat factory in Spain earns €800 per month, at least ten times the wage of a carpenter or builder in Rufisque. Youssou, a stayer, explained that 'this journey that the *clandestins* do is truly important, because if they send, for example, 100,000 francs [€152.50], that can help their mothers to repair the house, whereas here you can work for 40 years without being able to do this' (interview no. 55, Rufisque, 20 June 2008).

## Leaving Senegal

A decline in the fishing industry led fishermen to engage in the more profitable enterprise of trafficking. The captains often attempted to enter Europe clandestinely with the passengers. One fisherman in Mauritania explained that he was considering bringing people to the Canary Islands and seeking work in Europe, but he regretted that visas were inaccessible and that this risky route should be taken (interview no. 11, Nouakchott, 7 May 2007). A local imam explained:

> Diokoul is a traditional Lebu district and it's because of this that many young people have had the ability to get to Spain by *pirogue*. People often advise against this but here there is no work activity that can retain them.
>
> (interview no. 75, Rufisque, 8 July 2008)

In this case, the journey is on the migrants' doorstep. Skills, political clout or well-placed associates can lead people who are economically poor out of the continent, who might stay if there were sufficient local and regional options. Poverty and unemployment are therefore significant factors in this case and cause married men to leave their wives and children behind at great risk as well as the more predictable younger men. Poverty as a driver is distinct from *l'aventure*: rather than a rite of passage, it introduces an element of compulsion, returning to the problem of how to classify the migrants. Migrants in Rufisque frequently paid nothing for the journey if they were clandestine, and therefore required no financial means to emigrate. 'I didn't pay because I'm a fisherman,' explained Laye, who was repatriated upon arrival in Tenerife (interview no. 50, Rufisque, 18 June 2008). This phenomenon also disconnects from cultural explanations for mobility. A fisherman who was recruited in Saint-Louis obtained a free journey to Spain because his employer owed him money. He did not inform his parents until he had arrived (interview no. 62, Rufisque, 24 June 2008). Mrs Cissé was also not informed by her son of his clandestine journey: he explained that he was going to Tambacounda (in the east of Senegal), and then called her after some days to tell her that he was in Spain (interview no. 70, Rufisque, 2 July 2008). Parents were against departures by *pirogue* in Rusfique, and migrants were thereby clandestine from the outset despite migrating on behalf of the household. This secrecy is similar to other stepwise migrations, and predates the Thiaroye-sur-Mer drownings in 2006. Alioune described a friend who was amongst the first to leave clandestinely, before the repatriation agreements, and now he was sending money from Spain:

> He's very reserved, he didn't tell anyone his business, and no one could imagine that he'd try clandestine emigration, he didn't seem the type. You could stay a week in the house without seeing him because of his hours of entry and exit, and he tried clandestine emigration twice.
>
> (interview no. 66, Rufisque, 2 July 2008)

Secret departures led to fears in the district of others leaving without warning, and it was expected that most young people would take the opportunity if it came. Youssou explained: 'At times [mother] has phoned me at the building site to see if I have left or not' (interview no. 55, Rufisque, 20 June 2008). On the contrary, collective decisions dominated in Thiaroye-sur-Mer, where labour migration at its peak was imposed by families as a response to the economic crisis, and was largely led by mothers (Bouilly 2008a: 18). A fisherman from Thiaroye-sur-Mer, who was repatriated, claimed that his parents encouraged him to cross the Atlantic: 'They were convinced that it's easy to find work in European countries' (interview no. 28, Thiaroye-sur-Mer, 8 April 2008). A combination of early successful crossings from Thiaroye's beach and greater severity of poverty than in Rufisque probably accounts for the broader acceptance of sea crossings.

## Underdevelopment and migration in Mauritania

Although unmissable on a map of Africa, for its size of over a million square kilometres, Mauritania is considered to be a small country that has approximately three million inhabitants. Most of the land lies within the Sahara desert, moving southwards into the Sahel region. At least 7 per cent of the population are immigrants (Bensaâd 2008: 2). Its migrant populations are in flux, combining west (and sometimes central) Africans who are 'in transit' or turned back from Europe, with more established regional migrations and refugee movements (see Figure 4.3). In line with this book, the focus is on migrants who have travelled from sub-Saharan Africa.

'Free labour', as discussed in Chapter 1, signified freedom both from slavery and from ownership of the means of production. It also means freedom to enter the labour market, to sell labour power. The 'freeing' of labour, historically, is associated with coercive separation from the means of subsistence and with a degree of compulsion in entry to the labour market (Marx 1867/1970; Fine and Saad-Filho 2004). To further the discussion, this section will consider, briefly, the transition that 'freed' Mauritania's labour. This is to keep in mind the development of the political economy that continues to provide 'hopping' points for migrant labour.

Prior to colonial conquest, Mauritania was organised into emirates. It was most densely populated in the sub-Saharan region to the north of the Senegal River, where Tukolor and Fulani (both Pulaar-speaking, or Halpulaar'en), Soninké and Wolof groups constituted sedentary village communities. They would pay tribute to chieftains representing the emirs. In the Sahara region, pastoral nomadic production was organised through family ownership of herds and collective access to land, with pooled labour in activities such as sheep-shearing. The Bidan tribes, speaking Hassaniya Arabic, were hierarchically divided among those of Arab and Berber descent, black haratin (freedmen), and domestic slaves (Bennoune 1978; Seddon 2000; Bonté 1981). Bidan tribes are, historically, dominant in society and continue to hold the most political and economic power (Seddon 1996: 198). Power struggles between the ruling classes continue to characterise government politics.

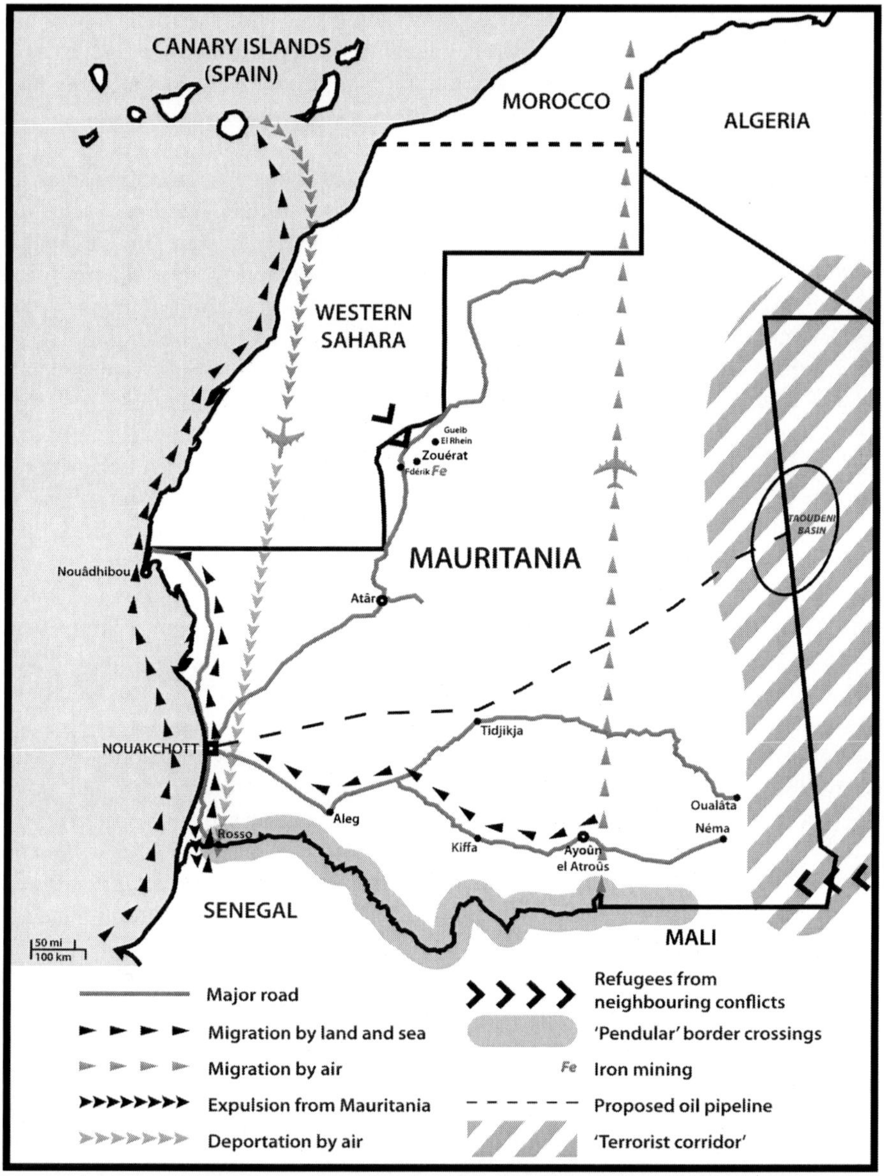


*Figure 4.3* Migrations, the 'terrorist frontier' and natural resources in Mauritania, 2008
Illustrator: Alex van Zomerplaag. Previously printed in Cross (2011)

As a protectorate in French west Africa from 1903, Mauritania had its colonial capital in Saint-Louis, Senegal. Mauritania's experience of primitive accumulation at the start of the twentieth century included a French-led programme of murder, rape, blackmail and bribery against resistant emirs in Adrar (Bennoune 1978: 35).

The French administration proscribed slavery and some slaves, particularly of the sub-Saharan populations, were able to escape into Senegal. However, both haratin and slaves remained in the Sahara and although the former could supposedly buy their freedom, the majority of haratin stayed with their masters.

Sub-Saharans living in southern Mauritania had to pay a head tax on every person over the age of 10 and joined the reserve of labour on groundnut plantations. Saharan groups had to contribute a proportion of their herds and crops to the colonial administration. Colonial administrators would impose 'native henchmen' at the apex of the existing hierarchy and accountability shifted from local councils to distant administrators, exacerbating divisions in the traditional order (Bennoune 1978: 35–8; Seddon 2000: 209). Ethnic cleavages were co-opted in Mauritania's development and provided a source of low-cost labour, which would, in turn, extend to the intercontinental labour regime (Baduel 1994: 14; Jourde 2007: 80–1; Bonté and Guillaume 1994: 4).

A lack of productive activity, which can be connected with Mauritania's strategic role as a 'vacuum' territory connecting French northern and western African colonies, limited the establishment of political movements preceding independence in 1960 (Bennoune 1978: 36). First President Moktar Ould Daddah, who held office until a military coup in 1978, appointed French Ministers of Finance and Economic Planning. The post-independence capital, Nouakchott, was constructed *ex nihilo* from 1957. Nouakchott's population expanded rapidly from under 6,000 inhabitants in 1961/2, to almost 400,000 by 1988 (Office Nationale de la Statistique 1995). The socio-economic landscape altered considerably after the severe droughts from 1969 to 1974, which accelerated urbanisation. Nomads, constituting three quarters of the population in 1960, today represent only between 3 and 5 per cent (Bensaâd 2008: 1). There was a massive transfer of cattle from traditional herders to traders in the towns. A network of *boutiquiers* was established, mediating between local producers and capitalist enterprises (Bensaâd 2008: 3). By 1970, around 23,000 Mauritanian traders were in Senegal (USAID 1980: 15).

The imposition of colonial taxes in cash and the opening of the market to French manufactured products had launched the population into the international economy. Having been recruited in the French army during World War II, Soninké labourers – in a region that straddles Mauritania, Mali and Senegal – could subsequently visit France and work, chiefly in automobile factories, before returning home (Dussauze-Ingrand 1974: 243). However, the Saharan population was primarily engaged in agriculture and herding up to the time of independence, with wage labour of secondary importance. Substantial mining activity, which began after independence, changed this. A railway from Zouérat to Nouadhibou was constructed to support a two-kilometre-long train, which would carry iron ore to the coast for shipment to Europe and the United States. Production grew almost tenfold between 1963 and 1973, exceeding 10.4 million tonnes of iron ore and surpassing agricultural production in national accounts (Bennoune 1978: 42). The combination of drought and heavy state taxes produced a labour reserve for the mines. Workers received 'starvation wages' and were heavily repressed, particularly in 1968, when deaths and injury by arms were the outcome of workers' strikes (Bonté 1975: 105; Bennoune 1978: 46). Production was managed at this time by the multinational Society of Iron Ore Mines in Mauritania (MIFERMA) with the backing of the French state. The Mauritanian government received 5 per cent of the profits (Bonté 1975: 94). Mining was nationalised in 1974, soon after the currency exited the franc zone to become ouguiya (UM), developed in Morocco. Mauritania's nationalisation aligned it more closely with Arab countries. The National Society of Mauritanian Industry (SNIM), which replaced MIFERMA, opened its shareholding to international investors in 1979. Ten years later, the Mauritanian government retained over 70 per cent of the share, followed by Kuwait's Foreign Trading, Contracting, and Investment Company (9.6 per cent), the Arab Mining Company (7.6 per cent), the Iraq Fund for External Development (6.2 per cent), the Bureau de Recherches et de Participations Minières of Morocco (3.1 per cent), the Islamic Development Bank (2.4 per cent) and Mauritanian private shareholders (0.2 per cent) (Ould-Mey 2006a: 170).

As well as incorporating black citizens from the south in production, Mauritania also attracted cross-border migrants. At the time of independence, Senegalese, Malian, Guinean and Beninese migrants filled labour shortages. By 1970, the population in Nouadhibou comprised 11,500 Mauritanians, 3,000 sub-Saharan Africans, 1,800 French and 1,000 Spanish immigrants, mainly from the Canary Islands (Choplin 2008: 75). Senegalese migrants entered the fishing zone, followed by Ghanaians from 1980 onwards. The latter began to salt and dry fish for export to the Gulf of Guinea.

During the 1980s and 1990s, the IMF and the World Bank guided macroeconomic reform that focused on liberalisation of trade and currency exchange before shifting the emphasis to privatisation after 2000. The Mauritanian currency was devalued with a 531 per cent depreciation of the ouguiya (UM) per US dollar between 1980 and 2002. Despite a global increase in iron ore demand in the 1990s and sustained fish production, export of goods and services declined from $253 million to $183 million between 1980 and 2000. In the same years, external debt increased from $843 million to $1,207 million (Ould-Mey 2006b: 349). The decline of subsistence production led to considerable economic dependence on external markets. Imports of goods and services represented more than 40 per cent of GNP by 1984 (Tandia 1994: 66). Ouguiya needed to be converted into dollars or other hard currencies to pay for imports.

In 1983, the traditional system of land management was abolished under structural adjustment programmes. Land was distributed according to clientelistic relations. Peri-urban settlements accelerated and financial speculation governed land transfer. A clandestine market grew and prices reached more than ten times the official price. Land reform also affected the Halpulaar, Wolof and Soninké groups along the Senegal River. Abolishment of the system of collective land ownership led to dispossession by ruling factions. The land was passed over to haratin for cultivation (Crousse and Hesseling 1994: 89–90; Koita 1994). The land disputes that continue today precipitated conflict between Mauritania and

Senegal, and within Mauritania between the Bidan and black citizens, including the haratin. Mauritanian herders would cross into Senegal and Mali annually to obtain water and pasture during the dry season, leading to a dispute over grazing rights as land was privatised (IRIN 2006).

From April to May 1989, and in the months that followed, villages in the Trarza-Est region were cleared out by the Mauritanian army. Residents, mainly Halpulaar and Wolof, were expelled to Senegal and Mali. In February 1989, almost half of the fishermen in Nouadhibou and Nouakchott were Senegalese. By August, Senegalese migrants did not appear in the registers and were replaced by Mauritanians, Nigerians and Ghanaians (Choplin 2008: 76). By 1991, 500 black officers in the armed forces were executed in response to a fake coup and hundreds of civilians were killed. Senegal also expelled Mauritanians, mainly traders, as a result of the same conflict (Koita 1994; Jourde 2007: 80; Charmes 1994: 77). The United Nations High Commissioner for Refugees (UNHCR) led the return of Mauritanians who had been expelled in the crisis. Sixteen years later, in August 2007, it began to repatriate 24,000 refugees from Senegal and the Kayes region of Mali (UNHCR 2007b; Pambazuka News 2009).

Neo-liberal reform impacted on the monetary economy and unemployment, previously irrelevant, reached 46.1 per cent by 1992 for urban 20–24-year-olds, giving rise to a strong informal sector (Charmes 1994:76). Price increases of foodstuffs between 1987 and 1997 reached an index of 231 per cent without proportionate salary and wage rises. Water, electricity and telecommunications were an exception to the liberalisation of domestic prices, as was petroleum until 2000 (Ould-Mey 2006b: 351). From 2006, the discovery of oil placed Mauritania more firmly on migrants' itineraries as well as the geostrategic map of the US. Approximately 48,000 workers, mainly from Mali, Senegal and Guinea, migrated to Mauritania in response to oil-led growth (Fargues 2009: 5).

Projections of cumulative oil wealth in nominal terms ranged between US$3 billion and US$10 billion, amounting to significant rents in comparison with GDP of $2.6 billion (Auty and Pontara 2008: 60). However, oil wealth was over-anticipated and failed to deliver its promise. The Chinguetti oilfield, operated by the Malaysian company Petronas, reduced its production at the end of 2009 as a result of difficulty in accessing multiple, unconnected oil deposits. The Taoudeni Basin provides more optimism, though it would require an expensive pipeline (see Figure 4.3) to be commercially viable. Oil exploration equipment costing $493.7 million was the largest single import in 2007 (EIU 2009c: 6). Despite a surge in growth from 5.4 per cent in 2005 to 11.4 per cent in 2006, Mauritania ranked 137 out of 177 countries in the Human Development Index in 2008 and the incidence of poverty reached 46.7 per cent of the population (World Bank 2009b).

The African Development Bank approved a US$175 million loan to finance the expansion of the Guelb El Rhein iron ore mine in September 2009 (AfDB 2009b). The World Bank promoted privatisation of SNIM in a report that only mentioned junta rule in passing. Privatisation, furthermore, of the water and electricity that is supplied free to residents in the mining neighbourhood of Zouérat was endorsed, which would result in higher overall tariffs (World Bank 2008a).

Auty and Pontara recommend direction of the economy towards 'market-guided wealth creation' and the cessation of employment subsidies in order to stimulate competitive interest in rural areas (2008: 69). These analyses of the oil and mining sectors hold the regime to account for poor management of resources, although this section has highlighted the role of currency devaluation, debt, privatisation and dispossession in Mauritania's underdevelopment, mediated by the state elites.

## Migrant labour in Mauritania

Mauritania was a net sender of migrants until the mid-1990s. This is related to its trade expansion into sub-Saharan Africa; labour migration from the south towards Europe; and expulsions at the end of the 1980s. Labour migration to the Mauritanian coast and cities has been a significant factor in its development and in west African livelihoods since independence, while its role as a stepping-stone to Europe is more contemporary.

According to World Bank figures for 2007, GNI per capita in Senegal was measured at €623.53, while in Mauritania income was slightly higher at €638.73; both, however, below the average of €723.90 for sub-Saharan Africa (World Bank 2008b; 2008c). The official figures, however, do not show the opportunities for saving that Mauritania has presented. Currency exchange on Mauritania's informal market appears to work in favour of migrants. Mauritanian merchants outside the large banks in the centre of Nouakchott will buy 10,000 UM for 20,000 F CFA, although the market value is 17,941 F CFA.

The southern borders of Mauritania, marked by the Senegal River, are often crossed daily by Senegalese or Malian 'pendular' traders, commonly owning mobile phone sim cards for both countries in which they live. Currencies are easily interchangeable and taxi drivers ferry remittances and goods, serving as an important line of communication between migrants and their communities, particularly among the Halpulaar in the Senegal River Valley. These crossings generate 'border rents' for traders, who play on differences in currency, price, availability of goods, political economy and customs tariffs between the countries (Gregoire and Labazée 1993: 10). A border guard on the Mauritanian side of the Senegal River explains:

> Several people from [here, Village A] leave every morning to trade in [Village B].
> *What do they sell?*
> They sell sugar, vegetables, meat, animals for livestock... People from [Village B] often come here to buy sugar and sometimes even seek work.
> *Is the merchandise that Mauritanians take to Senegal recorded?*
> No, because the stock coming from Mauritania is already paid for. These people don't carry much merchandise, to avoid paying a lot of money.
> *How much do they pay the customs in Senegal?*
> It depends on the value of the stock. Senegalese customs don't want to import Mauritanian sugar – it's illegal.

> *So how do they take the sugar?*
> They take it in the night, you know the border is very vague, very vague. There are also people who take rice from Senegal to here; many traffickers pass in the night.
>
> (interview no. 15, village on Senegal River, 20 May 2007)

While sugar is cheaper in Mauritania than in Senegal, rice is more expensive. A Senegalese migrant from Rosso, another border town that is split between Senegal and Mauritania on either side of the Senegal River, claims that Mauritanian food prices are higher in general (interview no. 8, Nouakchott, 7 May 2007). This indicates the complex interplay between migrants and borders, yet the latter have progressively been hardened, particularly since 2005, in connection with the security narrative in the region.

Aside from the *grands commerçants* who earn a living from international trade, border crossings also present the opportunity to save and contribute to other livelihood strategies, albeit as cheap labour. The average earnings in Mauritania are between €85 and €170 per month (Ndah Mohammed-Saleh 2008: 8). Furthermore, Aicha, a Senegalese migrant, explained: 'We can save here and not in Senegal, because you can have a salary of 5,000 francs CFA (€7.62) and spend it in ten days on ceremonies or with people who ask for help' (interview no. 30, Nouakchott, 14 May 2008). John added that the cost of living is higher in Ghana than in Mauritania in terms of spending on accommodation, food and transportation, but 'when the Ghanaians arrive here, whatever they are doing it is very easy for them to save' (interview no. 36, Nouakchott, 20 May 2008).

Similarly, women from Gambia, Senegal, Mali and Mauritanian villages gather outside the church in the Tevragh-Zeina district of Nouakchott and wait to be recruited as housemaids or cleaners. Near to the recruitment area for women, men gather under trees to seek employment as taximen, mechanics or builders. The women explain that it is easier to find work and the wages are better than where they live. They have families that depend on the cash or goods sent as remittances. Nyima, from Gambia, was sending home 20,000 UM (€54.70) every three months via her ambassador, and was saving to start her own clothing business (interview no. 1, Nouakchott, 7 May 2007). Suzanne and other members of her family had been migrating from Podor, a Senegalese town along the Senegal River that has experienced severe environmental degradation. 'We go and come back…when we have the money we want, we go back'. In Senegal, 'it's not difficult to find work but the wages are very low compared to here in Mauritania' (interview no. 4, Nouakchott, 7 May 2007). These examples illustrate the gains associated with crossing borders, and particularly into Mauritania.

Ethnic tensions have improved since the end of Colonel Taya's presidency, but there remains an absence of legal rights for workers from southern Mauritania, as well as for those who have crossed the border and this leaves people vulnerable to exploitation with no legal support if wages are unpaid (Cross 2011). For workers in Nouakchott and Nouadhibou, movement between borders is thus an established, though precarious, livelihood strategy, which contributes to household income. Mauritania has greater prospects for working and sending remittances than Senegal or Mali, but since the period of fieldwork, stability for migrants has deteriorated (Chapter 6).

The asphalted 465-kilometre road from Nouakchott to Nouadhibou, completed in 2004, contributed to Mauritania's popularity as a point of departure to Europe. The violent incidents in Ceuta and Melilla in 2005 also led more migrants to Mauritania, being discouraged from entry to Morocco. It is assumed that sub-Saharan men living in Nouadhibou all have failed to meet visa conditions and intend to embark on a clandestine journey to the Canary Islands. The port, for example, was heavily guarded by armed police in the spring of 2008, which is a popular time of year for attempting the journey. A Ghanaian living in Nouakchott for five years, John, explained:

> People from Cameroon, Nigeria, Ghana, Liberia, also the poor ones you see from here, their intention is to get over to Europe. Those people, they are trying, they have made several attempts but they cannot proceed so they just stay, but if you bring three ships, you put them here now, you say Europe, right here you won't meet anybody, even those who are here for 50 years, you will not see anybody, everybody will have tried to go.
>
> (interview No. 36, Nouakchott, 20 May 2008)

The most expensive sea route to Europe from Nouadhibou departs on the large fishing boats from China, Japan, Greece, Germany, Spain, France, Portugal, Korea and other countries, which head to the Canary Islands or the Iberian peninsula. Sometimes the tickets have been pre-paid to Portuguese captains by Bissau-Guineans, costing between €2,500 and €3,000. A less secure route is by *pirogues* tied to trawlers, costing around €500 and particularly dangerous because captains have been known to throw migrants overboard if patrols are in sight (Ba and Choplin 2005: 4–5). More commonly for 'stepwise' migrants, captains of *pirogues* would often offer a free passage to coworkers, mechanics, medics, friends and recruiters, then charge up to €500 to the rest. *Pirogues* pose the same hazards as other smuggling operations. A Senegalese fish trader in Nouakchott explained, for example, that he and all other passengers had been thrown overboard by a captain who subsequently kept the payments. He was able to swim to shore, but others drowned (interview no. 10, Nouakchott, 7 May 2007). *Pirogues* carried an estimated 20,000 clandestine migrants from Nouadhibou in 2006. The Catholic Mission and the Mauritanian Red Crescent estimated human losses between 20 and 30 per cent, reaching 40 per cent between February and March 2006 (Choplin 2008: 85). In the first seven months of 2008, more than 7,000 migrants successfully reached Spain by boat.

## Conclusion

It is evident in this chapter that communities were not thrown into 'completed forms of dependence' during the colonial period (Amin 1972a: 106), but instead, the labour reserves are in flux and new forms of dependence are created, while at other times they are challenged. The exclusion from global economic development that communities face is selective and inconsistent rather than absolute. People are actively thrown out of the global economy in particular moments (Harvey 2003: 164). This abjection is combined with restricted forms of migrant labour, sometimes as re-incorporation in a controlled labour market.

The two Lebu communities studied in this chapter reveal a contemporary dependence upon emigration. Dispossession has 'freed' a new generation from artisanal fishing and is the key dynamic in attempts to migrate to Europe. Remittances are a coping strategy for these processes, which have caused residents to lose land and livelihoods. There is a strong orientation towards Europe as a result of the vast difference in earnings, which is then activated by its labour regime. If we return to Bryceson's (2000: 199) negotiations between peasantries and global trade networks, we see that fishermen in these communities had access to productive resources in the form of *pirogues* and fishing materials. However, they lacked extractive claims on their labour product, and the level of externally provisioned social and productive service infrastructure was limited to established members of the community. In addition, production bears risk. It fails to sustain households, leading people to migrate. In Rufisque, the decline of industry and the public sector are another change that leaves young people in the unreliable professions of carpentry and building, while their parents' occupations were more dependable.

This chapter has also presented the background to Mauritania's migrant labour regime, which will be examined closely in Chapter 6. This country shows some characteristics of *l'économie de traite,* particularly because social strata and classes have received external political support, which has allowed them to appropriate lands and organise internal migration from the regions left in poverty (Amin 1972b). However, it also diverges from the west African region, partially belonging to the Arab world, and it has a distinct informal economy that has accommodated migrant labour in historical patterns and, more recently, from newly displaced people.

# 5 Regulating migrant labour

## Clandestine emigration and the EU

This chapter examines the dynamic relationship between EU migration management and west African migrants, with the purpose of identifying the EU's role in the migrant labour regime. The political element of this regime comes to the foreground, having examined the economic factors in displacement. The territorial logic prevails and is expressed through processes of securitisation by which migrants are dealt with as a threat, but this chapter also examines the EU as an economic endeavour, whose remit includes the management of labour markets to enhance competitiveness and the institutionalisation of unfree mobility through formalised mechanisms.

The postcolonial period was associated with the expanded circulation of people, and in some cases, this movement extended to centres of production in Europe. The British Commonwealth and French *Communauté* that succeeded the demise of colonial empires had relatively liberal immigration and citizenship policies during the 1950s and 1960s (Sutcliffe 2004: 267). However, from the start of the 1970s, political and economic crises led to mass expulsions and the collapse of industries. Populations struggled against the global trade architecture that, in Africa, was balanced against the autonomy of producers and the general subsistence needs of households in the neo-liberal era (Cheru 2002; Ferguson 2006).

This chapter is concerned with clandestine emigration because this is the juncture where stepwise migrants meet EU borders. Clandestine migrants leaving directly from the coast can also be considered as stepwise because their migration is unorganised and is likely to involve itinerant work in different European towns if successful. The Atlantic voyage may also shift to stepwise migration in north Africa if the boat is intercepted, breaks downs or runs out of supplies, or if the migrant is sent to the 'transit zone' after arriving in Spain. The first section reviews developments in European migration policy from the mid-1980s to 2005. It will show that European integration was realised through the incremental dismantling of its internal borders and a stronger focus on external control. This was combined with intergovernmental decision-making that would evade democratic scrutiny from the European Parliament. The control emphasis deepened as part of the general securitisation of policies that followed attacks on the US on 11 September 2001. The next section will examine the EU's Global Approach to Migration and Mobility (GAMM), in development since 2005, which has a

[p]articular emphasis on Africa and the Mediterranean and paves the way for further co-operation with 'third' (non-EU) countries. EU policies seek, as part of the GAMM, to address the 'root causes' of migration, but the motivations and intentions of migrants are not referred to (see previous chapter). It is precisely these issues, however, that would be of practical value to an immigration policy that is not dominated by the self-perpetuating logic of securitisation or by efforts to control the migrant labour market.

This chapter highlights the exclusion from labour, visa and asylum policy that west African youth face, pushing them into cheap labour roles, with the outcome of being forced into the category of 'illegal immigrant' and criminalised before leaving African shores. The fourteenth ECOWAS – EU Ministerial Troika meeting of 23 November 2008 issued the following statement:

> Turning to country specific situations in west Africa, the parties discussed the consolidation of peace and democracy in Côte d'Ivoire, Guinea, Guinea Bissau and the Sahel region. In a number of these countries scourges such as terrorism, organised crime, trafficking of drugs and small arms as well as human trafficking are causing growing concern.
>
> (Council 2008)

The crime that has been associated with the securitisation of migration is connected primarily with the countries that have experienced conflict and serious refugee and humanitarian crises – not Gambia, Ghana, Mali or Senegal, which are the principal senders of clandestine migrants in sub-Saharan Africa (de Haas 2008b: 32). However, this journey to the Canary Islands is usually the outcome of crisis. This is particularly true of Gambia, where political exile has been an important cause of emigration, but it also applies to the other sending countries that are categorised as politically stable. Irregular, transit and asylum migration can be approached as a continuum. People in need of international protection increasingly take the irregular route, entering the country illegally and aiming to apply for asylum. They may remain undocumented if this is rejected (Papadopoulou 2005). The earlier chapters showed that there is often a lack of alternatives to the decision to emigrate, the place to emigrate to, and how to reach this destination. This account from an unsuccessful migrant reveals the stakes in attempting to enter Europe:

> Some of the illegal immigrants, some of them have been to Spain and they have been repatriated four times, some of them have had accidents, the others died . . . even if they construct a wall, if they want to enter Europe they will pass . . . they take a route, they go one week, they lose fuel and everything and they die.
>
> (interview no. 32, Nouadhibou, 17 May 2008)

## Development of EU immigration policy

The period from 1945 to the mid-1970s was the 'Golden Age' for labour migration. Guest-worker rotations in Austria, Germany and Switzerland or neo-colonial worker regimes in the UK, France and the Netherlands guided labour migration. Workers from the south were welcome to contribute to postwar reconstruction in Europe and received formal contracts. European states recruited labour in Spain, Portugal, Greece, Turkey and the Maghreb countries or in former colonies (Samers 1999: 187; Guild 2005: 103). The recessionary impact of the oil price crisis, and de-industrialisation associated with the completion of postwar reconstruction, led to a decline in foreign workers and the start of 'Fortress Europe' by the mid-1970s. European restrictions included the curbing of intra-continental migration, including the closure of German, Swiss and French borders to Spanish workers. In Germany and France, the number of foreign workers significantly fell between 1973 and 1980 (Sassen 1999: 102).

The ending of guestworker programmes contributed to Spain's transformation to a labour-receiving country. Departures, mainly to northern Europe, fell from around 100,000 emigrants per year between 1961 and 1974, to around 20,000 per year from the mid-1970s, shrinking to 2,000 annual emigrants at the end of the century (Ortega Pérez 2003). Economic growth in Spain contributed to the reduction of departures when cross-border movement within Europe was facilitated. However, European consolidation would intensify the inequality between Europe and Africa by transferring border security from European countries to the African frontiers. Europeans could easily circulate and enter Africa but Africans would need to fulfil increasingly prohibitive criteria in order to enter Europe. It was a process that Ankie Hoogvelt calls 'imploding globalisation' (cited in Anderson and Shuttleworth 2004: 5), a means of creating labour reserves in the periphery, which capital can dominate by means of flexible border management.

France, the Federal Republic of Germany and the Benelux countries were the initial group to dismantle their boundaries by signing the Schengen Agreement in 1985. This establishes an area of free movement and has provided the basis for deeper co-operation on immigration and asylum. The 1986 Single European Act further provided for the free movement of people, services, goods and capital in Europe. The dismantling of intra-European border and migration controls left a 'security deficit' as institutions of border management and immigration were abandoned, moving the focus to their external borders (Den Boer 2001: 296; Huysmans 2000: 759). This meant that 'unwanted' migration was framed as a threat.

The Maastricht Treaty on European Union in 1992 sought to formalise immigration and asylum by connecting it with Justice and Home Affairs (JHA) issues. As a result, the Commission, the European Court of Justice and European Parliament were largely excluded from this policy area. Decision-making was in the hands of the Council, which is composed of interior and justice ministers. Legal output was limited, but there was significant development of a security-oriented understanding of immigration and asylum (Geddes 2001: 25; Huysmans 2000: 751).

The Schengen *acquis*, implemented in 1999, incorporates the Schengen Agreement as part of the EU framework and now includes all member states with some exceptions. The UK and Ireland have maintained their borders and have only partial participation in the *acquis* (they participate in police and judicial co-operation but separate visas are needed for visitors from outside Europe) and Denmark can opt out of certain border-related measures. Accession states must adopt the external border control *acquis*, though a Council decision is required to lift border controls with European states. Institutionally, the Treaty of Amsterdam in 1997 set the protocol for the *acquis* and led immigration towards a narrower policy area. JHA became an 'area of freedom, security and justice' (AFSJ). Concerns about the formal incorporation of the Schengen agreements are based on their opaque construction, which took place outside of the democratic and legal framework of the EU. Guild *et al.* (2008) note three processes that have been decisive in the construction of the AFSJ: firstly, securitisation, 'the discursive construction of wider categories of persons and practices as threats'; secondly, the application of technology to resolve issues constructed as threatening; and thirdly, a move towards intergovernmentalism as a response to common security problems (2008: 2).

The Schengen Information System (SIS), central to the Schengen mechanisms, was established; a system of information exchange between border authorities that gives access to reports on people and objects. This system, followed by SIS II, further Customs and Visa Information Systems and Europol systems, is one component of the technological approach. Data-protection issues have subsequently arisen as a result of the institutional complexity of the Amsterdam Treaty (Guild *et al.* 2008: 4). This Treaty extended Community powers to external relations, leaving the Community in a position to create agreements between member states and third countries (Mitsilegas *et al.* 2003: 39). This process has raised concerns because it would strengthen the role of states' executive actors and it produced a framework of control. The basis for decision-making would remain intergovernmental and thereby excluded democratic consultation (Geddes 2001: 25–6; Jeandesboz 2008: 2). These mechanisms for external relations have supported the intensification of 'policing at a distance' (Bigo and Guild 2005). Furthermore, agreements between member states and sending countries have been markedly focused on the objective of excluding unwanted 'third country nationals' from entering member states' territory. Following the Amsterdam Treaty and the incorporation of the Schengen *acquis* into the EU, the Tampere summit on 15 and 16 October 1999 called for a common immigration and asylum policy with a 'root causes approach' (Geddes 2005: 797). This was reinforced in the Seville European Council in 2002, where emphasis was placed further on the root causes of migration and the impact of migration processes on the EU and countries of origin (Balzacq 2008: 18). The 'root causes' approach is, however, limited in scope because the objective is predetermined and inflexible.

Security has been described as a 'self-referential practice' (Balzacq 2005: 177). This is evident in a discourse in which the problem with illegal immigration is that it challenges states' abilities to maintain their borders and to regulate the number of people entering the country. Furthermore, illegal migrants are expensive to process and provide with necessary albeit poor and short-term facilities (Mitsilegas *et al.* 2003: 42). Box 5.1 shows the significance of borders to some migrants in Senegal, Mauritania and Spain. It reveals that borders deter migrants in particular times and places with saddening, sometimes violent, consequences; but at the same time it is known by all that they do not prevent the continuity of migration. From the perspective of European forums on immigration, the extensive use of border technology is not expected to stop unwanted immigration but is useful in order to obtain finance, social power and legitimacy (Bigo 2005b: 78).

**Box 5.1** Borders and migrants

There are Mauritanian, Moroccan and Spanish police at the frontiers. If we could get the visa we wouldn't do this, but while they maintain their position, we are not going to give up even if they put bombs in the sea.

(fisherman who plans to migrate, interview no. 6, Nouakchott, 7 May 2007)

I know people who have left from this beach but now it's forbidden and if someone is caught, they are imprisoned.

(fisherman, interview no. 12, Nouakchott, 7 May 2007)

From the African world, people cannot just enter Europe like that... they don't like black people to enter in Morocco because it's the law of the Spanish government; they don't like migration so they are catching people and sending them back, and they were killing people.

(Nigerian migrant, interview no. 16, Salt, Girona, 23 February 2008)

They cannot stop people. They will try to control it but they cannot stop it, it's impossible. Before, there was nobody in Mauritania taking that risk, they'd go from Morocco. But when they blocked Morocco, people started in Mauritania, and if they block Mauritania, people will start from Libya, and when they block Libya, the people will travel to Tunis, and when they block Tunis, the people will start from Algeria.

(Nigerian migrant, interview no. 31, Nouadhibou, 17 May 2008)

They started to bring helicopters and boats to control the people. But according to the Spanish delegate that came here, seven or eight boats arrived in the Canaries yesterday. Almost 200 people were in the boat from Saint-Louis and then up to 70 from Nouakchott and Nouadhibou but as the helicopter and patrol boats started, they could catch no more people. The Red Cross can take up to 150 people but they cannot keep them there because the next week or the next day people are coming; there is not much control.

(Ghanaian migrant, interview no. 32, Nouadhibou, 17 May 2008)

> If you're Senegalese, you're returned to Senegal. The Spanish authorities check people's declared nationalities by sending messages to the declared countries of origin but most of these countries have disabled these requests from Spanish marines. In the case of Senegalese, if one group of *clandestins* is repatriated, the next group will get through.
>
> (attempted clandestine migration five times, interview no. 49, Rufisque, 18 June 2008)
>
> Although the EU is against clandestine emigration, Spain has a lot arranged for receiving *clandestins*. The Senegalese coast is too large and, as a consequence, you can leave from anywhere. It's enough simply to avoid passing the navy.
>
> (unsuccessfully attempted Atlantic journey to Canary Islands, interview no. 63, Rufisque, 24 June 2008)

If the objective of security is to perpetuate itself, Amsterdam and subsequent Lisbon Treaty reforms provided mechanisms with which to 'reason' with its dominance over migration policy. They gave higher jurisdiction powers to the Court of Justice and the Parliament (Mitsilegas *et al.* 2003: 36; Perkowski 2012: 20). However, there has been continuing competition among member state authorities and networks, for example in the Treaty of Prüm, signed on 27 May 2005, initially by seven member states. This treaty has the objective of furthering EU co-operation in exchange of information, particularly in combating terrorism, cross-border crime and illegal migration. One argument is that Prüm's intergovernmental arena excludes the European Parliament, thereby lacking democratic scrutiny and transparency (Guild *et al.* 2008: 5). Illustrating the implications of undemocratic decision-making structures, the Parliament in 2004 rejected a proposal by the UK, Germany and Italy that would keep the majority of refugees in north Africa (Baldwin-Edwards 2006: 320).

The above account of the development of European immigration policy demonstrates that the events of 11 September 2001 did not change the direction of policy, but they did lead to a 'state of exception' in which the rights of foreigners could be subsumed by constructed security imperatives (Bigo 2005b: 72). This meant that states could control migration at the gate and in the interior with reduced accountability, diminishing the effectiveness of the EU's renewed and growing emphasis on fundamental rights. The Hague Programme, agreed by the European Council on 4–5 November 2004, referred to a 'new urgency' of security in the EU and its member states and professed the firmer establishment of the ASFJ. This followed 9/11 and the Madrid bombings on 11 March 2004 (Council 2005). To this end, under the Finnish presidency, the Council agreed on the common definition of Integrated Border Management (IBM). On 4–5 December 2006, the Justice and Home Affairs Council defined the IBM model as comprising: (1) border control, including border checks and surveillance, risk analysis and gathering of intelligence; (2) detection and investigation of cross-border crime; (3) a four-tier access control model, including measures in non-EU countries, co-operation with neighbouring countries, border controls and controls within the area of free movement; (4) interagency and international co-operation for border management; and (5) co-ordination and coherence among the member states and with EU bodies. The IBM model aims to 'fight against' illegal migration, but also discusses co-operating and building links with non-EU countries (Jeandesboz 2008: 3).

The IBM adopted the Schengen Borders Code and further developed the *acquis* on internal and external borders, also establishing FRONTEX. This code incorporates the European Parliament in decision-making procedures and includes 'a wider set of guarantees and rights in the event of refusal of entry on to EU territory' (Carrera 2007a: 71). Repatriation agreements, however, remove these rights as the responsibility of refusal is shifted to the sending government or governments in countries of transit. The next section examines the EU's Global Approach to Migration and Mobility (GAMM), which originates partly in the violence of 2005, when Moroccan forces shot at people attempting to enter the heavily militarised Spanish enclaves of Ceuta and Melilla.

## The global approach: security, development and labour mobility

The European Council adopted the 'global approach' to migration in December 2005, now the renewed Global Approach to Migration and Mobility (GAMM) with a focus on Africa and the Mediterranean. This focus was catalysed by pressure from EU southern member states, which requested more financial and human resources after being on the frontline of clandestine immigration (Wolff 2008: 257). The 'global approach' combines development and security and was reinforced by Franco Frattini, European Commissioner for Justice, Freedom and Security in 2006, who stated that 'we need to address legal migration, combat illegal migration and deal with subjects covered by the migration and development agenda' (2006). The declaration of the Euro-African Ministerial Conference on Migration and Development was adopted in Rabat on 11 July 2006 and committed participating states to 'work together following a comprehensive, balanced, pragmatic and operational approach and respecting the rights and dignity of migrants and refugees' (UNHCR 2008: 1)

In the communication on 'the Global Approach to Migration one year on', the objective was set out to agree on 'mobility packages' with non-EU countries (Commission 2006: 7). These packages, which changed to 'mobility partnerships' in 2007, are strongly tied to the continuation of the EU security agenda and, concurrently, to the control of labour. The commitments from third countries, in a typical mobility partnership, include: identifying and re-admitting their own nationals; re-admitting third-country nationals and stateless people who arrived in the EU through their territory; initiatives to discourage illegal immigration; efforts to improve border control and/or management, supported as appropriate by operational co-operation with member states and/or FRONTEX; improving the security of travel documents with biometrics where appropriate; exchanging information with relevant authorities in EU member states; and initiatives to combat migrant smuggling and promotion of productive employment and decent work. Along with these commitments, the labour mobility in these partnerships is based on the labour market needs of EU member states and emphasises the mobility of students, researchers, young professionals and volunteers (Commission 2007a, 2011). Senegal was a prime candidate for a partnership. It entered into a secret agreement with the Commission, which was expected to be similar to that of Cape Verde by reinforcing the role of FRONTEX and 'fighting against illegal migratory flows'. Furthermore, Senegal would act as a 'gatekeeper' by restricting flows of west Africans as well as Senegalese migrants (Chou and Gibert 2010: 9–10). These negotiations have stalled.[1]

The interim progress report on the 'Global Approach' to migration referred to several meetings and summits in Rabat, Tripoli and Lisbon, between the EU and the African Union, the Economic Community of West African States, and the countries of Cape Verde, Ghana, Mauritania, Senegal and Ethiopia. The Migration and Development Agenda aimed to integrate migration issues and concerns in Poverty Reduction Strategies and to establish micro-projects aimed at the use of remittances for income generation. Border controls, at the same time, were to be stepped up and the Rapid Border Intervention Team (RABIT) Regulation was adopted on 11 July 2007 (Commission 2007b). External border protection was a priority of the German presidency for the first half of 2007. RABITs were introduced as a means of providing rapid assistance to member states facing 'urgent and exceptional' pressure at the external borders, to be managed by FRONTEX. The Executive Director makes the decision and he explains the outcome only to the Management Board. The team is permitted to use weapons (Monar 2008: 115; Perkowski 2012: 19).

The French EU presidency built on the global approach with the European Pact on Immigration and Asylum, adopted by the European Council on 15 and 16 October 2008. The Pact has five key elements: (1) to organise legal immigration to take account of the priorities, needs and reception capabilities determined by each member state; (2) to control illegal immigration by ensuring the return of illegal immigrants to their country of origin or a country of transit (strengthening co-operation between countries of origin and transit); (3) *to make border controls more effective – by which co-operation with countries of origin and transit will be intensified to enable them to improve control of their own borders*; (4) to construct a Europe of asylum; (5) to create a comprehensive partnership with countries of origin and transit to encourage synergy between migration and development (Ministère de l'Immigration, de l'Integration, de l'Identité Nationale et du Développement Solidaire, France 2008 – italics added by author). The Pact and EU strategies are in conflict, where the Commission calls for 'clear and transparent rules for the entry and residence of third country nationals' and for fair treatment of migrants; both excluded in the Pact (Carrera and Guild 2008: 7).

The italicised Part 3 of the Pact reflects that the frontier 'relates more and more to the act of leaving one's country of nationality than getting into another' (Bigo and Guild 2005: 234). The frontiers are located less and less at the state borders:

> ...they are less visible and they structure the world into two spheres: one composed of people allowed to travel and a second one, of people who are banned from it without any possibility to protest since they have no appeal against the decisions and are miles away from the border, because they cannot even board a plane or leave their own country.
>
> (ibid.: 235)

The paradox of fighting against illegal migration and protecting the human rights of migrants, when the organisers are the migrants themselves, pervades west African–European migration management. With often violent results, responsibility for protection is transferred outside European boundaries and Africans are turned back, resulting in an *Afrique humiliée* (Traoré 2007a; Chapter 6).

In 2008, meetings on legal migration, combating illegal migration, and migration and development were held in Rabat, Ouagadougou and Dakar respectively. Agreements simultaneously offered the provision of visas for labour mobility, co-development and protection of asylum, whilst controlling illegal immigration. The next sections examine, separately, visa arrangements, co-development, FRONTEX and repatriations as means of controlling migration.

## What legal provision for labour migrants?

Within the Community framework, labour migration is based on the principle that the individual has the right to choose whether or not to migrate for economic reasons (Guild 2005: 127). External labour migrants, in contrast, are subjected to the requirements of the labour market. The first commitment of the European Pact on Immigration and Asylum is to organise legal immigration to take account of the priorities, needs and reception capabilities determined by each member state (Ministère de l'Immigration, de l'Integration, de l'Identité Nationale et du Développement Solidaire 2008). Furthermore, the legal logic for the EU visa follows a principle in which no third-country national can access EU territory if considered a risk to a member state. National police databases, Interpol and the Schengen Information System (and linked database of Sirene) contain information about people who have tried to enter the EU or are 'undesirable' for other reasons (Bigo and Guild 2005: 238).

Following the restrictions on immigration that have been consistent since the mid-1970s, immigrant labour in the EU can be characterised by recruitment to the upper and lower extremes of the labour market (Guild 2005: 114). On one hand, therefore, there have been concerns about 'brain drain', especially concerning medical professionals at the upper end, and on the other, exploitation of cheap labour. It is observed by Amin and El-Kenz that Europe has sought an 'immigrant labour force' but not an 'immigrant society', leading to the establishment of quotas and seasonal contracts (2005: 119). This is clear in the GAMM (Commission 2011: 3), which reports that demographic factors mean 'some of the additional and specific skills needed in the future could only be found outside the EU'. It aims to polarise legal and illegal labour, stating that 'the portability of social and pension rights could also be a facilitator for mobility and circular migration, as well as a disincentive for irregular work and should therefore be improved' (Commission 2011: 4). An 'adaptable' workforce is required to enhance the 'vitality and competitiveness' of the EU. This is evident in the Blue Card, which is aimed at highly skilled immigrants. It provides enhanced freedom to access labour markets and offers equal treatment in working conditions, social security, pensions, recognition of diplomas, education and vocational training. In contrast with the US Green Card, it can be withdrawn if the member state decides to give priority to EU citizens as a result of changes in the labour market (Niessen and Kate 2008: 56). Furthermore, it may be withdrawn when holders are unable to support themselves or families without social assistance for more than three months or more than once during the validity of the card. This is a clear example of separating the means of renewal and subsistence, with the Directive also incorporating 'pre-departure measures focusing on upgrading skills and proficiency in EU languages' (Commission 2011: 13), thus saving on some of the training expenses as well as indirect benefits.

In December 2005, the Commission issued a Communication on a Policy Plan on Legal Migration, which would divide economic migrants into categories of highly qualified workers, seasonal workers, remunerated trainees and intra-corporate transferees. For seasonal workers, it proposed the provision of a residence/work permit allowing the person to work for a certain number of months per year for four to five years. The report stated that 'even in the presence of high unemployment, this category of immigrant workers rarely conflicts with EU workers as few EU citizens and residents are willing to engage in seasonal activities' (Commission 2005: 7). However, migrants frequently note that visas are not distributed according to embassy rules. There are claims in Mauritania that the visa cost is raised for black migrants or they are sold on the informal market (interview nos 6 and 11, Nouakchott, 7 May 2007). Nigerian migrants have claimed that the money they paid for visas was retained without the appearance of a visa (interview no. 16, Salt, Girona, 23 February 2008; interview no. 38, Nouakchott, 20 May 2008).

From March 2007 to the end of 2008, around 500 Senegalese workers were recruited on temporary visas to work in Spain's fishing and farming sectors (IRIN 2008b). When asking the youth about contracts and visas, the response was frequently that you need *bras longs* (long arms – friends in high places) in order to benefit. Cheikh, the head of an association of repatriates on the outskirts of Dakar, claimed that the state gave the visa to members of the PDS (then the ruling Senegalese Democratic Party) (interview no. 29, Colobane, 8 April 2008). Boubacar added, 'the Spanish government wanted to grant visas in the fishing domain but the Senegalese state gave them to their close relations, people who hadn't mastered the sea at all' (interview no. 40, Thiaroye-sur-Mer, 3 June 2008).

Rufisque, however, possesses households with such political connections, owing to its historical role in Senegal's political development (Chapter 4). Both illegal and legal forms of emigration are yet insecure for the migrant and, by extension, the migrant's family. Mrs Sakho's daughter, with the help of her uncle, received a rural work contract for two years. This predated the agreement between Senegal and Spain. Mrs Sakho explained: 'Now the contract is finished...she is staying, it's difficult to take the risk of staying in the country without money or anything, but she will try to find something else' (interview no. 58, Rufisque, 24 June 2008). Mrs Diop had two sons who tried clandestine emigration. They were both fishermen, and one obtained a free *pirogue* journey to Spain through colleagues. The other sold his *pirogue* and then gained 'a contract from President Wade' (interview no. 64, Rufisque, 2 July 2008). During the eight-month term, he sent remittances via Western Union. It expired a month before the interview, and Mrs Diop explained:

> These days, he goes to the port to seek work...he's not with any acquaintance, he's alone because he resigned from his work before the end of his contract, to avoid them taking him back to Senegal just after it ends.
>
> (ibid.)

Mrs Diao's son also travelled to Spain with a work contract for nine months, after an attempt to reach the Canary Islands in a *pirogue* was halted by a storm.

> He sent but not big sums because he was saving at the time, in preparation for the end of the contract. Now his contract is finished and he's without work, it's very hard for him. Now he has left the countryside to find work in the towns. Contrary to what is thought about the contracts, emigration of the recipients hasn't changed a great deal.
>
> (interview no. 71, Rufisque, 2 July 2008)

This is because the time abroad required to secure household funds, beyond daily consumption, exceeds the terms of the visa. An emigrant working in a factory in Spain would earn €800 per month, at least ten times the wage of a local carpenter or builder. However, showing one example of an expense that is not covered by workers' subsistence, one returned migrant explained:

> Travelling to Europe is firstly to meet the needs of the house. Emigrants must also think of investing to prepare for their retirement. For investment, emigrants will have to do 15 years abroad.
>
> (interview, Rufisque, 24 June 2008)

Showing more ambivalence to the contracts, Mrs Cissé stated that her son, who successfully reached Spain by *pirogue*, was sending fewer remittances now because Senegalese state contracts reduce clandestine immigrants' chances of finding work (interview no. 70, Rufisque, 2 July 2008). While migrants 'want' to do their time abroad for a temporary period, the scale of dispossession does not allow for such circulation, nor does the legal framework. The fundamental shortcoming of the contracts is that they are unfree labour, which leaves migrants exploited and households lacking their presence. Anna complained that as her husband was away in Spain, she had to stay at home and look after the children. He entered with a fishing contract:

> He worked on the big boats but people sell the places. The owner of the boat does not keep the personnel. My husband knew very early that this employer didn't manage personnel well. It's why he abandoned it before the 'thank you'.
>
> (interview no. 60, Rufisque, 24 June 2008)

This suggests that consideration of 'cheap labour economics', which places household reproduction at its core, is another component of labour migration that has been lost in aggregation and individualistic approaches, explored at length with reference to southern Africa (Bush, Cliffe and Jansen 1984).

## Development as deterrent?

Non-European labour migration is institutionally opposed within the EU framework. It is undesirable unless it meets the specific demands of member states. Co-development is an approach that may soften the impact of prevention by means of border security and legal enforcement. It can assist the return and reintegration of undocumented migrants by supporting job creation in sending regions. It can also encourage migrants to stay at home by developing infrastructure, education and market access (Martin *et al.* 2002: 90–1). Labour migration from Africa to Europe can have negative consequences in sending communities. The pursuit of work across borders can be necessitated and reproduced when sending communities are dispossessed of the means to sustain themselves, i.e. historically by the imposition of taxes and conversion of land by colonial administrations, or by more contemporary forms of predation. The implications of displacing labour in this way are that a 'labour reserve' is created from which workers must sell their labour in vulnerable conditions, undermining development in situ. Box 4.1 reflected the desire in migrant communities to prevent the need to emigrate as cheap labour, difficult as this prevention is, amongst other measures. Failed clandestine journeys led President Wade to pledge the REVA (*Retour vers l'agriculture*) plan for 'zero clandestine emigration' and to 'respect the dignity' of youths aiming to go to Europe, with domestic production of crops such as biofuels to meet the demand of industrialised countries (Ministère des Affaires Etrangères 2006). It aimed to address the import-dependent food economy in which households are vulnerable to price hikes. With strong contributions from Spain and France and a large number of meetings under the rubric of co-development, few results were seen (Schmitz 2008: 6). One reason for the failure of this plan was said to be the lack of interest in agriculture from youths wishing to migrate, many of whom had grown up in cities and gained skills and qualifications unrelated to farming (Ba and Ndiaye 2008: 8). More representative of the communities informing this book, Alioune, a repatriated migrant in Rufisque, considered REVA and the subsequent GOANA (Great Agricultural Offensive for

Food Security) plan to be unrealistic and inaccessible to those who stood to benefit (interview no. 66, Rufisque, 2 July 2008).

From the perspectives of sending households and European politicians, encouraging potential migrants to stay in Africa can reconcile the mutual aims of keeping people in Africa and at the same time out of Europe. Spain has engaged in partnerships that aim to encourage development and manage borders, and these tend to have a relatively robust inclusion of human rights. Spain became the largest donor to ECOWAS (the Economic Community of West African States) in July 2008. The €10 million ECOWAS–Spain Fund on Migration and Development incorporates control of irregular migration and trafficking with the promotion of free movement in west Africa, management of regular migration, and support of the rights of migrants, asylum seekers and refugees (ECOWAS 2008; AECID 2012). One undervalued issue that arises in the use of development as a deterrent is, however, the often explicit and insensitive goal of preventing Africans from reaching Europe – a rejection that is common knowledge amongst households in Senegal, Mali, Burkina Faso and in other west African countries that have a history of mutual dependence with Europe on labour migration.

As described earlier, the European Pact on Immigration and Asylum, developed under the French EU presidency, set out that 'co-operation with countries of origin will be developed to discourage and combat illegal immigration' (Ministère de l'Immigration, de l'Integration, de l'Identité Nationale et du Développement Solidaire 2008). This was not a new initiative. In 1994/5, the PDLM (Programme Développement Local Migration) was launched between France and Mali, Senegal and Mauritania. The programme financed micro-projects in regions of prevalent emigration around the Senegal River Valley. It was criticised for its coincidence with reform of the French Office for Protection of Refugees and Stateless Persons (Ofpra) and a hardening of the politics of asylum (Gubert 2008: 49–50). France also has bilateral agreements with Gabon, Cameroon, Burkina Faso, Congo-Brazzaville, Benin, Tunisia, Mauritius and Cape Verde, which involve the hindrance of 'illegal' migration to Europe. President Nicolas Sarkozy was strongly connected with *refoulement* (turning people away) after returning African immigrants on 'Sarkozy charters' when he was Minister of the Interior. The Malian government stalled co-operation with France in deportation agreements, which would include the delivery of development aid and labour contracts (BBC 2009). The remittances gained from Malian emigrants were of too much importance for their government to rush this politically sensitive issue, which had long been a sticking point in French–Malian relations (Martin *et al.* 2002: 90).

Additionally, when French Foreign Minister Bernard Kouchner reinforced the use of development aid to curb migration in 2007, this met with concerns in part because it was seen as a continuation of neo-colonial clientelist relations described as *Françafrique* (*Economist* 2007). This suggests that co-operation continues to be a 'euphemism frequently used to describe/disguise... crude self-interest', suggesting 'a voluntarism that may or may not in fact exist' (Yates 1996: 6–7). It brings into question both the motives and the benefits of development aid in the context of migration (see Bracking 2009).

## FRONTEX, *refoulement* and west African migrants

The number of *pirogues* entering Spain is relatively small, despite an emphasis on this type of migration in FRONTEX operations. Between 1990 and 2007, 3,641,669 immigrants entered Spain, of which 34,915 arrived by *pirogue* (Institut Nacional d'Estadistica 2007). Most 'illegal' immigration in Europe is via airports. The importance of clandestine entry is not, however, 'created' (see Carrera 2007b; Jeandesboz 2008). In 2003, Spain halted clandestine migration in the Straits of Gibraltar with the SIVE (integrated external surveillance system), which was strengthened after co-operation with Moroccan mixed patrols. Following this, there was more emphasis on irregular migration via Morocco or the Atlantic, increasing from 2,506 detected people in 2002, to 19,176 people in 2003, of which over three quarters were Senegalese (ACCEM 2006: 13). In September 2005, thousands of west and central Africans approached the Spanish enclaves of Ceuta and Melilla in northern Morocco, where Moroccan security forces and the Spanish Guardia Civil were deployed. On 29 September, in Ceuta, bullets were fired and five migrants were reported dead. Similar events occurred in Melilla in the night of 5–6 October (Traoré 2007a: 118).

The Canary Islands, as a zone of transit, became the next front line of the migratory relationship between Europe and Africa (Godenau and Zapata Hernandez 2008: 16). Approximately 6,000 African migrants died at sea or went missing on the journey from the west African coast to Canary Islands during 2006, and 600 bodies were picked up on their shores. At least 31,000 migrants successfully reached the islands in that year and fewer than 5,000 were intercepted. Almost as many Africans reached the Canaries in 2006 as in the previous four years combined, according to Spanish immigration officials (BBC 2006a). In the same year, Spanish authorities and the Mauritanian government installed a detention centre in Nouadhibou for 'illegal' migrants (Chapter 6). Food and other support such as access to telephones are provided by the Red Cross of Spain and also of Mauritania. Between October 2006 and June 2008, 6,745 people were held in the centre (Lamazou 2008). Aminata Traoré, former Malian Minister for Culture and Tourism, argued that Africa was becoming a prison in which violence is subcontracted to countries of origin and transit (Traoré 2007b). As one report noted (Adamou *et al.* 2010: 15), while arrivals in the Canary Islands decreased by 93 per cent between 2006 and 2009, the repression of migrants continued in Mauritania through arbitrary arrests and detention, not based on Mauritanian law but on European pressure. Over half of those arrested were Senegalese and the rest were mainly from Mali and Gambia.

In November 2006, the European Commission called for reinforced management of the EU's southern maritime borders and to maximise the capacities of FRONTEX. Established as an Agency in May 2005, FRONTEX tasks are governed by a management board, in which delegation members are all border chiefs or in a similar position. Its purpose is linked with the prevention of deaths at sea, leading to calls to gear up the patrols and enhance the capacity of third countries, 'from which unseaworthy, overloaded boats set sail for the Canary

Islands, Greece, Lampedusa and Malta' (Bertozzi 2008: 1). Although the UK can opt out of aspects of the Schengen *acquis*, it has contributed funds, security staff and airport facilities to FRONTEX. This is on the basis of the UK's leadership role in strengthening border control by 'creating a new offshore line of defence, by checking individuals as far from the UK as possible and through each stage of their journey, using new technology, particularly biometrics and new approaches to managing risk and intelligence' (Home Office, Border and Immigration Agency 2007: 4).

'Border security is a constant compromise between the freedom of movement of EU citizens and third-country nationals who enter the EU', argued Lt Gen. Minze Beuving, the FRONTEX Management Board Chairman (Beuving 2008: 4). This highlights the tension and contradiction between freedom of movement within the EU and *refoulement* of those wishing to enter; their processing at the borders constitutes a threat to ease of movement for EU citizens. It is argued that FRONTEX is not a product of securitisation, but on the contrary aims to harmonise and regulate the border practices of member states. The development of a core curriculum for border guard training and the Common Integrated Risk Model illustrates a technocratic 'move away from the political spectacle of the security emergency' (Neal 2009: 348). Carrera, however, argues that FRONTEX is overly politicised and that 'compliance with the principle of legality may be open to debate' (2007b: 27). Legal issues with FRONTEX accord with Bigo's (2005a) description of post 11 September securitisation, which 'constructs a group as abnormal, justifying the solution of changing the law, and affecting justice, citizenship and the norms of liberal regimes', including mobility. The agency is an institutionalised and formalised securitisation measure, which has increased its ability to take the exceptional measures that are linked with securitisation. It is, in another sense, apolitical, aiming 'to prevent illegal border crossings regardless of the motive' (Beuving 2008: 8).

The priority is placed on reinforcement of security at common EU external territorial borders (Carrera 2007a: 68). The European Border Surveillance System (EUROSUR) proposal, following two feasibility studies conducted by FRONTEX, set out the long-term objective of developing common tools and instruments for border surveillance. It particularly focused on the southern maritime borders of EU member states, which surpass 34,000 km in length. It sets out several options, however, which range from maintaining the *status quo* to interlinking existing surveillance systems, developing new technologies such as unmanned aerial vehicles and earth observation, and establishment of a 'common pre-frontier intelligence picture', which reinforces externalisation and bilateral agreements with non-EU countries (Jeandesboz 2008: 10). The development of EUROSUR and the expansion of FRONTEX's competences would change the scope of FRONTEX activities: the agency would participate in the Schengen evaluation mechanism and would be able to run pilot projects with non-EU countries, giving more autonomy to the EU's external relations (Jeandesboz 2008: 11–12). The implications of this enhanced role for the fundamental values of the EU are challenging, as seen in FRONTEX's joint operations in the Canary Islands.

Operation HERA I was based on a request from Spain and started in July 2006, during the year in which *pirogue* disasters peaked. FRONTEX aimed to determine the countries of origin of 'irregular' migrants, with experts from France, Portugal, Italy and Germany, and two subsequent groups. HERA II ran from August to December 2006 and involved the facilitation of technical equipment for border surveillance. In the zone between the Atlantic coast and the Canary Islands, the *pirogues* were to be intercepted, and then the authorities of the sending country would deal with the immigrants and their return: the boats would only be escorted to the Canaries if they were intercepted over 24 miles away from the west African coast. Operation HERA III followed, combining the first two operations of identification and interception. This represents, therefore, the externalisation of EU border control with a legal basis in bilateral agreements between the EU member state and third countries in Africa, in this case between Spain, and Mauritania and Senegal. These agreements were secret, thereby challenging European principles of democratic scrutiny and transparency, embodied in the First Pillar under which FRONTEX was created (Carrera 2007b; Jeandesboz 2008). A satellite system at the start of 2009 linked Spain, Portugal, Senegal, Mauritania and Cape Verde, with its centre in Gran Canaria. The EU-funded Sea Horse operation allows police to track migrant vessels on the Atlantic coast and past the Canary Islands and to draw shared maps of routes (Tremlett 2009).

These more repressive measures of keeping Africans within their own borders, seen in shootings in the enclaves of Ceuta and Melilla (Traoré 2007a), the Mediterranean and the Atlantic and in detention centres, depict a fortress in north and west Africa. Routes of migration have dispersed, however, challenging this fortress. As patrols close in on Senegal's beaches, migrants will go further afield, to Gambia or Guinea, and the journeys become more perilous. In October 2006, boats were leaving from the Gambian beach of Tanjeh after Senegalese and Mauritanian beaches were patrolled (BBC 2006b). Boats still were leaving Senegal in small numbers, however, in 2008, once from Yarakh beach in July, despite Spanish reports that Senegalese migration has ceased.

## Removals and repatriations

The Council Decision to co-ordinate joint removals by air of migrants who are the subjects of individual removal orders, established in 2004, was also adopted by the UK and Ireland. Re-admission agreements are a key part of the Schengen *acquis* and of the conditionality applied to candidate states. The agreements oblige the contracting states to re-admit their nationals if they do not fulfil the conditions for entry, presence or residence. The Council meeting in Seville in June 2002 called for a speeding up of re-admission agreements, and re-admission became integral to the 'comprehensive plan to combat illegal immigration' (Balzacq and Carrera 2005: 30–1).

Spain signed agreements with Cape Verde, Gambia, Guinea Conakry, Guinea-Bissau, Mauritania, Nigeria and Ghana for re-admission (IOM 2008; Cross forthcoming). The repatriations did not evidently reduce migrations by sea and migrants were sent either to transit countries or to countries of origin. Table 5.1 shows that a large proportion of migrants embarked on the journey to Spain in transit countries (Mauritania, Morocco and other north African countries).

*Table 5.1* Immigrants to Spain by region of departure and mode of transport, 1990–2007

| *Origin* | *Number of people* | *Of which* pirogue | *Of which* pirogue *is from country of transit as distinct from place of birth* |
|---|---|---|---|
| EU27 excl. Spain | 1,246,101 | 258 | 258 |
| Morocco | 415,451 | 27,587 | 21,435 |
| Rest of African countries | 134,342 | 7,070 | 6,118 |

Source: Figures from Institut Nacional d'Estadistica 2007

Repatriation is a misnomer. Senegal's repatriation agreements with Spain and Mauritania have led to the 'return' of west Africans who are not Senegalese, often at the Senegal–Mauritania border town of Rosso on the Senegal River. The following description illustrates the messiness that occurs in dealing with migrants between northern and southern countries:

> When we were in Morocco, the Spanish signed an agreement with Morocco on taking charge of the *clandestins*. But since there was no plane, they decided to lead us to the Mauritanian border. During this, the Mauritanians refused us, then we were returned again to Morocco . . . For our return to Senegal, things started truly to drag out, then Morocco decided finally to lead us to Senegal.
>
> (interview no. 47, Thiaroye-sur-Mer, 7 June 2008)

Beginning in September 2006, more than 4,600 Senegalese, and people of other nationalities who embarked in Senegal, were repatriated by aeroplane to Saint-Louis by the request of state authorities (Willems 2008: 278). A repatriated male who was a trained architect explained:

> Not long ago, a *pirogue* left for Spain and someone was able to escape because he declared he was Kenyan nationality, because he had mastered English very well but for the other Senegalese *clandestins*, it didn't work. All other *clandestins* enter Spain without problem except the Senegalese. This is because the president of Senegal signed agreements with Spain . . . as soon as the authorities there know that you are Senegalese, they hold you and let the others go.
>
> (interview no. 63, Rufisque, 24 June 2008)

Alioune added: 'The Senegalese state requested the repatriation of Senegalese . . . the Spanish police regrouped us all to prevent escapes. That's how we returned to our home country' (interview no. 66, Rufisque, 2 July 2008). Migrants considered that President Abdoulaye Wade had requested their return. To accompany the repatriation agreements, President Wade and Spanish Prime Minister Jose Luis Rodriguez Zapatero signed agreements in December 2006, which would allow 4,000 Senegalese to work temporarily in Spain. Spain also pledged €20 million to Senegal to fund job training and create economic opportunities for youth (BBC 2006c). This meant the 'unwanted' migrants who had invested heavily in their journey with personal risk and the destruction of the household were swapped for those who could be selected by the Senegalese state and then directed towards labour shortages in Spain.

## Conclusion

There has been a fast and continuous growth of EU-led procedures that formalise and reinforce the prevention of south–north movement. These mechanisms have included restrictive visa and asylum policies, the deployment of patrols to intercept clandestine migrants, agreements with sending countries for repatriation, and the prevention of emigration through development. The expansion of FRONTEX and new technologies leads migrants to detention, longer and more dangerous sea voyages to avoid patrols, and to 'repatriation' to unstable transit countries. Its formulation has been uncompromising in its efforts to prevent 'unwanted' immigration from Africa, following a logic that is apparently territorial.

There have been recent Commission attempts to mitigate against the flows of prohibited migrants using less coercive means, in recognition of human rights. These measures include co-development, strategies for job creation and the creation of legal means of entry, all salient in sending communities and going some way to acknowledging the context of entry. At the same time, there are two key failings in these efforts to broaden border management, which reside in the political and economic priorities of the EU. The first issue is that migration policy has sidelined regulation by the supranational institutions and has been developed by the interior ministers of member states, who take a notoriously hard line on immigration and, in many instances, have been responsible for stimulating the discourse of illegality and criminalisation. This constrains the possibility of tackling the problems that lead to clandestine migration. The condition of stepping up security in order to receive development aid challenges democracy and the aims of development. The second problem and the second set of conditionalities are centred on the labour market, similarly constraining the possibility of a reciprocal labour migration arrangement. There is an absurd imbalance in the 'exchange' found in the GAMM, by which people who can meet labour shortages in the EU are granted mobility on the condition that unwanted migrants in the EU are sent back – it is unsurprising that negotiations have stalled. The two priorities of illegalisation and controlled labour are the modern incarnation of the dual labour market, existing in a single policy document (Meillassoux 1975: 122).

## Note

1 Interestingly, President Macky Sall's administration, elected in April 2012, have announced the reciprocation of visa charges to visitors from the countries that impose them, starting in July 2013. This would incorporate EU countries (Jean-Matthew 2012).

# 6 The projection of borders

## The EU and Mauritania

Whether or not Mauritania is 'naturally' a transit country has been challenged. Representations of knowledge have continuously disengaged the Sahara from broader understandings of 'Africa' (Ahmed-Salem, 2005: 492; 2010; McDougall 2007: 23; Lydon, 2005: 293). Reflecting that this separation is an external construction, labour law, dating back to 1974, had been lenient in the number of work permits issued until recently (Bensaâd 2008: 1; Fargues 2009). In recent years, this separation has materialised in legal and military form as a result of US and EU strategies to control the movement of people. Mauritania has become one of Europe's frontiers, with the consequence of fundamental change in its labour regime.

This is because indebtedness has driven a foreign policy that depends on rents gained from its strategic position as well as natural resources. Mauritania can be classified in broadest terms as a rentier state because it receives 'on a regular basis substantial amounts of external economic rent'. This term mainly applies to Arab oil-exporting states that nationalised neo-colonial petroleum exploitation in the decades following independence, leading massive amounts of foreign currency and credit to flow into state accounts (Yates 1996: 11–12). It links external rent with economic stagnation and political authoritarianism. Mauritania has been grouped with rentier economies because around a quarter of its revenues derived from exports of iron ore and around a third of revenues were gained from customs duties from the mid-1960s. Public consumption was strongly linked with foreign trade. Fishing royalties were also an important source of revenue, while taxation was limited. Furthermore, foreign gifts and loans were credited to special accounts, largely from Arab oil-producing countries. They were intended to fund industrial projects, including oil and sugar refineries, whose profitability came into question (Oulalou and Jaidi 1987: 188–9). For the rentier state, 'it is far easier for dominant classes to secure access to ready-made wealth in the form of rent, and for the state in those circumstances to become increasingly autonomous from society at large' (Bush 2007: 133).

A rentier economy is associated with a lack of productive activity but the predominance of revenue as rent does not necessarily constitute a rentier state. The disjuncture between booms in revenue and the lack of macroeconomic growth or poverty reduction in rentier states can be understood as rentier politics, which reveal the social relationships that constitute the state. It can emerge where 'the balance of class forces shaping state policy pursues the "easy" route of revenue generation from resource rents, often because there is little popular control over the state' (Bush 2007: 133). It is suggested that similarities between Arab and African rentier economies constitute an international problem, which emerges as a result of globalised production rather than being the outcome of states' particular characteristics (Yates 1996: 6). This indicates the importance of rentier politics in determining the migration regimes of other transit countries such as Libya and Algeria.

This is critical in analysis of Mauritania's post-independence trajectory, in which foreign rents underpin the articulation of the state and its borders. Mauritania was under junta control during much of its post-independence history. General Mohamed Ould Abdel Aziz directed the *coup d'état* on 6 August 2008 and subsequently won the presidential election in 2009. The coup was triggered by a series of military dismissals. It was blamed on rising food prices and a lack of transparency over the use of finances. In contrast with the coup of 2005, of which General Abdel Aziz had also been a protagonist, condemnation initially followed from the United States, the African Union, Nigeria and the European Union (*Economist* 2008). Negotiations for the 18 July presidential election were held in Dakar and attended by the ruling junta, ousted President Sidi Ould Cheikh Abdallahi and Ahmed Ould Daddah from the parliamentary opposition (Afrol News 2009). Two journalists reporting on the elections were assaulted in May. Mohamed Ould Zeine, editor of the Arab-language daily *El Wattan* was beaten and left for dead. A reporter from Agence Nouakchott d'Information was manhandled by activists from Daddah's Rally of Democratic Forces party. This followed a complaint about practical support extended to opposition parties by the US embassy, which Daddah revealed in an interview (Reporters Without Borders 2009). According to Moussa Ould Ebnou, adviser to the former president, the United States hardened their position towards the members of the junta when General Abdel Aziz requested the departure of the Israeli ambassador in Nouakchott (Ebnou 2009). The next section examines more closely the role of external interests in determining Mauritania's borders and in undermining established patterns of mobility. In addition to iron and oil rents, the state regime is maintained by geostrategic rents gained as a result of the War on Terror and migration management. Furthermore, 'terrorism rents' enable regimes to crack down on opposition groups and other expressions of civil society democratisation, as well as providing military aid (Keenan 2009: 206). The War on Terror also generates a security emphasis that enables migration to be managed as a threat rather than as a humanitarian crisis.

Clandestine migration to Spain, membership of the Arab Maghreb Union, and departure from the Economic Community of West African States (ECOWAS) place Mauritania strategically in these overlapping regions of the Mediterranean and Middle East. The US-led War on Terror and EU-led efforts to restrict migration both include border security and the prevention of uncontrolled migration. The United States incorporates Mauritania in its Trans-Saharan

Counter-Terrorism Partnership (TSCTP), which expands from the Sahara to the Sahel region of west Africa. EU plans have incorporated Mauritania, along with Libya, Tunisia, Algeria and Morocco, into its migration regime as a 'buffer zone' between Africa and Europe (Baldwin-Edwards 2005a: 4). Mauritania joined the Euro-Mediterranean Partnership in 2007 – now known as the Barcelona Process: Union for the Mediterranean. The Barcelona Process partners Mediterranean, Middle Eastern and, more recently, Balkan states with the EU. The 5+5 dialogue is part of that arrangement.

Hosted by the International Organisation for Migration in 2004, the 5+5 further detached Mauritania from the south. This conference on migration management included countries north and south of the Mediterranean: Algeria, France, Italy, Libya, Malta, Mauritania, Morocco, Portugal, Spain and Tunisia. In 2010, the EC commissioner in charge of expanding the EU, Stephen Foley, attended the 5+5 meeting in Tunis. He stated that, 'it is crucial to have an intensive codification of illegal immigration and a classification of legal immigration; and we can assure you there is agreement on this matter' (Magharebia 2010). Echoing the perception of many migrants who set out to enter Europe, Amin and El-Kenz described the Euro-Mediterranean Partnership as primarily a 'defence' agreement and one that 'protects the EU against possible social, political and cultural "overflowing" from the countries on the southern side of the Mediterranean' (2005: 82). Senegal's President Wade contested that, 'Europe's strategy is crystal clear. It consists, through the establishment of the Union... of cutting off North Africa from the rest of sub-Saharan Africa' (Pana 2009). Mauritania's incorporation in European border management sets it apart from sub-Saharan neighbours. Xenophobic discourse is argued to have strengthened as a result of the construction of migrants as a security threat. Militant nationalists, in a letter to the former president, claimed that: 'the return of Mauritania to ECOWAS by nature would compromise the future of our country, in which national unity is still very fragile' (Choplin 2008: 88).

## The securitisation of migration in Mauritania

In its migration component, the Union for the Mediterranean emphasises co-operation in the management of migration flows. It underlines a 'comprehensive, balanced, integrated and holistic approach', which will protect the rights of migrants (Commission 2007c). However, Mauritania's political economy and involvement in the War on Terror have precluded the inclusion of human rights in bilateral arrangements, and instead they focus on repressive measures. From the early 1990s, the use of anti-terrorist discourse enabled Mauritania's neo-authoritarian regime to be sustained by external western support, thereby resisting pressures for democratisation during President Ould Sid-Ahmed Taya's leadership (Jourde 2007: 77, Bonté and Guillaume 1994: 3–4). From 1993, the Mauritanian government began to arrest political opponents for alleged ties with transnational Islamist groups, and in 1994 it staged the arrests, confessions and releases of Islamist plotters (Jourde 2007: 87). President Taya further cracked down on Islamists in 2003 and strengthened ties with Israel towards the end of his 21-year rule in order to gain US support (Africa Confidential 2003).

Speculation that adverse conditions such as poverty, weak governments and unmonitored borders provide a 'breeding ground' for terrorists has supplemented economic interests since 9/11 and has guided US military support to north and west Africa (African Terrorism Bulletin 2005). Control of African territory, 'both urban and rural, and its land, sea and aerial borders' is promoted for making countries, and American targets, safe (Cilliers 2003: 102). Prior to this, Vice-President Dick Cheney published a report in May 2001, which forecast that by 2015 a quarter of US-imported oil would come from the Gulf of Guinea. As a result of the Cheney Report, President Bush defined African oil as a 'strategic national interest'. Chiefs of staff from Chad, Mali, Mauritania, Morocco, Niger, Senegal and Tunisia took part in a meeting in March 2004 at the US European Command (EUCOM) headquarters in Stuttgart. The meeting reflected US interests in establishing a military presence in the Sahara and the Sahel (Koch 2005: 25).

This led to the creation of the Pan-Sahel Initiative (PSI), represented by Mali, Niger, Chad and Mauritania. EUCOM Deputy Commanding General Charles Wald stated that, 'Africa is becoming a strategic area, whether we like it or not – a large population, many resources, lots of potential instability' (Koch 2005: 25). Thus, in an overall strategy that has been compared with military operations in the Persian Gulf and the Caspian Sea region, when they were defined as national security interests, the US began to establish military bases in Africa (Klare and Volman 2006: 302). The bases would provide low-key facilities and would be maintained by local troops, partly to avoid popular resistance but also because an offshore naval armada was available for deployment to oil-rich regions and would produce the most likely intervention scenario.

The suggestion that US involvement in Africa could be a 'new Cold War' for the region (Besteman 2008) holds weight in Mauritania, from where over 54 per cent of total exports are directed to China, followed by France with just over 14 per cent of exports (EIU 2009c: 6). Furthermore, Washington returned to practices associated with police aid during the Cold War. A threat-driven foreign policy towards central America had established programmes in the 1960s with the purpose of developing covert intelligence networks and offering 'anti-terrorism assistance'. US policy was, however, 'guided first by threats to US investments, and then by the communist threat', which resulted in the USA supporting authoritarian dictatorships whose actions deepened poverty, inequality and repression (Hills 2006: 632). The resurrection of Cold War practices post-9/11 includes the broadening of the US Agency for International Development (USAID) into a quasi-security agency, which contributes resources to the Trans-Sahara Counter-Terrorism Initiative (TSCTI).

The TSCTI – to become the TSCTP – followed the PSI in 2005. Now it includes Algeria, Burkina Faso, Morocco, Tunisia, Chad, Mali, Mauritania, Niger, Nigeria and Senegal, while Libya is no longer listed as a partner. Its objective is to reinforce capacities to fight terrorism by consolidating and institutionalising co-operation between the security forces in the area. It receives military support from Operation Enduring Freedom Trans Sahara, which is the US government's third priority counterterrorism project. The Partnership 'strengthens counterterrorism and border security, promotes democratic governance, reinforces bilateral military ties, and enhances development and institution building'. The US Department of State, Department of Defense and USAID contribute resources to the TSCTP (US AFRICOM n.d.).

The PSI stated its aims to 'protect borders, track movement of people, combat terrorism, and enhance regional co-operation and stability' (Keenan 2008: 17). Regional co-operation in the Sahara and Sahel can also be connected with a wider US strategy, in place since the launch of the Eizenstat Initiative in 1999, to encourage trade and investment and to reduce barriers to trade between north African states (Zoubir 2006: 2). The free movement of capital and goods, combined with highly restricted movement of people, is inbuilt in the US's global strategy. It means that external actors and local capitalist elites attempt to control labour-power in the region. Following 9/11, in particular, the European and US security agenda 'seeks to keep African labour in the continent for fear that it will contaminate order in Europe' (Bush and Keenan 2006: 175).

The EU's Global Approach to Migration and Mobility (GAMM) steered policy from a security-oriented understanding of immigration towards 'holistic' and 'integrated' border management, still security-oriented but paying heed to the root causes of migration and incorporating co-development and the selective encouragement of labour mobility (Chapter 5). However, the inflexible goal of keeping migrants south of the Mediterranean was obvious and, in return, policy offered the 'concession' of extracting workers who could meet the needs of member states' labour markets. Similarly, development entered the common parlance of US military engagement in Africa in the same year. It is argued that the 'security-development' discourse was exported by Tony Blair's Commission for Africa, which tied aid to security and connected poverty and underdevelopment with danger to state security and the international community (Bush 2007: 47). Development and security were entangled in the UK Department for International Development's strategy to 'fight poverty to build a safer world', which would integrate the IMF and World Bank in security assistance (UK DFID 2005). The shift from EUCOM to AFRICOM (US Africa Command), which became an autonomous and operational military command in October 2008, reflected this entanglement. However, military violence appears to have increased since this shift in paradigm and, furthermore, there has been a marked increase in terrorism in Mauritania.

Initial TSCTI training sessions took place in 2005 in the south-eastern town of Bassikounou. During this time the GSPC (Algeria-based Salafist Group for Preaching and Combat) allegedly attacked a remote military garrison in the north and this event was used to justify the training programme, despite questioning of the government's version of events by non-government organisations (Jourde 2007: 92). There are high gains both for leaders who wish to suppress minority groups and opponents, and a US security policy that places natural resources in its midst. The TSCTP returns Mauritania to an emphasis on Islamism and the

Tuareg insurrection in neighbouring Mali, both of which have featured in its politics as a postcolonial state (Bonté and Guillaume 1994: 3). External military operations in north Africa have included intelligence-gathering for Chadian forces engaged in combat against Algerian Salafist guerrillas, and deployment of a cargo plane in Bamako to supply the Malian counter-insurgency against Tuareg forces (Volman and Mintner 2009). The latter conflict has led refugees to Mauritania, and when this escalated in 2012, 15,000 people entered in the second half of June, followed by hundreds per day into July (UNHCR 2012b).

Since December 2007, murders of foreigners, the cancellation of the Paris–Dakar rally, attacks on a nightclub and the Israeli embassy, a suicide bomb and kidnappings have more firmly entrenched Mauritania within the War on Terror. Violent outbreaks have included a 'pitched gun battle between Mauritanian security forces and several suspected terrorists holed up in a house' and decapitations of soldiers (US Department of State 2009). Approximately 90 terrorist suspects were arrested during 2007 and 2008, including 60 in connection with the killings of four French tourists. In June 2009, an American NGO worker was murdered in Nouakchott. A French aid worker was killed in July 2010 after Mauritanian attempts for his release were reported to have left six militants dead and there were further confrontations on the Mauritania–Mali border in 2011 (*Guardian*, 24 August 2010; US Dept. of State 2012).

The development and security discourse has shaped the response to terrorism. Mauritanian authorities announced that the suicide bomber, who detonated himself outside the French embassy in August 2009, was from a poor neighbourhood in Nouakchott and had been trained in camps in the desert regions between Mauritania, Mali and Algeria. Army chiefs-of-staff from Algeria, Mauritania, Mali and Niger then reportedly planned to mobilise 25,000 troops to the border regions. France sent a military delegation to discuss co-operation and the US aimed to ensure that AQMI does not receive grassroots support (EIU 2009c: 17). Political opponents have been arrested under the War on Terror regime, including former minister Isselmou Abdel Kader, who accused the presidential guard of behaving like a militia. Amnesty International reported systematic torture 'as an essential element of the security system' of successive Mauritanian governments (2008: 30). It noted the presence of Moroccan security forces in the formal and secret prisons, possibly resulting from co-operation between the Euro-Mediterranean 5+5 dialogue, which implicates the European migration regime in human rights abuses. As a result of sanctions imposed following its *coup d'état*, Mauritania was excluded from proposals in foreign military financing, education or training. It still is, however, included in the TSCTP. For the 2010 defence budget, President Barack Obama requested $278 million to fund the TSCTP and AFRICOM (Volman 2010).

The terrorist incidents in Mauritania that followed its membership of the TSCTI supports the claim that US military involvement in the Sahel and Sahara exacerbated regional discord in a similar trajectory to US involvement in the Caspian Sea region (Besteman 2008, citing Michael Klare). Reports of incidents in Mauritania constructed poverty and underdevelopment as dangerous

(Abrahamsen 2004). The War on Terror poses the greatest threat to opponents of the state regime and to Muslim or Islamist groups but it is also infringing on labour migrants and refugees in Mauritania. It provides a framework in which Europe is able to practise the repressive component of immigration policy without incorporating the softer elements of development and employment generation, with which it bribes more stable clients.

The presence of Françafrique neo-colonial relations, European and Spanish migration control apparatus and US strategic command does not appear to have induced conflict or contradiction between these powerful external security interests. France's 'deafening silence' on the War on Terror can be linked with the 2002 establishment of an intelligence centre in Paris with the US at the time of planning for the Pan-Sahel Initiative (Keenan 2007: 42). A prohibited military zone was established along the land borders and expansion planned for the northern part of the country, between western Sahara and Mali, covering a third of Mauritania's land mass (Mandraud 2010). This is connected with French military assistance and economic interests. The US Navy and sea patrols have also co-operated on the west African coast. Mauritania, along with Senegal, Benin, Togo, Sao Tome and Gabon, was included in discussions about a joint naval and coast-guard initiative in May 2007. The aims of boosted naval presence were to combat terrorism, illegal migration and drug trafficking, as well as securing oil interests from the Gulf of Guinea. A US Vice-Admiral also stated, more specifically, a commitment to stemming the flow of west African migrants going to the Canary Islands (Flynn 2007). This is indicative of their securitisation. In August 2006, Spain granted two patrol vessels to the Senegalese Navy and US Navy visitors repaired a Senegalese vessel in October 2008 (Jane's Information Group 2009). US and European security interests can coexist and have common goals. In Mauritania, they are concerned with different border regions and different sectors of the population, but converge on the coast. The War on Terror thus provides favourable conditions for a 'buffer zone' to Europe. But migrants are not just caught in the crossfire of imperial conflict and geostrategic rents: they are another valuable resource for employers of labour.

## Labour migration and governance in Mauritania

The governance of migration is entrenched in Mauritania's political economy. Migration control in north and west Africa and from Mauritania, in particular, occurs within a network with shared interests in preventing international mobility. Mauritania's partial integration into the European fortress results in a dual role as receiver of 'returned' migrants and, in turn, returner of migrants from sub-Saharan Africa who may try to proceed to Europe (see Figure 4.3). The European Council's definition of return is 'the process of going back to one's country of origin, transit or another third country' (Cassarino 2006: 2). In other words, European states can 'return' migrants to Mauritania who belong to any African nationality, and also Mauritania can 'return' sub-Saharans just outside its borders. This means that most foreign workers in Mauritania can be arrested or directed to the border by simple suspicion of irregularity (Samy 2008; Yessa 2008: 1). In 2003, a total of 50 migrants were sent back to the border, rapidly growing to 11,637 in 2006 (Ndah Mohammed-Saleh 2008: 2).

The French Minister of the Interior, Overseas and Collective Territories, Michèle Alliot-Marie, stated that: 'we must further mutualise the way that we project European borders outside' (Alliot-Marie 2008). Enacting this policy, the IOM, the Mauritanian Ministry of the Interior, Post and Telecommunications and the French International Service of Technical Police Cooperation (SCTIP) established border posts in Mauritania and arranged visits for Mauritanian officials to French posts in Modan, Lille, Strasbourg and Perpignan. It also began to assess the use of biometric controls at the borders (Confidential document, anonymous international organisation). The SCTIP prioritises international terrorism, organised crime and the 'expansion' of illegal immigration as threats, again linking terrorism with migration. Border posts were established in 2010 at the Mauritanian frontiers with Senegal, Mali and western Sahara. The Mauritanian Minister of Defence, Hamadi Ould Baba Ould Hamadi, connected the posts with AQMI, illegal migration, drugs and arms trafficking, claiming that security was the top priority and more important than development and democracy. An opposition leader claimed that 'this fuss about security has been used to justify [President] Aziz seizing power' (Mandraud 2010).

The naturalised conception that politicians are in charge of border controls belies the impossibility of directing millions of individual decisions (Bigo 2005b: 49–50). Border guards and other gatekeepers can be compared to nightclub bouncers, 'with a social function that far exceeds his job' (Crowley 2005: 152). The management of migration ultimately lies at the hands of the guards, and Mauritanian management is known to be oriented towards a *corruption ambiante* (Yessa 2008: 6). Whether directed by policy or simply a means to extract rents, customs officials at the checkpoints along the border with Senegal and Mali and on the road to Nouadhibou are known to demand cash from potential *clandestins*, or outsiders, more than from citizens or itinerant traders. For example, on a journey from Nioro in Mali to Ayoun el-Atrous in Mauritania, three young Malian men had to pay the guards 3,000 francs CFA (€4.57) at least five times, whilst others in the bush taxi were not charged (see Figure 10.1). Lillian, a Nigerian migrant living in Nouakchott, explained:

> I wouldn't advise many people to come here because it's not that easy for anyone, 'ah this is a Nigerian, this is a Senegalese', instead of collecting 2,000 UM [€5.42] like the others, they will ask for 10,000 [€27.08], just to put the stamp on the passport.
>
> (interview no. 38, Nouakchott, 20 May 2008)

When asked about how Lillian's family felt about her leaving, she explained, 'I was 18 and thinking I have the free will to leave if I want... I wanted to go out and see what is outside and, you know, learn what will happen' (ibid.). Unlike most of the migrants encountered in Nouakchott, she ascribes her journey to choice and not displacement. However, as soon as she reached the Mauritanian frontier, her freedom was compromised. Thus external intervention in the management of borders, for example in the French training programmes with IOM, disrupts migration patterns and adds to the turbulence of migrants' experiences.

Spanish authorities and the Mauritanian government installed a detention centre in Nouadhibou for migrants who attempt to leave Mauritania's shores, which came to be known as 'Guantánamito', in 2006. The overcrowded conditions and reported ill-treatment in this old school led to this reference to the notorious detention centre in Cuba. Imprisonment of migrants in unacceptable conditions may be unsurprising to concerned residents in western Europe, but the centre also has to be connected with the externalisation of European borders to African shores, which criminalises the intention of emigration from Africa. In February 2008, the Mauritanian Information Agency reported that 172 clandestine migrants of different sub-Saharan nationalities were 'repatriated' from Nouadhibou, including 55 people who were stopped by the police in the town, said to be preparing for the journey to Europe. They were held in the detention centre before being sent back (Pana 2008). Mauritania signed an agreement with Spain in July 2003 that concerned not only readmission of its nationals but also of those who are presumed to have transited in the country. As boats leaving the west African coast pass Mauritania *en route* to the Canary Islands, the agreement undermines Mauritania's challenging relations with west Africa as it becomes a European frontier. It takes approximately four days to reach Nouadhibou by *pirogue* from the Cap Vert peninsula in Senegal, during which time supplies can run short or problems are encountered with the boats, leading to breakdowns. One such case occurred in August 2006, when two *pirogues* from the Casamance coast in the south of Senegal were rescued by Mauritanian gendarmes. At least 14 were found dead and 179 survivors from the two boats were taken to hospitals and then repatriated (Agence France-Presse 2006).

Repatriation, as the previous chapter has explained, is not to be taken literally, and in Mauritania this frequently means being escorted to the border, after which migrants often re-cross and try again, paying the border guards a second, third or fourth time. In October and November 2008, 289 clandestine emigrants were held in Nouadhibou or 'repatriated' via the towns of Rosso and Gogui, which border Senegal and Mali respectively (Agence Nouakchott d'Information 2008; Agence de Presse Africaine 2008). Charles, a Ghanaian migrant living in Nouadhibou, explained that sub-Saharan migrants are deported to Rosso, which straddles the Senegal River with Mauritanian and Senegalese sides: 'From Mali, from Ghana, from Nigeria, from Côte d'Ivoire, they go to Senegal, people get to the border, and then they come back. They pay 10,000 ouguiya [€27.51] to come back' (interview no. 32, Nouakchott, 17 May 2008). Maxwell, a Ghanaian living in Nouakchott, was able to take advantage of this ineffectiveness:

> *How long were you in Europe?*
> [Laughs]. When we were there, we were discovered and I think we stayed there for just four days, then on the fifth day we went back.

*So you were repatriated to Ghana?*
No, Senegal.
*So did you have to make your own way to Ghana from Senegal?*
No; from Senegal we were released and had to go back home.
*Why were you sent to Senegal?*
Ok, they asked that. I myself told them I don't want them to send me to Ghana so they decided to fly me. I told them I want Senegal. I chose Senegal myself.
*Did you go back home after that?*
No, no, no. I didn't go back. I didn't go back home, it is difficult to go back; if I have to come back then I will make sure that I have money. I cannot return with just an empty hand.
*Did you work in any other countries after that or did you come straight to Mauritania?*
I came straight to Mauritania.

(interview no. 35, Nouakchott, 20 May 2008)

In an extreme case of chaotic migration management, *Marine One*, a shrimp trawler from the Gulf of Guinea carrying nearly 369 migrants, was discovered in international waters off the coast of Mauritania by the Spanish coastal patrols in January 2007. The migrants were from Pakistan, Burma, Sri Lanka, Afghanistan and sub-Saharan African countries. After the ship had been at sea for weeks, on 12 February, Mauritania allowed Spain to tow the ship to Nouadhibou on the condition that Spain flew the migrants out within four hours. Most of the migrants, believed at the time to be Pakistani or Indian, presented no identity documents and subsequently were held in a warehouse for at least a month. The IOM eventually began to assist their return, while 35 were sent to Spain to apply for asylum. Following this debacle, both Spain and Mauritania expressed regret about their involvement and neither admitted responsibility for the conditions of the warehouse (IRIN 2007; Yessa 2008: 8).

It is possible that fishermen and other traders will be given the opportunity to set out towards Europe, not having intended to go on the voyage; equally, there are 'transit' migrants who decide to stay in Mauritania after understanding the risks. In the busy markets of Nouakchott, migrants from both 'conflict' and 'labour-exporting' countries can be found running small businesses such as restaurants, barbers and textile manufacturers. Gerard explained:

When I reached Mauritania, I found there are many things here such as fish . . . people travelling from here, but I found the journey from here is very very difficult. I was not tempted to enter the *pirogue* although it was my desire . . . Even if I want to go to Europe, taking the *pirogue* to enter the water, no, my life is most precious. I discovered that when people get to Europe they face hard times, even more than in Africa, because they don't have work, they don't have things to do, they don't have papers, and they are hiding from police, not good, not good. Some people have liberty of

> movement, they go wherever they want to go but it's more or less I'm a prisoner, that's why I prefer not to go to Europe.
>
> (interview no. 31, Nouadhibou, 17 May 2008)

Given the precariousness of entering or leaving Mauritania, many migrants are discouraged from a dangerous and possibly fruitless journey. Jacob, a Nigerian from the Delta region, would not attempt to reach Europe by *pirogue*. He claimed that 'some people take the *pirogue* here to go there but unfortunately they end up in Morocco . . . they catch their *pirogue* by the Moroccan seas. They are there begging, not working' (interview no. 37, Nouakchott, 20 May 2008). Thus they remain in the Mauritanian 'holding zone' by choice and not only as a result of forced return by interceptors. The west African peninsulas of Bissau, Dakar and Nouadhibou have been points of departure towards Europe, but they also attract skilled fishermen. It was noted by Mauritania's labour ministry in May 2008 that there is high demand in the fishing and mechanical sectors in Nouadhibou (Ministère de l'Emploi, de l'Insertion et de la Formation Professionelle 2008). The port in Nouadhibou is divided into quarters representing different nations including Ghana, Guinea, Mali and Nigeria and with each quarter processing a different type of fish. Charles explained that in Nouadhibou:

> There are so many fish you can buy and take to your own country like Nigeria . . . the sea is rich and with certain African fish when you sell them to your country, you can get about 50 per cent profit . . . the migrants will be searching for them and drying them, smoking them, they'll get jobs to do and those fish can go. In my country, Ghana, we need fish meal for chickens, they can lay more eggs.
>
> (interview no. 32, Nouadhibou, 17 May 2008)

Charles had been in Nouadhibou for seven years and was in the process of opening a restaurant for immigrants. He also offered safety advice to *piroguiers* about food, water and other supplies, and liaised with NGOs in Spain. 'Transit migrants' like him have undertaken dangerous journeys as a result of dispossession and conflict. There is a thriving parallel economy in Mauritania, which continues in spite of efforts at subjugation, and is sometimes strengthened by them. However, since the fieldwork period, Mauritania has launched an initiative to enrol Mauritanian citizens and foreign residents in a national electronic database, using biometric technology which is meant to identify people at ports of entry. A new government agency has been established, the National Agency of the Population Register and Secure Documents, and this has verified the identity of 100,000 individuals since May 2011. The EU and the Spanish Guardia Civil joined in a ceremony to mark a US$2.6 million investment in 'Project Western Sahel', which introduces new technology for border screening and training for border guards (US Dept. of State 2011).

## Conclusion

By showing how the 'holding zone' is constructed, we can see the important role of EU border security in establishing the separation between migrant workers and those with more substantive freedom. This chapter has indicated the importance of rents to Mauritania's development and the impact this has on the character of the state and its contemporary positioning as a securitised buffer zone to enclose sub-Saharan migrants who aim to enter Spain. This follows the geopolitical logic of EU and US interests in expanding capital, mobilising cheap labour and asserting territorial integrity. The migrant is, however, an essential factor in labour mobility, who challenges the demands of economy and territory that are sometimes in conflict. This is evident in transit migrants' decisions to stay in Mauritania when their livelihoods develop successfully within the vibrant African communities in Nouadhibou and Nouakchott. Mauritania's informal economy offers opportunities that are not encountered in neighbouring states, but the position of workers veers towards unfree labour because their circulation may be restricted according to the will of security personnel.

Since the fieldwork period, this has become an acute problem. The EU and US have installed an 'efficient' system of border management. They have brought 'legality' into the movement of people; yet this is superimposed on a legal system from which southern Mauritanians and foreign workers are excluded, in a country where the EU has externalised most of the violent and arbitrary elements of its border regime, and where the US has instigated a vast military zone. Rapid measures to irregularise cross-border movement in Mauritania with Spanish and French assistance have resulted in arrests, detentions and extortion of migrants at border posts. This has added tension to established patterns of migration from Sahelian communities, disrupting the existing labour reserves as new processes of accumulation take over. With the rents that Mauritania has gained from this renewed regional order, its labour market is likely to continue attracting west African workers who have nowhere else to go, and to absorb their labour in an unfree regime.

# 7 Keeping labour costs down

## Global pressures and west African migrants in Spain

This chapter aims to bring us closer to the dynamics of west African labour migration by addressing four questions in turn. These are, first, What is the role of migrant labour in Spain's political economy? Second, Why and how do west African migrants enter Spain? Third, How does the state then manage them? Fourth, How do migrants interact with the labour market in Spain? This book has explored theoretically the importance of unfree immigrant labour in economic growth and has empirically examined the displacement of labour. Now the four questions will examine the extent to which this has evolved in Spain for west African migrants.

A reversal of Spain's migratory balance began in the early 1970s and developed more markedly from the 1990s (see Table 7.1). Like in Senegal, this transformation was part and parcel of its political economy – but in this case the shift was from a negative to a positive balance. These changes support the argument that the landscape of migration has changed in the 'global' era. The dynamics of these changes are, however, less clear. Is there a reconfiguration of labour-exporting and labour-importing countries, none the less maintaining the general patterns of postwar migration; or are the changes more profound than geographical shifts? This chapter will show that dispossession is a potent factor in west Africans' decisions to enter Spain clandestinely. It will, moreover, describe migrants' circumstances of entry and stay. Spain subsequently has a reliance on labour that is reproduced at a cost to sending communities rather than to the employers. Thus we see characteristics of this south–north movement that suggest the persistent centrality of unfree labour in capitalist development. However, on examining migrants' modes of organisation and strategies for coping with change, struggles emerge that challenge the role of 'labour-import' that is assigned to them by global labour policy and the state economy.

Efforts to deter 'unwanted' immigration to the EU include member states' partnerships with the governments of sending countries, which emphasise co-development combined with coastal patrols, or temporary visa arrangements to meet Europe's labour needs. For migrants that successfully leave their countries without papers, interceptions and repatriation agreements have led to immediate flights either home or to transit countries, or simply into other countries in Africa, after days at sea. Spain halted clandestine migration through the

Strait of Gibraltar in 2003 and into the enclaves of Ceuta and Melilla in Morocco during 2005. It significantly reduced illegal entries to the Canary Islands after the number of fishing boats from west Africa peaked in 2006. More recently, it is dealing with another wave of injured sub-Saharan migrants in Isla de Tierra, an uninhabited Spanish rock close to the Moroccan coast. From here the Guardia Civil transferred some, especially women and children, to Melilla while it sent others to Morocco, from where the migrants were sent on to Algeria (El País 2012). Shootings in Ceuta and Melilla, deportations of migrants in north Africa to remote desert areas, and shipwrecks arriving in Spain from as far away as Guinea reveal a danger created by security forces as well as the natural hazards of desert and sea. This chapter focuses on the migrants who bypass all of these deterrents, either by exceeding the period or terms of legality, or by crossing the border without documentation.

## Informal labour and economic growth in Spain's political economy

In our case study of Spain as a receiving country for west African migrants, it is important to note two things: firstly, that it was a country of emigration only 25 years ago (see Table 7.1), and secondly, that it has been considered as a marginal state in the EU due to its high unemployment and a large underground economy. Spain converged with the GDP per capita of OECD countries and experienced higher than average growth by 2005. It is still, however, considered to be in a marginal position *vis-à-vis* Europe (Amin 2010). Supporting this perception, it fared worse than the OECD average in the global financial crisis in 2008 with a steeper rise in unemployment and a more pronounced dip in GDP growth (EIU 2009b: 20).

*Table 7.1* Net migration, growth and unemployment in Spain

| *Period* | *1965–70* | *1970–75* | *1975–80* | *1980–85* | *1985–90* | *1990–95* | *1995–00* | *2000–05* | *2005–10* | *2010–15* |
|---|---|---|---|---|---|---|---|---|---|---|
| Net migration rate (per 1,000 population) | –1.3 | 0.1 | 0.6 | –0.7 | –0.4 | 1.7 | 4.0 | 12.0 | 7.9 | 6.1 |
| Net migration (1,000s) | –43 | 3 | 23 | –26 | –15 | 65 | 159 | 501 | 350 | 280 |
| GDP growth (%) | 1965<br>6.3 | 1971<br>4.6 | 1975<br>0.5 | 1980<br>2.2 | 1985<br>2.3 | 1990<br>3.8 | 1995<br>2.8 | 2000<br>5.0 | 2005<br>3.6 | 2010<br>–0.8 |
| % of labour force unemployed | — | — | — | 11.1 | 21.0 | 16.0 | 22.7 | 13.9 | 9.2 | 20.5 |

Source: UN DESA 2009c; World Bank 2010; EIU 2009b

Between 1850 and 1950, 3.5 million Spanish workers left for the Americas from Galicia, Asturias and the Canary Islands. Argentina received the most Spanish immigrants at 1.5 million, followed by Uruguay, Brazil and Cuba (Ortega Pérez 2003). These new-world migrations from Spain outnumbered the conquistadors and settlers who entered Spanish America during the colonial period (Moya 1998: 1). Also, by the end of the nineteenth century, there were 94,000 Spanish emigrants in north Africa. After the establishment of the Spanish protectorate in Morocco between 1916 and 1919, a quarter of a million Spanish emigrants were counted here, including residents in Ceuta, Melilla and Tanger. Most originated in Andalusia and the Levante, thus flowing in the opposite direction to contemporary migrations (Alscher 2005: 6). Until the 1930s, 80 per cent of Spanish emigrants headed to the Americas, but this shifted from the 1950s to the mid-1970s, when three quarters of migrants chose instead to go to northern Europe, at which time Spain was also a transit country for migrants heading north from Africa (Ortega Pérez 2003).

Until 1975, Spain was a 'labour-frontier' country for Europe. This is distinguished from a labour reserve because the frontier engages in capitalist relations of production, thus enabling free movement for workers (Skeldon 1997: 145). This helps to explain why remittances from Spanish workers were said to have a significant role in addressing the trade deficit (Harrison and Corkhill 2004: 147) but have been less effective in countries where workers cannot meet their reproduction needs (Meillassoux 1975: 95). Furthermore, Castles and Kosack (1973), writing in the 'golden age' of labour migration, noted that high levels of remittances towards the countries of southern Europe and north Africa did not alter the balance of payments situation in these countries over time. Workers did not leave in sufficient numbers to alleviate unemployment or to raise wages. Thus the development aid moved from the poor countries to the rich ones (1973: 418–20). Spain's growth can therefore be connected with its full integration in Europe, which polarised its positioning in the labour market from that of Morocco.

Before the mid-1980s, most immigrants in Spain were not workers but tourists and retirees from the UK, Germany and other countries of northern Europe. Shortly after joining the European Community in 1986, Spain transformed from a country of emigration to one of immigration (see Table 7.1). It was not only economic development in Spain that led to this switch towards positive net migration; but there was also lower demand for foreign labour in western Europe following the oil-price hikes. At this time, the working-age population increased faster in Spain than elsewhere in the EU. From 1964 to 1994, the Spanish labour force grew by more than 3.5 million or around a quarter, and employment generation could not keep pace (Harrison and Corkhill 2004: 149). The recession in Spain between the mid-1970s and mid-1980s was accompanied by a tripling of the unemployment rate, an expansion of the informal economy and an increase in the number of immigrants (Amuedo-Dorantes and de la Rica 2005: 8; Mendoza 1997: 51). It transformed thus to a labour importer while the labour frontier moved south to the countries of northern Africa. Immigrant workers from Morocco, Latin America (mainly the Dominican Republic) and Asia (mainly the

Philippines and China) constituted the largest inflow. By 2000, 60 per cent of foreigners in Spain were from non-EU countries (Cornelius 2004: 388).

As discussed earlier, the EC was heading towards increasingly restrictive policy towards non-EC entrants from the 1970s onwards. Spain's first immigration law in 1985 was modelled on Germany's legislation for guest workers as it entered into the Schengen Agreement. It focused on controlling access to the labour market and ultimately hindered stable residency for the foreign-born population, thus creating a large undocumented population (Ortega Pérez 2003). Between 1996 and 2004, while José María Aznar's Partido Popular (PP) was in government, the number of immigrants to Spain grew from half a million to 2.5 million (Balfour 2005: 157). During the first term, until 2000, Prime Minister Aznar's centre-right government pursued moderate policies, enjoying a lack of far-right opposition. Spain's post-Franco democratisation discouraged the development of right-wing populist tabloids and racist discourse (van Dijk 2005: 20). Immigration policy recognised the structural role of migrant labour. It protected the rights both of legal and illegal workers and included the provision of healthcare, education, legal advice and interpreters.

Convergence with the EU line developed, however, after Aznar's electoral victory in March 2000, which came the month after violent incidents in the southern region of Almeria. In the town of El Ejido, days of rioting broke out between Moroccan and Spanish residents (BBC 2000). Aznar's second term saw a reversal of the earlier policy, now denying fundamental rights of assembly and association to undocumented migrants. Following the EU path, the government dichotomised legal and illegal migrants, ensuring integration of legal immigrants and restriction of those who were unauthorised, thus constructing the double labour market. It also paved the way for co-operation agreements with sending countries. Aznar's EU chairmanship in 2002 constructed immigrants as a threat to the EU. The term 'illegal' immigration was repeatedly used in connection with public safety and was explicitly connected with crime. It was argued that international solidarity with all human beings would enable more illegal immigration. This was 'a classic case of preformulation of racism by the elites', developed in order to dominate non-whites (van Dijk 2005: 20). Aznar stimulated anti-immigrant sentiment as an acceptable element of political discourse in Spain, with particular xenophobia against Arabs and Berbers. Furthermore, the rise of far-right support elsewhere in Europe led the PP leadership to justify stringent border controls. Preference was directed towards 'culturally closer' Latin American and eastern European migrants over those from the Maghreb, giving rise to tensions in Andalusia (Alscher 2005: 13).

The EU then became a moderating factor in Spanish policy, blocking Tony Blair and Aznar's proposals to punish third countries that failed to regulate migration to Europe (Cornelius 2004: 392; Gillespie 2005: 206). Prime Minister José Luis Rodríguez Zapatero's socialist government from 2004 displayed a more accommodating policy towards immigrants than its predecessor. One migrant reported that under the Aznar administration, the police had persistently and slowly circulated the areas of the park where he would meet friends and associates but this no longer happened under Zapatero (interview no. 76, Barcelona, 21 February 2009). His government oversaw a significant increase in foreigners with residence permits, increasing from 1,647,011 in January 2004 to 3,740,956 by September 2007 and reaching 11 per cent of the Spanish population (Rius 2008). However, illegal labour continued to be significant. In January 2008, three quarters of registered Senegalese migrants lacked residence permits (González-Enríquez 2009: 3). The conditions for migrants deteriorated again when the PP returned in 2012 under Mariano Rajoy's leadership. This administration began to dismantle healthcare provisions for 'illegal' migrants, declaring that registration would no longer be enough to enable medical access. This measure met with strong opposition from the health services including the pledge from 2,000 doctors that they would 'conscientiously object' to what one doctor called a 'genocide for reasons of social discrimination' and would treat all people who needed it (El Mundo 2012).

Most immigrants in Spain are from former colonies in Latin America, followed by Europeans, Africans and Asians (see Table 7.2). Distribution of migrants across the country, however, is unequal. At the end of 2008, 17.5 per cent of the working population in Catalonia was foreign-born (Pajares 2009a: 4). Furthermore, Catalonia became the main contributor to Spain's growth, followed by Madrid and Andalusia (OECD 2009b: 18). In Girona, to the north east of Barcelona, Moroccans and west Africans comprise the largest immigrant population (INE 2008).

*Table 7.2* Foreign population in Spain and selected regions, 2008

| | *Spain* | *Barcelona Province* | *Girona* | *Lleida* |
|---|---|---|---|---|
| Total foreign population | 726,009 | 128,843 | 20,276 | 10,462 |
| Europe | 254,316 | 31,048 | 6,401 | 4,381 |
| Africa | 146,735 | 22,778 | 6,430 | 3,709 |
| Asia | 60,005 | 23,273 | 2,093 | 457 |
| Americas | 264,340 | 51,630 | 5,346 | 1,914 |

Source: INE 2008

Spain's growth was the result of 'increased labour utilisation and capital accumulation' (OECD 2009a: 104). In the decade between 1996 and 2006, while growth increased steadily, salaries decreased from 5.3 per cent to 3.1 per cent annually during the same period (Martín Urriza 2007: 16). Growth was principally in the construction and tourism sectors, which utilise cheap labour with temporary workers and a foreign labour force. In 2006, the Spanish Workers' Commissions (CC OO) calculated labour costs in Spain at 54.5 per cent of each product unit, below the Eurozone average of 56.5 per cent and lower than Italy, Germany, France and the United Kingdom (ibid.: 21).

Barcelona had a higher growth rate, at 8.4 per cent from 2006 to 2007, than the Spanish average of 3.9 per cent, and employment was also higher. The Catalonian city had experienced industrial decline in the late 1970s and 1980s, reaching an unemployment rate of 21.4 per cent in 1986. The awarding of the 1992 Olympic Games in that year, however, provided a 'springboard for the development of a strong brand for Barcelona based on an entrepreneurial spirit and a high quality of life' (OECD 2009b: 16). As an analysis of preparations for the 2012 Olympics in London also found (Cillo and Perocco 2008: 22), Olympic development in Barcelona depended on informal labour. The greatest beneficiaries of Olympic activity were the companies with more than 500 employees, 70 per cent of which participated, whilst only fourteen per cent of small companies were involved. The large enterprises underwent a process of decentralisation, subcontracting and shrinkage, leaving a stable core of employees and unstable workers at the margins as construction boomed (Miguélez and Carrasquer 1995: 5).

Times both of growth and of recession in Spain show the continuous role of cheap labour in accumulation and an increased emphasis on low production costs where capital accumulation is strained. Spain's comparative advantage in labour costs generates a large and growing pressure to pay the labour force at a lower rate than its competitors. Numbers of clandestine migrants and their degree of employment elude the official and speculative data. Most of the shadow economy is related to the formal economy, and downturn can therefore lead in absolute terms to a contraction in employment. The easing of formal employment also has the effect, however, of growth in some sectors (Cillo and Perocco 2008: 38).

Unemployment levels in the global economic downturn at the end of 2008 mainly affected construction, with 228,300 job losses, followed by industry with 168,100 and services at 107,100, whilst agricultural jobs rose by 14,000 (EIU 2009a: 14–16). As residential construction and private consumption ceased to drive growth, Spain was subjected to pressure from international organisations to improve its productivity at lower costs (IMF 2009: 4). The ILO (2009), finding the global labour market in 'severe distress', claimed that increased productivity would be the key to poverty reduction: 'the poor do not suffer from an absence of work, but rather from low productivity and the resulting low remuneration' (ILO 2009: 15). It argued that although not guaranteed, higher output per worker could lead to increased wages or shorter hours. We will see, however, that wages and terms of work are overdetermined by a competitive and segmented labour market.

## 'Illegal' entry to the Spanish labour market

Colonial labour regimes converted land and economy in favour of supplying export goods to the imperial powers and labour from this milieu could then increase the value of capital. The 'marginal mass' of unemployed or poor people that colonialism created was thus associated with the postwar economic boom (Löwy 1981: 104). This meant that Spain could be provided with the subordinated labour force required to accumulate capital (Brandariz García and Fernández Bessa 2009: 151–2). In Senegal, conversion of land use to meet external demand

*Figure 7.1* Catalonia
Illustrator: Alex van Zomerplaag

and international fishing agreements that undermine fishing communities' livelihoods have partially driven postcolonial emigration. We have seen in Thiaroye-sur-Mer and in the accounts of migrants in Mauritania that ongoing accumulation propels people out of west African countries and towards Spain. The flow of resources from Africa to Europe is an underlying cause of (restricted) emigration and is not merely a philosophical contradiction between movement of goods and people. Kheraba Drame, a Senegalese migrant living in Barcelona, argues, 'All the time African resources come – diamonds, gold, bauxite, uranium; every day African things come here to Europe. We want to be dispossessed of our things?...and this does not affect anybody?' (interview no. 76, Barcelona, 21 February 2009).

However, explaining migratory movements in terms of inequality between sending regions is unsatisfactory, as most people do not migrate (Hammar and Tamas 1997; Chapter 2). Therefore, we now seek explanation of migrants' entry to Spain in particular. Furthermore, this examination of Spain's management of new entrants will identify some of the forces behind this movement and consider whether or not it is 'free'.

Another explanatory factor for transnational migration besides inequality 'pushing' people from one region and 'pulling' them to another is the facilitation of movement that globalisation signifies. Senegalese migration is frequently associated with modern communication and transportation, which enables the development of 'transnational livelihoods' (Crespo Ubero 2006; Zohry 2005). For example, Mourides from Senegal are known to trade items including CDs and handbags in Spanish tourist areas, within networks that span Spain, north America and other northern countries. Therefore, there is an emphasis in this narrative on mobility rather than restriction. However, when available to migrants, inventions of mass transportation and communication do not substantively alter their dynamic relationship with controlled labour mobility.

The majority of 'irregular' west African migrants in the EU enter legally by air (de Haas 2008b: 48). Illegal entry is the less common route to irregularity, but is possibly more significant than anticipated. Immigrants who do not have residence papers or who have entered illegally and received expulsion orders may register on the *padrón* (municipal register). Because this entitled migrants to healthcare, it was thought that the figures for 'illegal' immigrants were reasonably accurate (Sandell 2006, cited in de Haas 2008b: 34). A report by ACCEM (Spanish Catholic Commission on Migration), however, estimated 1,500–2,000 unregistered migrants in Salt, a municipality of Girona in which African telecentres, restaurants and other businesses are prominent. The overall foreign population there increased from 6.1 per cent in 2000 to 37.5 per cent in 2007 according to the town census. The majority was from Africa and the study found that almost half of the unemployed migrant population was not registered (Benabid 2008: 2–3). They were likely to have entered the country without detection and either to fear repatriation – preferring to borrow identity papers from compatriots – or to be unaware of the opportunity to register.

A 'chain of work' can replace push-and-pull factors as an explanation for migrant networks. The migrant labour network between the Dominican Republic and Spain has been described as 'a job network that enables people to circulate from a more peripheral area to one that is less so', in order to produce goods and services akin to commodity chains (Ubaldo Martínez Veiga 1999: 110). The place of origin supports the circulation and mobility of the workforce, while the place of arrival 'constitutes the centre of contact between supply and demand', in this case the Corona Boreal Square in Aravaca, where Dominican women exchange goods and news of opportunities (ibid.). Similarly, the ports and transit towns in west and north Africa offer areas to exchange information, seek work and pool resources.

Examination of journeys from west Africa to Spain reveals trajectories that are barely touched by the spread of information and technology that globalisation signifies. Treks through ancient desert routes interspersed with manual labour and ending in small fishing boats, un-networked or via precolonial networks, individual and improvised, characterise a common journey to Spain. Migration through Morocco or the west African coast can thus be considered as a *regional* movement from adjacent countries rather than a *global* migration (Baldwin-Edwards 2004).

Take the case of Abada, a Cameroonian who was living in Catalonia (interview no. 22, Barcelona, 26 February 2008; Figure 7.1). He left Nkambe in Cameroon when he faced difficulty in meeting household needs. His elderly parents had enough land and cattle to survive, but they were no longer able to make profit from the crops by the mid-1980s, when he was in secondary school, and at this time the school fees increased. He would undertake odd jobs, such as fetching firewood, to pay for books and fees, but eventually left under pressure to help his sisters and parents. He worked in a sawmill for two years and as a boxcar driver for eight months. His father and others from the village had migrated itinerantly to Nigeria, transporting limestone, but he decided to go to Europe after seeing people return successfully. The whole journey took him around five years, often delayed by long treks to avoid checkpoints or by stops in border towns, where he would earn the money to pay smugglers in north Africa. It is a typical 'stepwise' journey (Conway 1980; Albert 2008), which allows us to examine why and how he entered Spain.

> *So you went overland to Morocco? How?*
> From Cameroon I had to enter Chad, from Chad to Libya, Libya to Algeria, Algeria to Morocco.
> *And this was all by bush taxi?*
> Some places I had to trek; like, for example, from Chad to Libya. I never had the money for going through. And the region where I was in Chad . . . sometimes we had all these scorpions and people died. So I saw some people that transport camels from Chad to Libya. They take three months to six months.
> *How long did it take you from Chad to Libya?*
> It took us five months, six months. I thought Libya would be better. So I went to Libya. So when I reached Libya it was OK and immigration took me and they asked for my passport, and I told them I don't have any passport with me. They said then that they have to send me back to my country. I was kept in a detention centre maybe for two weeks. It's not too bad – you cannot go out but they give you food, they give water . . . when they released me I went to town. I had to ask if I can see other Africans, maybe the black Africans, from around central west Africa, some Cameroonians, Nigerians. Two, three days after, I found a company, one South African company, where they do construction, so I worked for them just as a labourer . . . I did that for three months . . . I worked mixing the cement until I could have again some small monies . . . so I sent some small monies to my mother.
> *How much did you send?*
> I sent her $200. Secondly, I had to send to her again, maybe $200 . . . if there is sickness or any other thing they can buy drugs, can buy oil.
> *So what happened after Libya?*
> So after Libya I had to think of going to Italy because my main aim was that I had to do all that, from the word go, that was my goal, because Libya is not free . . . Maybe you are on the street just walking, police just come and stop you . . . I had to just stay quiet, do what I could do, I had to work hard in order to leave the country. I discovered that was the system. When I came to Algeria, I saw that Libya was better than Algeria, I think, and from Algeria to Morocco, I discovered that Algeria was again better than Morocco [laughs].
> (interview no. 22, Barcelona, 26 February 2008)

Abada spent almost a year each in Algeria and Morocco, moving frequently to avoid the police. The Moroccan police apprehended 27,000 migrants in 2004, over half of whom were west African (de Haas 2008b: 32). Abada particularly feared being deported in Algeria to the extremely isolated border town with Mali of Tin Zaouatene, from where it would be difficult to re-enter Algeria without money. He occasionally worked in construction sites for around €7 per day. Eventually he paid €1,250 for a chaotic, crammed boat journey that included Ivorian and Congolese refugees: 'The boat is supposed to carry 35 or 40, maximum. The women with pregnancy, the small children – I'm not counting the children, I'm only counting the others, who were in number around 78' (interview no. 22, Barcelona, 26 February 2008). A young boy from Mali jumped overboard and a woman died. Abada was trying to calm the young captain as the engine failed. The boat was escorted to Almeria by the Spanish coastguard, arriving on 20 November 2007.

Thus we see in Abada's case how he was propelled between Cameroon and Spain: he frequently had to avoid police under fear of deportation. He was arrested, and he worked for a very low wage. He was able to send money home and, in this sense, was successful, but the journey was at times a struggle for survival. However, the experiences of migrants also show, on the flip side of precariousness, that luck plays an important role in the journey to Spain. Bakary, for example, found favour with security personnel. He was a Gambian university tutor who left Serekunda as a result of intense government surveillance, eventually being 'informed by the intelligence that the best thing was to leave the country' (interview no. 17, Salt, Girona, 23 February 2008). A 'Herculean' journey, taking almost a year, followed:

> Sometimes you have nights somewhere, some different places, like from Senegal back to Mali, Mali to Morocco, you spend some days there...I stopped at some points, sometimes you work for some time, usually on farms, to support you on the way...I was fortunate because at that point in time they had some soldiers there, Moroccan soldiers, in Tanger...those are the guys who helped us across.
>
> *So you paid them?*
>
> Actually I didn't pay – because of my knowledge in language, they had the desire to communicate with some of the people there, so I could speak for them and then help them to communicate...so actually my knowledge paid the villains!
>
> (ibid.)

Lamin, also from Gambia, was a groundnut farmer who was driven to migrate when his crops would not sell. 'My family did not want me to leave. I wanted to go to Europe to help the family and get them out of suffering' (interview no. 19, Barcelona, 25 February 2008). He sought work in Mali, Mauritania, Morocco, Guinea and Senegal, working as a seaman, until a friend notified him that there would be a ship to Spain. He left from Diogué, at the estuary of the Casamance

River in Senegal and close to the border with Guinea-Bissau. Migrations from this area escalated following increased patrols to the north of Senegal after the peak of boat migration in 2006.

> *Did you feel danger?*
> I felt danger. A French trawler escorted us for around two days, giving us food to prevent us from being detained in Morocco. They decided that they can't leave us in the sea to die and they can't let us go to jail in Morocco. They brought us near to the Spanish coast and called the Spanish people.
>
> (ibid.)

Thus Lamin, firstly, gained the opportunity for a successful passage to Europe and, secondly, benefited from the exceptional generosity of passers-by. Therefore, chance is an important force in the entry of migrants to Spain, and also we have seen that periods of informal employment support geographical mobility. Similarly, in the case of migration from north Africa to Europe, compared with colonial links and demographic 'push', the most important factor in 'illegal' migration is the influence of large underground economies, which support and require the employment of immigrant labour. In these economies, 'labour costs are minimised and production, which might otherwise be internationally unviable, continues' (Baldwin-Edwards 1999: 13). Thus the underground economies that supported the journey continue at the destination. A large proportion of 'illegal' immigrants to advanced industrialised countries enter low-paid service or agricultural jobs, releasing their employers from legal responsibility.

## How does the state manage migrants?

Illegality is a structural factor in the Spanish labour market. Migrants with deportation orders are incorporated in Spain's development, particularly in the agricultural sector (Cillo and Perocco 2008). Returning to the case of Abada, we see how Spain's political economy creates 'illegal' migrants:

> When we came to Almeria, they gave us some clothes to change and after we changed they took us to the commissariat. So we had to spend some days in the commissariat but the next day they took our matter to the court and the court issued a paper which was a deportation paper. I couldn't understand, all was written in Spanish. What I understood is that they... had to keep us for 40 days and see our nationalities... they decided now to send us to come here in Barcelona.
>
> (interview no. 22, Barcelona, 26 February 2008)

Lamin also was issued with an expulsion order after detention in the Barranco Seco camp in Gran Canaria. Similarly, Olivia migrated from Ibo State in Nigeria, arriving in Las Palmas de Gran Canaria in 2001:

> I came here through Libya. Libya through Algeria. Algeria through Morocco. I came through the patera, we call it, in the sea, in 2001. The journey almost took me one year on the road. When I came here I was talking to the police and they interviewed me, they separated everything when we were in Las Palmas; after, they let all of us come, some people they deported. It depends on the luck. If you have the luck.
>
> (interview no. 16, Salt, Girona, 23 February 2008)

Thus the 'lucky' migrants are subjugated in Spanish society because they carry papers that state their illegality. The Red Cross revealed for the year 2006 that 32,917 people in the Canary Islands were supported in the Relief and Emergency plan (Cruz Roja 2007: 2), although the outcome for these thousands of migrants is unpublished. There are some indications, however. A government delegate in Barcelona stated that during 2008, 980 out of 4,700 cases of expulsion had been enforced, constituting about 20 per cent (El Periódico de Catalunya 2008). See the number of apprehensions of unauthorised migration in Spain, compared with removals, in Table 7.3. Not to be confused with the raids upon migrants staying in the UK, removals in Spain are normally expedited within 72 hours of detection and have mainly affected Moroccans who are apprehended at the borders (Alscher 2005: 15). Table 7.3 shows that despite a significant increase in apprehensions from 2002 onwards, reaching more than 95,000 people in 2006, the number of removals did not exceed 34,000. It is likely that the increase in apprehensions reflects enhanced detection methods in Gibraltar, Morocco and west Africa, respectively, as well as increased numbers attempting to migrate. However, we can see an increase in unauthorised migrants in Spain because 'removal' methods were not developed as robustly as apprehensions. Table 7.4 shows apprehensions and removals by country of citizenship: note that identifying citizenship is problematic (Chapter 5). It is likely that deportation of over 5,000 Senegalese migrants in 2006 influenced the reduction of entrants in 2007, but also this would increase the likelihood of destroying identity papers.

*Table 7.3* Apprehensions and removals of migrants in Spain or at the borders, 1997–2007

| *Year* | *Number of apprehended migrants* | *Number of removals* |
|---|---|---|
| 1997 | 11,212 | 27,773 |
| 1998 | 11,511 | 22,723 |
| 1999 | 10,574 | 23,840 |
| 2000 | 6,579 | 23,942 |
| 2001 | 12,976 | 26,801 |
| 2002 | 56,130 | 26,434 |
| 2003 | 55,164 | 26,757 |
| 2004 | 77,017 | 26,432 |
| 2005 | 62,812 | 25,370 |
| 2006 | 95,765 | 33,235 |
| 2007 | 72,559 | 25,443 |

Source: Spanish Ministry of Interior 2009

*Table 7.4* Apprehensions and removals by countries of citizenship (top five)

| | *2004* | *2005* | *2006* | *2007* |
|---|---|---|---|---|
| Apprehensions of migrants | Morocco 22,340<br>Romania 9,526<br>Ecuador 5,285<br>Mali 4,966<br>Algeria 3,352 | Morocco 20,574<br>Romania 9,829<br>Algeria 2,928<br>Brazil 2,650<br>Mali 2,479 | Morocco 19,350<br>Senegal 16,224<br>Romania 12,554<br>Algeria 4,986<br>Bolivia 4,970 | Morocco 18,204<br>Bolivia 10,623<br>Brazil 5,916<br>Algeria 4,212<br>Senegal 3,984 |
| Total removals | Morocco 15,716<br>Romania 3,112<br>Nigeria 1,042<br>Ecuador 983<br>Colombia 778 | Morocco 16,396<br>Romania 3,493<br>Algeria 894<br>Nigeria 663<br>Brazil 528 | Morocco 15,168<br>Senegal 5,357<br>Romania 4,450<br>Algeria 1,713<br>Brazil 1,055 | Morocco 13,820<br>Senegal 2,820<br>Algeria 1,618<br>Brazil 1,460<br>Bolivia 426 |

Source: Spanish Ministry of Interior 2009

Having examined illegal entry to Spain, it is also possible that migrants who enter with documents will become illegal if they fail to obtain a residence permit. Even with a residence permit, a migrant may not have the right to work (Jahn and Straubhaar 1999). There are limits to the timeframe and extent of legality, and there are also different shades of employment, which include day-to-day casual recruitment and seasonal agricultural labour. Around 90 per cent of immigrants who were legal residents in 2005 had previously experienced a period of non-legality in Spain. Furthermore, administrative delays that take up to 12 months can cause legal migrants to lose their position. Processing times led 200,000 migrants to become 'irregular' in 2004 (González-Enríquez 2005: 10–11).

However, amnesties have featured in Spain's migration politics since it became a labour-receiving country and thus migrants gain the opportunity to enter legality. Table 7.5 shows the major regularisation programmes that have been enacted since Spain's first immigration law in 1985. The programmes target particular groups of migrants, such as those who have lost legal status in 1996, and agricultural workers in 2005. For the latter programme, just over 90 per cent of sub-Saharan applicants were successful in Barcelona Province (Sabater and Domingo 2012: 200). These programmes were limited in their numbers, time-frames, type of permit and role, often 'segmenting' workers into agricultural or domestic work and then returning them to an 'illegal' status.

*Table 7.5* Regularisation programmes in Spain, 1985–2009

| *Year* | *Population affected* | *No. of permits granted* | *Notes* |
|---|---|---|---|
| 1985–6 | Illegally resident workers and families. Must have job offer | 23,000 | Connected with 1985 Law on the Rights and Freedoms of Foreigners, viewing immigrants as temporary workers who need to be regulated. |

| | | | |
|---|---|---|---|
| | | | Total 44,000 applicants. Short-term legalisation; difficult to renew and slow bureaucratic process; 50–75% of eligible migrants did not apply (lack of infrastructure). |
| 1991–2 | Illegally resident workers and families; rejected/pending asylum seekers | 109,135 | Total 135,393 applicants. Permits restricted to economic sectors; three years later 26–50% estimated not to have renewed permits. |
| 1996 | Immigrants who have lost legal status (59%); family members of immigrants with permits (34%) | 21,300 | Total 25,000 applicants. 13,800 gained work and residence permits; 7,500 gained residence permits. |
| 2000–1 | 1. Work permit or residence permit in previous 3 years | 153,463 | 247,598 applicants; beneficiaries worked in agriculture, domestic service or construction. |
| | 2. Prove settlement or 'roots' in Spain | 221,083 | 350,000 applicants; beneficiaries mainly in domestic service and construction. |
| 2005 | Normalisation programme | 575,000 | Work permits, one year (renewable). 10,100 Senegalese applicants were successful. |
| | Registered for at least six months and offered work contract of at least six months/ three months for agriculture | (84,027 in Barcelona) | 90.6% success rate for sub-Saharan Africans in Barcelona. |
| 2006 | Illegal residents | 100,000 (20,000 in Barcelona) | Work permits; must return to country to obtain visas. |
| 2006–9 | Settlement programme | | |
| | Labour settlement: must have lived in Spain for at least two years and can prove existence of a labour relationship | 79,433 | 43.7% success rate for sub-Saharan Africans in Barcelona (mainly Gambian and Senegalese applicants). More than a third of these failed to change from Labour Settlement permit to ordinary work permit. |
| | Social settlement: has lived in Spain for three years, can produce a work contract and has proven links with the local community | (21,458 in Barcelona) | Lapsing into illegality was found to be frequent in this programme. |

Source: Mendoza 2000: 6–7; Rius Sant 2006a; Rius 2008; Levinson 2005: 48–50; Sabater and Domingo 2012: 196, 200, 207

ıaller regularisations have also taken place. Plaza Catalunya is a metro n and square. It is at the apex of Barcelona, leading on to La Rambla. At the start of 2001, 133 sub-Saharan migrants staying here were regularised by agreement between the city council, the Generalitat (government of Catalonia) and the Spanish government. The cohort was living under non-enforced expulsion orders (Rius-Sant 2006b). Eight months later, 120 sub-Saharan migrants were forcibly evicted in an early morning raid (Noguer and Costa-Pau 2001). This shows again that migrants enter an unstable existence that nevertheless can be overturned in Spain more easily than in other EU countries. Furthermore, labour quotas have responded to shortages in the Spanish labour market, for which most applicants have already entered Spain without documents. In 2002, the government set a quota of 32,079 workers, which some labour unions considered to fall short of the needs of agriculture. It was, however, reduced again by 10,000 in 2003 (Ortega Pérez 2003). When short-term visas were issued to Senegalese workers, the migrants would be likely to overstay the period, even leaving their position early and moving on to prevent deportation (Chapter 5). It was also evident in the Senegalese case that past regularisations of illegal entrants, or emigrants' ability to send money home even without legal residence, was a significant driving factor in new attempts to reach Spain by boat.

Ultimately, the circulation of labour is controlled by these fluctuations in legality. As much as President Sarkozy's 'returns' and anti-immigration discourse effectively repelled west African workers from France, Spain's regularisation programmes have attracted them (Levinson 2005; Reyneri 2003: 8). Saskia Sassen points out that inequality is not sufficient to explain movement from one country to another, or there would be significantly larger migrations towards Europe. Instead, this inequality needs to be 'activated' through organised recruitment, neo-colonial bonds or, more generally, the economic, political and social conditions in the receiving country (1999: 136–7).

To conclude this section, we return to the discussion in Chapter 2 about the dialectical relationship between the political and the economic (Harvey 2003; Ashman and Callinicos 2006: 111–16). Spain promotes a territorial logic of power by criminalising, detaining, apprehending and returning migrants. The capitalist economy then promotes an economic logic of power by absorbing 'illegal' foreign migrants into production. Thus the state and economy have opposing aims, but they are interdependent. This is because the state is pressured to continue with a model of growth in which cheap labour adds value to production; that value can be added if labour is subjugated by carrying the threat of expulsion.

## Interaction between migrants and the labour market: segmentation and opposition

Migrants are more mobile and therefore able to fill labour demands in different regions. Between 2004 and 2007, around 3 per cent of the Spanish population migrated internally each year, whilst the figure was between 10.8 and 11.8 per cent for foreigners (Pajares 2009b: 119). This mobility is mainly geographical, however.

The segmentation that occurs for foreign workers into particular sectors and roles limits their labour mobility (Miles 1987: 9). For migrants, this is the product of race relations. As the state legitimates inferior treatment of foreigners, employers are spared from demands for improved conditions (Meillassoux 1975: 120–2). Kheraba explained in a discussion about African migrants: 'You can be an engineer and you will be working as a gardener, you know, they don't value us for what we know. It's just the physical part' (interview no. 76, Barcelona, 17 August 2008). Migrants in Spain experience little convergence with native workers over time, and are restricted to unwanted, unskilled work. Immigrants initially face higher unemployment rates than native workers but eventually the gap closes or even surpasses Spanish workers so that the former have a higher participation rate. The gap of over-education and the incidence of temporary contracts for migrants, however, has been found to remain constant over a five-year period (Fernández and Ortega 2006). While a survey made in 1994 found around 60 different professions among immigrants, their employment in Spain was limited to domestic and agricultural work, sales, construction and four or five trade professions in a process of 'disqualification' (Martínez-Veiga 1999). Immigrants of different nationalities, furthermore, enter particular segments, so that high concentrations of Dominicans or Filipinos can be found in domestic service, and Moroccans or Gambians in agriculture. Olivia moved between the sectors known to employ immigrants:

> When I came, I worked in taking care of the old people . . . then I changed my work in Mataró, where they kill pigs . . . then I had to work in a restaurant where they were selling pizzas, and now I am cleaning houses and plates, washing plates every day, that's how I survive.
>
> (interview no. 16, Salt, Girona, 23 February 2008)

Similarly Angel, a Nigerian living in Salt, Girona, obtained a three-month visa in Lagos and flew to Spain with his brother in November 2005. He explained that poverty was the driving factor of migration from his region of Edo state. He worked in a telecentre in Salt for five months, which was owned by an associate, then lost his legal status. He had to seek work with an agent and entered into agricultural work (interview no. 18, Salt, 23 February 2008).

In the agricultural sector, particularly, activity is seasonal and depends on an 'army of reserve manual labour' that is always available and can be laid off without consequences (Martínez-Veiga 1999). From the 1970s, the farming sector in Spain experienced natural decrease, as farmers began to enter better-paid manufacturing and service jobs and the workforce aged over 55 expanded, while the number of farmers aged below 25 decreased by 139,949 between 1982 and 1989 (Hogart and Mendoza 2000: 5). In Girona, the rapid expansion of tourism in the 1990s drew Spanish workers towards the accommodation and restaurant sector, which shares the peak season with farming. It can be expected that agriculture, for its strength in past times of recession, and domestic work in view of an ageing population, will continue to attract informal labour, while construction and industry tend to contract in times of recession.

The OECD and the IMF have promoted the further easing of employment legislation, including a reduction of severance pay for workers with permanent contracts, in order to hamper the negative effects of a segmented labour market (OECD 2009a; IMF 2009: 4). Lower dismissal costs for workers were also promoted in the 1990s with little effect on Spanish fixed-term contracts, which have remained for around a third of the wage and salary workforce (Amuedo-Dorantes and de la Rica 2005: 7). Although this strategy could reduce polarisation between stable and unstable workers in a dual labour market, it is unlikely to improve labour mobility equally within services, industry, agriculture, or domestic and other sectors, and is more an effort to expand the labour reserve. 'Irregular' migrants are obscured in growth strategy and analysis from the global neo-liberal institutions, but at the same time their restricted circulation is a structural factor in economic competitiveness. A major structural economic reform in Spain's austerity era, during which youth unemployment has soared to 47 per cent, is to merge the double labour market by relaxing labour laws so that it is easier and cheaper to fire workers (*Economist* 2012). Despite this, the demand for migrant labour will continue because migrants are excluded from receiving any 'indirect wages' in the form of family allowance, pensions, unemployment benefits and sickness cover. Their sending households will cover these costs.

Migrants' engagement in the unfavoured side of the double labour market occurs because they have been displaced from the sending community by means of dispossession. In order to send money home, Senegalese emigrants are known to drastically reduce spending in reception countries, considering them to be 'like a field, that is to say a space of work, a place of activity' (Tall 2008: 53, translated by author). This is evident in the case of Frank, a migrant from eastern Nigeria (interview no. 25, Barcelona, 28 February 2008). He entered Spain by legal means and by air like the majority of west African migrants (de Haas 2008b: 48). His situation changed from relative wealth in Nigeria, which he could no longer sustain, to destitution in Barcelona. Despite this, Frank would consider his migration to be 'successful' if eventually he could fund his children's education. He reckoned that he would probably wait for two years to have residence papers and find work, and then he would be able to return to his family (interview no. 25, Barcelona, 28 February 2008).

Migrants oppose the limitations of the role that the state and capital assign to them. We return to Abada, whose entry into work reveals social cohesion between immigrants, challenging the restrictive nature of an illegal status:

> So from Barcelona I first came to Tarragona and worked for a Spanish man. When I started to work, he paid me to work maybe 15 hours.
> *What kind of work?*
> Just renting bicycles . . . since I speak French and English, he said it was an advantage. Because a lot of the tourists that come there, they speak English, French. So I started in the morning at 8:00 and I had to close at 9:00 [p.m.] and I had no time to rest . . . I had to take a bus early in the morning from where I lived, at 6:15 . . . I had to pay €2.25, I was paid just as I worked the

> whole day, he gave me €35. I had to pay for transportation, everything. He told me I have to extend it to 10:00, 10:30, I told him it wasn't possible because the buses in Tarragona close . . . What time am I going to cook? What time am I going to eat?
>
> (interview no. 22, Lleida, 21 August 2008)

He therefore left and moved to Lleida, staying in an apartment with other Cameroonians and babysitting for a housemate who was working daily. He was able to seek work and could be accommodated during this time despite entering Spain alone and encountering destitution. He would work occasionally, but claimed that many people had arrived from other parts of Spain after hearing that there was work available and this limited his employment. Documented workers earn €6 or €7 per hour, but those without papers earn €4 after the agent has taken a cut. It is expected that the indigenous population prefers unemployment, training or education to low wages, leaving companies to rely on immigrant labour in order to be internationally competitive (Baldwin-Edwards 1999: 3). Abada illustrates, however, that immigrants without rights may also opt out of employment terms that fall below a certain level, and are thereby able to challenge over-exploitation in the labour market.

To consider resistance to the control of migrant labour, we return to Mamadou Diouf's (2000) exploration of the relationship between globalisation and the mobility of Mourides. The destruction of peasant livelihoods in central Senegal by slavery and military assault created an opening for the development of the brotherhood, which interacted distinctively with the colonial groundnut economy. Diouf's analysis of contemporary engagement between Mourides and the global economy showed the importance of accounting for the 'creativity involved in the slow and shrewd deployment of the local in global space and time' (ibid.: 702). This provides a narrative of trade networking that places it in the context of displacement; thus the international and 'cosmopolitan' nature of immigration is not detached from its causes and the state's role in managing the experience of migration (Grillo 2007). This description by Khalifa, a 54-year-old electrician who returned to Senegal after working in Spain for several years, reveals the strategies he employed to overcome illegality (interview no. 61, Rufisque, 24 June 2008). As cosmopolitan as Khalifa's experience was, his existence was unstable:

> As soon as you set foot in Spain, you're confronted with a problem of communication which obliges us to learn Spanish. Secondly, if you don't have a speciality, you have to do walking trade, bags, shoes, you have to play hide-and-seek with the police. The other problem is that you have to use others' papers and if you don't have them, or if the residence paper has already lasted five years and the inspector asks you for it in Spain, you must understand and be able to respond. There are risks for both fraudsters; the papers of the one who lends his residence papers can be changed, and they expel or repatriate the one who has borrowed them. The conditions of living and lodging are an issue because, at times, we overtake the number of tenants

> required by the landlord. To justify this large number, we say to him that our tradition is to eat in a group, and after the meal they will leave. Most of the time, *clandestins* without papers do small trade to sort themselves out. There is also the Red Cross who helps them.
>
> (ibid.)

Khalifa's explanation of coping strategies demonstrates the resourceful response to an 'irregular' status. This is also demonstrated in the labour of Kheraba, a migrant from Ziguinchor in the Casamance region of Senegal (interview no. 76; 17, 18, 20 August 2008). At the time of fieldwork, he occupied a house with an adjoining unused restaurant, which included occupants from Equatorial Guinea, Uganda, Senegal and Gambia. He also used the store room of a local food company to run reggae nights, which had strong local support. He would lend his residence papers to undocumented migrants. He explained that ten years ago, people came legally, but now most Africans he met had arrived on the *cayucos* (fishing boats). He employed newcomers in an organisation he started in 2003, which utilised his past trade networks in Benin, Senegal and Guinea. With these networks, he sent used tyres for making shoes or for carrying water.

> We try to take the material practically thrown away from here and try to make it useful in Africa. It can be all sorts of material, as we have a lack of many types of industrial... and necessary products... we get all sorts of materials you know, like computers, which we took from the street, from the garbage, computers... we are helping our brothers to go back to Africa. That is what the project is about, this recycling project... gathering materials that will be useful there.
>
> (ibid.)

Kheraba welcomes and co-ordinates new African migrants. In addition to numerous west African languages, including Jahanké, Mandinka, Bambara, Pulaar and Wolof, he also speaks Spanish, Catalan, Portuguese, French and English. He converses in all of these languages frequently in a park in Barcelona, where Africans from several countries, joined by Catalans and other Europeans, gather during the day. Occasionally he sends remittances to Senegal, the last time amounting to €600. He was asked about the use of his remittances:

> *So your family is OK now?*
> It's not that my family is OK, it's that life is not only about food and drink, we like to build more things and do more things, and we could do if we got the chance.
> *So now you only have food and drink?*
> Yeah, we don't have other things, we are all packed together in one place... I'm sending money to pay dues to my family.
>
> (ibid.)

Since the fieldwork, Kheraba has been in the national press when a factory that he established as three separate junkyards was threatened with eviction. There were 300 people living in the industrial complex including recent arrivals, and hundreds more would come and go (*el Periódico* 2012). The role that Kheraba created for himself in Barcelona was exceptional, but also it is a reflection of social and political organisation among west Africans in Spain, which varies in formality. *Tontines* are groups that are linked by family, kinship or friendship, in which members contribute to a regular fund that can then assist members in difficulty through the provision of loans or grants. This financial arrangement could be found among mothers of disappeared youth in Thiaroye-sur-Mer, Senegal, and has also funded clandestine boat journeys (Chapter 4). In Catalonia, there are *tontines* of up to 70 members, which include Guinean Women of Lleida, Gambian Women in Mataró, Mixed Cameroonians in L'Hospitalet and Senegalese Women of la Segarra (Sow 2007: 40). Furthermore, in 2006, groups including the Nigerian Association of Tenerife, Senegalese Serer and Diamba associations and Côte d'Ivoire Group demonstrated against violent racism in the Canary Islands (Angel de Lucas 2006).

It is evident that migrants' resourcefulness overcomes the limitations of carrying expulsion orders and experiencing an 'irregular' status in the host country of Spain. However, this cannot submerge what it takes to succeed and send money home, nor does it discredit structural approaches to migration. As a result of migrants' risky existence in Spain and their exclusion from labour and asylum policies, an NGO, the Spanish Commission for Aid to Refugees (CEAR) and the largest trade union, CC OO (Workers' Commissions) have both incorporated support for illegal migrants in their policy. CEAR has linked illegal migration from Senegal and Mauritania with unfavourable European fishing and petroleum agreements, and more generally with European imperialism and neo-liberalism (2007: 36–7). CC OO promotes the rights of irregular workers, although as might be expected, it proposes regulation of migration flows to be determined by the needs of the labour market (CC OO 2008). This shows a comprehension of the connections between forced and labour migration, which is missing from the more powerful political and economic regimes.

## Conclusion

The continued flow of undocumented migrants is the consequence of a 'message' to Africa that although labour migration to Spain is unstable, there is the chance to gain legal status and ultimately to send remittances. The perception among Senegalese youth that Barcelona holds the answer to their lack of mobility is therefore grounded in reality. The most important question that arises from this situation is centred on the reason for 'choosing' this lifestyle, given that the migration is 'voluntary' (Fine and Saad Filho 2004). It is often regarded as a collective delusion, but the evidence from Thiaroye-sur-Mer and Rufisque showed that people knew the implications of this journey, hearing detailed accounts of people's lives in Spain, being repatriated or even witnessing drownings. Examination of the dynamics of entry have revealed a compulsion to migrate and the viability of doing this with few means at the disposal of the migrant.

In turn, cheap, productive labour plays an essential role in Spain's agricultural and industrial development. Competitive labour costs have been lauded and encouraged by the IMF and OECD without regard for how this is attained. A dialectical relationship has emerged between the state and the economy that regulates the entry of undocumented workers, limits their circulation and channels them into unskilled, physical work roles. The 'successful' migrants live under the threat of expulsion and other vicissitudes of the immigration regime and the labour market. Imprisonment, homelessness, undesirable work and long waits for legality are built in to migrants' conditions of entry and residence. At the same time, migrants have carved out livelihoods within these constraints using collective strategies that are particular to west Africa. A further challenge to the role of unfree labour emerges in the growing masses of dispossessed Spanish workers, who have evidently resisted efforts to separate them from migrant workers in the dual labour market.

# 8 Remittances and underdevelopment

## Why formalising remittances will not alleviate poverty

> My worst experience was my repatriation from Europe. I like to think that some people will make it.
>
> (Ghanaian migrant repatriated from Spain – interview no. 35, Nouakchott, 20 May 2008)

Like the last chapter, this one mainly focuses on the 'successful' migrants and the broader outcomes of their success. The use of remittances as a poverty-alleviation strategy has been explored in research reports commissioned by international development, financial and policy institutions such as the United Kingdom's Department for International Development (DfID) (Addy *et al.* 2003), the International Monetary Fund (IMF) (Bouhga-Hagbe 2004), the World Bank (Ratha and Xu 2006) the International Labour Office (ILO) (Ammassari 2006) and the Migration Policy Institute (Ratha 2007). Global remittances increased from around US$30 billion annually in the early 1990s to $318 billion in 2007, with three-quarters of this amount directed towards lower middle-income and low-income developing countries (Vargas-Lundius *et al.* 2008: 14). Although there was a dip in remittance flows in 2009, this figure is expected to increase to $615 billion by 2014 according to World Bank estimates. The figure for remittances to developing countries in 2011, at $372 billion, was higher than the *global* estimate for 2007 (Ratha and Silwal 2012: 1). The dramatic rise of emigrant transfers can, however, be attributed to improved measurement and increased scrutiny of financial flows, reduction of remittance transfer costs and depreciation of the US dollar, as well as growth in migrant stock and incomes (Ratha 2007: 2). The gains from international migration nevertheless represent a growing portion of GDP compared with state development aid or direct foreign investment (Ammassari 2006: 18).

Thus the developmentalist approach to remittances focuses on their 'sheer volume, stable growth over time, and anti-cyclical nature', which locates them as an important source of external development finance (Addy *et al.* 2003: 3). In contrast with the statist optimism of the 1950s developmentalism, this resurgence of interest in remittances has adopted a neo-liberal agenda (de Haas 2007: 3; Cross 2008/9). It is chiefly financial and is founded on the belief that detectable, measurable growth equals development, and the role of the state is to facilitate this growth. Dilip Ratha, a senior economist at the World Bank, led a report for the Migration Policy Institute, which established the International Remittances Agenda. The Agenda aims to assist the flow of remittances towards poverty reduction with the implementation of monitoring, analysis and projection; retail payment systems; financial access for individuals or households; and the leveraging of remittances for capital market access of financial institutions or countries. The report promotes Washington Consensus policies: Ratha argues that rather than directing remittances to taxation or to specific development uses, the development community should instead make remittance services cheaper and more convenient through deregulation. These flows, he suggests, can also be leveraged to enable financial access for migrants, beneficiaries and financial intermediaries in countries of origin, offering 'financial education' to poor migrants and increasing their countries' creditworthiness (Ratha 2007: 12). The report is partially premised on the high costs currently implemented with money transfer operators such as Western Union, MoneyGram and Dolex, which charge regressive fees, in which the smaller remittances sent by migrants cost more per dollar sent. A move towards formalisation through banking is also promoted in the International Migration Policy Programme, an inter-agency group that includes the UK DfID, the World Bank, the International Labour Organisation and the International Organisation for Migration. The report states that macroeconomic environments in developing countries may pose obstacles to remittance transfers, and that by entering the banking system they become more secure, earn interest and make fresh money available for business loans (Addy *et al.* 2003: 14–15).

It is estimated that informal transfers, which bypass the money-transfer operators, the banks and, usually, the state are between two and ten times greater than officially reported global remittance flows. For example, around 70 per cent of remittances from France to Mali and Senegal moves through informal channels (Pieke *et al.* 2007: 351). One exploration of informal insurance arrangements in Ghana illustrates that as well as the 'altruism' that studies ascribe to remittance transfer (Bouhga-Hagbe 2004), monitoring and enforcement are key to the success of informal transfers. Migrant's remittances provide families with insurance against 'events' such as illness or funerals. At the same time, the migrant is also insured by the family in the case of arrest or being fired (Mazzucato 2006; cf Cooper 2008; Potts 2011: 39). This description of a system of insurance and money transfer that both works within a particular social structure and has built-in safeguards against abuse of funds is but one illustration of low-cost, effective and group-specific methods of remittance transfer. Hawala (Hindi for 'trust') networks are another, which operate from the west to Pakistan, India and Dubai. These systems of informal money transfer declined by as much as three quarters after the US government claimed links between Hawala networks and terrorism.

Pieke *et al.* (2007) argue that post-9/11 security concerns drive the move towards regulation of money transfers, rather than the notion of intervening in markets to support development and poverty reduction. Top-down formalisation of remittances could be detrimental to security, they add, as licensing a few select agencies may push informal agents underground (ibid.: 363). However, there is a third motive in formalisation – profit-seeking for the benefit of ever-expanding financial markets. DfID responded to the International Remittances Agenda with a detailed report into transfers from the UK to Ghana, which was prepared by Developing Markets Associates Ltd (DMA and DfID 2011). The report shows that the popular cash-to-cash methods of sending money are cheaper than other UK corridors, convenient and easily accessible, and operators build a loyal relationship with customers. However, they are 'traditional by nature' and the profit margins are low (ibid.: 2–3). Therefore banks should compete with them and develop the remittances market, fostering 'financial literacy and inclusion' in the UK and potentially in Ghana (ibid.: 27). It is primarily concerned with the competitiveness and expansion of the remittance market.

A linked premise for discouraging informal channels of remittances is driven by a loss of developmental value caused by lack of investment in the formal sectors considered to be productive. Examination of the efficiency and productivity of remittances features in IMF and World Bank reports (Bouhga-Hagbe 2004; Ratha 2007). In seeking financial means to harness and channel remittances into property, investment and enterprise, consumption without investment is seen as an unproductive use of remittance income.

Mazzucato's (2005) study of remittances sent by Ghanaian migrants in Amsterdam counteracts a denunciation of 'wasteful' spending with the example of a funeral. At the cost of €6,500, seven times the monthly income of the migrant, the impact of funeral costs on different economic sectors was significant. Forty per cent of the money benefited businesses in Accra, including printing press, mortuary, coffin-maker, video-production company, paint-seller and others. Businesses in Kumasi, including a tailor, rental companies and transport services, gained another 20 per cent; and a local bar in the village gained the equivalent of its average annual income (Mazzucato 2005: 6). Ironic criticisms of mere consumption and encouragement towards investment, by neo-liberal institutions, highlights a fundamental question in the values attached to development. The economic approach is arbitrary, as migration and remittances impact on a broad range of societal issues (de Haas 2007). The strong presence of IFI funding in migration research determines a market-driven analysis of remittances to the exclusion of examining how poverty is created and what it entails (Cameron 2005).

Approaches to the relationship between remittances and development can thus be summarised as follows: for the developmentalist position, remittances contribute to household strategies to raise income, insure against risks and reduce constraints in production and investment (Addy *et al.* 2003: 3). Adopting this position, one study argued that remittances to Ghana increase the number of children in a family going to school, thus enhancing the human capital in the household and therefore decreasing poverty (Gyimah-Brempong and Asiedu 2009). However, an opposing perspective is that the loss of migrant workers may outweigh the value of remittances, as human and capital resources are drained (Bracking 2003: 636). A significant illustration of 'brain drain' can be seen in Africa's annual loss of 20,000 healthcare personnel to Europe and America

(Blanchet and Keith 2006). For labour migration, be it formal or informal, countries lose their most dynamic and driven youth for varied periods of time. The impact of this loss on local production depends on variables such as type and patterns of migration, migrant characteristics, household structures and local conditions of agricultural systems (Vargas-Lundius *et al.* 2008: 31). In addition to the effects of loss of labour, the way that remittances are channelled can also have a negative impact. One rigorous study on behalf of the African Development Bank concluded that 'international remittances have a strong, statistically significant impact on increasing inequality in Africa' (Anyanwu 2011: 9). This was based on data from five eight-year windows between 1960 and 2006. The report argued that this happened because the remitters' households were not poor in the first place. This is on the macroeconomic level, but at the same time, it is more likely that the smaller remitters will use informal channels, possibly in higher numbers even if the quantities are lower, and in this respect research into the local dynamics of remittances and inequality have also been useful. Sarah Bracking (2003: 267) related this inequality to the phenomenon of remittance-receiving households undermining the spending power of households that do not receive remittances. Furthermore, remittance income from successful migrants can feed into the social and economic structure that helped to form their migration choice, leading to dependency on migration and reproduction of the causes.

Recent studies have explored the relationship between remittances and the global financial crisis. A working paper from the IMF concludes that African nations have been cushioned if they receive most of their remittances from the region, but they will gain in the longer run if they send more labour outside Africa (Barajas *et al.* 2010). The World Bank recognises the instability of labour markets in destination countries and that there are political pressures to reduce the amount of immigration, which might depress remittance flows (Ratha and Silwal 2012: 2–3). A further chapter in a World Bank volume asks whether remittances to sub-Saharan Africa are a source of resilience or vulnerability: it concludes the former because remittances are 'relatively stable' (Naudé and Bezuidenhout 2012: 346). They are considering the flow of remittances but exclude the fact that people are sending them, who are separated from their families and criminalised. West Africans have few stable options to find work abroad, and face physical, as well as economic, threat if they attempt to do so. Furthermore, various forms of coercion have led to the disposition to seek wage labour in distant locations – not only historically but in more contemporary forms of expropriation. A similar kind of tunnel vision guided the developmentalist approach to rural income diversification in west Africa, obscuring the relationship between a deficient market environment and strategies to 'make do' (Bryceson 1999). The promotion of safe migration and suggestions for how this may be achieved do not feature in the prescription of global development institutions (Ratha 2007; Addy *et al.* 2003: 3); instead, further migration and 'transnationalism' is encouraged.

## Remittances to Senegal: prospects for development

As in other west African countries, migration from rural to urban areas or to neighbouring countries has been the most significant in Senegal. Due to a vast gap in salaries between Africa and Europe, however, the largest source of remittances is France. There has also been a growing emphasis on migration to Europe as economic crisis restricts opportunities for work within Senegal or in the region. In recent years, however, effective restrictions of particular routes and destination countries have led to a dispersal of networks, routes, destinations and outcomes, leaving shortcomings in data.

It is often heard in Senegalese households that the country is 'lucky' because it lacks natural resources in comparison to its resource-rich and less stable, 'resource-cursed' neighbours. However, Senegal amongst other African countries has been a significant exporter of people throughout the history of European merchant capitalism (Bond 2006: 89–91). Supporting the continued export of labour, international financial institutions, in collaboration with academic research institutes, governments and NGOs, have reached agreement that migrants' remittances have the potential to contribute significantly to development. Emigration is periodically a driver of development in Senegal, evident in the towns, villages and industries that have decentralised, modernised and expanded with the help of migrant remittances. Senegalese emigrants originate as much in urban settings as rural, unlike other west African countries, and represent different social classes. This section will show that despite an ultimate diversity among remittance-receiving households, integration of migration as a household strategy into state policies and development agendas can expect more broadly to maintain structures of dependence and inequality.

As 'aid which reaches its destination', remittances have helped households to overcome crises (Sakho 2007). The waves of deflation and compression of public spending in structural adjustment programmes of the 1980s led to high levels of unemployment and the pauperisation of urban dwellers. The international migrant could save money and protect himself (usually male) and the household against political and social changes. A broad collection of studies carried out via research institutes in Dakar enables quantitative data to be overlaid with qualitative research, which reflects variation in migration and remittance behaviour across the country. In a debate attended by representatives of the Ministry of the Exterior, the National Agency of Statistics and Demography, Mouride representatives, the African Meeting of Human Rights, the UNDP and the Institute of Research Training in Population, Development and Reproductive Health, at the Université Cheikh Anta Diop, it was agreed that around 2.5 million Senegalese remit approximately 600 billion CFA (€914.7 million), of which half is by formal channels and half informal (Sakho 2007: 16). Compared with other economic indicators, the group found that official transfers represented a quarter of imports and a third of exports (Sakho 2007: 11). France was the largest source of remittances, sending €449 million in 2005 (of which 63 per cent was from Paris), followed by Italy with €350 million, Spain with €180 million, €108 million from the US and €99 million from Africa (African Development Bank 2009a: 15). Earnings from migrants in the USA or in European countries are doubled as a result of the devaluation of the CFA franc. Their buying power is augmented in the face of economic crisis: migrants' revenues do not submit to the hazards and instabilities of the national economy. However, the following interview excerpt highlights the instability of remitting and the complex economics involved, illustrating the limitations of rating them by volume alone. In this case, the conversion rate is an important factor, and informal trade between Senegal and Mauritania offers the most stability:

> *What do you do for work?*
> I'm a trader. I've travelled in many countries of the sub-region such as Gambia and Mauritania to buy things since 1975. I'm used to this work so I can't stay in the house without doing anything, and I do all of this to meet the needs of my family. My children try to do it in my place so I can rest, but for the moment they don't have the means.
> *Does your son in France send money?*
> Yes, but not regularly, because his work isn't so profitable. We're counting on him to change the situation we're in.
> *Are there other emigrants in your family?*
> Yes, there is another in Mauritania. He works there as a trader. As you know, staying here with no *métier* is no good; it's why I forced him to work. Sometimes he brings merchandise to his wife so that she has work.
> *Who earns the most? The one in France or Mauritania?*
> My son in Mauritania because, for example, if we have 50,000 francs (€76.22) we could buy lots of merchandise in Mauritania or even convert the francs to *ouguiya* to gain more. But it's not beneficial to convert the French francs into Mauritanian money.
>
> (interview no. 72, Rufisque, 2 July 2008)

Although the African Development Bank (2009a) and Senegal's Ministry of Finance (Diagne and Diane 2008) promote the formalisation of remittances for poverty alleviation, there is strong evidence across Senegal's diverse migrant groups that the money is directed towards development, investment and saving as much as possible. In the Ouro Sogui region, for example, a study found that migrants' investments were directed at water provision, schools, mosques and health centres respectively. In connection with these projects, employment was generated by the wealth of emigrants for people who stayed (Fall 2008: 203). Remittances have sparked the development of property, building, construction and artisanal sectors, creating both formal and informal labour demand. Emigrants constitute half of the proprietors in some quarters of Dakar (Grand Dakar and Parcelles Assaines) and contributed to 60 per cent of construction in Kebemer from 2002 to 2007, giving a 'second breath' to property development (Sakho 2007: 12). In the rural setting, the impact on food prices and communications can also be positive (Tall 2008; Fall 2008). Papa Demba Fall noted a 50,000 franc CFA (€76.22) investment in a 'life shop' in the village of Sédo-Sébé, funded by remittances, where essential goods were available at lower cost and could offset frequent stock market ruptures (2008: 207). Transfers from emigrants have covered education and medical expenses, provided for basic household needs and have allowed families to acquire tools for income generation and property. Migrants have successfully integrated themselves in the global economy. They have gained property and means of production, and therefore are no longer motivated to struggle for the lowest possible reward. These cases indicate why capitalism reproduces the separation of the producer and his/her means of production with a continuous geographical expansion because the appetite for displaced workers persists (Marx 1867/1970: 714; Perelman 1983; Fine and Saad-Filho 2004).

Remittances are less likely to put an end to coercive labour migration for households in the rural setting. A study commissioned by the Senegalese Ministry of Finance (Diagne and Diané 2008) examined the impact of remittances on poverty in 565 households in Dakar, other towns and in rural areas. The study found that in Dakar, remittances increased expenditure per head by 95 per cent compared to those households without these funds, while there was an increase of only 5.9 per cent in rural areas (Diagne and Diané 2008: 13). The study ascribed this difference to the greater severity of poverty in rural areas. Remittance transfers reduced the number of households living under the poverty line by almost a third; the same number of households would be poor if they stopped receiving money from distant locations (ibid.: 19). In rural Sahel zones, 97 per cent of remittance funds are used for household expenses and thus are said to have ameliorated the food crisis (Willem 2008: 295). However, the following interview with an emigrant from Podor, in the north of Senegal, illustrates the critical level of dependence upon remittances in her district. Suzanne (see Chapter 4) is seeking work as a housemaid in Nouakchott:

> *Do you send money home?*
> I send it, but not very often, it depends.
> *How do you send it?*
> I give it to those who are going back to the village
> *Do you see many people who go back home?*
> Yes, but I don't send it every time.
> *When you send the money, who takes care of this?*
> My father is dead, it's my mother who'll take of that. She is with my two children.
> *How will they use it?*
> It's just to feed them.
> *Do lots of people in the village use remittances?*
> Many people in the village are eating only the remittances . . . they live on the remittances but some don't have anyone to give them money. These people are eating only little.
>
> (interview no. 4, Nouakchott, 7 May 2007)

The broader benefits of remittances to Senegal are contested. Bertrand argues that the accumulation of migrants' savings has intensified social relations, reflecting the 'paradox of resource abundance' (cited in Tall 2008: 52; Fall 2008: 205). This means that the families who do not receive funds have less buying power, inequality expands and there is a decline in industrial enterprise (Daffé 2008: 127; Barro 2008). Furthermore, it has been claimed that remittances may negatively affect the productive efficiency of a household because they cause 'moral hazard', meaning laziness (Azam and Gubert 2006: 455). Dependence on foreign revenues, including remittances, may produce a 'rentier mentality', in which 'reward becomes a windfall gain and not the result of systematic hard work; it is situational, hence vulnerable and opportunistic' (Beblawi and Luciani 1987: 14). This combination of vulnerability and opportunity pervades the trajectories of migrants and sending communities, though it is important to consider, regardless of wage differentials, the hard work of the migrant who *belongs to the household* and who was raised in the household. Moreover, the loss of household members is likely to increase the volume of non-wage labour such as housekeeping and general maintenance. Although the community may gain windfalls in the form of new public buildings; the sending household's revenues do not grow on trees. Furthermore, the evidence from Senegalese coastal communities is that migrating is the effect of a lack of productive means, rather than the cause of a decline in hard work by household members.

The account of Mrs Cissé shows how emigration takes hold and is reproduced. Her oldest son was able to fund two years of technical training for his younger brother, paying 75,000 F CFA (€114.34) per semester. Her youngest son, however, 'refuses' to take up his baccalaureate for the following year, because 'all that interests him now is trying clandestine emigration like the oldest did' (interview no. 70, Rufisque, 2 July 2008). Mrs Ndiaye, a member of the Collective of Women for the Fight Against Clandestine Emigration, claimed:

> The influence is very strong in this district, in effect if a young person sees his peer leave, immediately he prepares himself to go. In our country, a person can live until old age without seeing a modest living. It's why over there is better.
>
> (interview no. 42, Thiaroye-sur-Mer, 6 June 2008)

Illustrating the cyclical nature of migration and remittances, it is argued that the vast importance of money transfers pushes further young people into leaving for Europe (Mbow and Tamba 2007: 13). Also constraining development, returning migrants to Senegal do not usually utilise the skills that they have gained abroad, which have commonly been developed in shoe factories in Italy or the automobile industry in France and cannot be applied in their local context (Tall 2008: 61). For the Lebu, emigrants often work in informal trade, agriculture or fishing in Spain, with methods of production that cannot be applied in their communities.

This cycle of migration and underdevelopment is compounded by the uncertainty of migration. The number of legal and illegal emigrants from Diokoul is roughly equal, and both can be found in a single household. Both forms of emigration are, however, insecure for the migrant and by extension the family that benefits. The Gueye household received payments from émigrés in Italy and the US, the former working informally as a trader and the latter teaching Wolof. The trader in Italy remitted infrequently and could return to Senegal for a holiday once after leaving in 2000. The teacher in the US, however, experienced difficulties due to lack of social security: his co-tenant left without warning; his teaching contract finished, and his wife fell ill, thereby unable to continue her work (interview no. 56, Rufisque, 24 June 2008). The vulnerability of the son living in the US illustrates an element of instability that remains with the legal migrants and extends to their families.

As for illegal migration, failed voyages towards the Canary Islands led the mothers of disappeared youth to form the Collective of Women for the Fight Against Clandestine Emigration, composed of more than 350 women. Each member pays 1,000 francs CFA (€1.52) per month. The money is collected in a *tontine*, an informal form of saving and credit. Credits of up to 50,000 francs CFA (€76.22) are then made available to the most vulnerable women in the group to fund them in income-generating activities (Chauzy 2006: 7). They also lend over €15,000 per year to repatriated migrants so they can re-establish themselves (Gano 2012). The Collective processes cereals, fruits, vegetables and seafood, then sells them nationally and also to neighbouring countries and to some in Europe (Sow 2012). It raised interest from the media and development agents. It became the central office for arranging visas granted by the Spanish government. The Senegalese state, having been reticent, signed an agreement of migration management with Spain. This agreement included the reinforcement of FRONTEX controls, repatriation of clandestine migrants, the granting of 4,000 work visas for targeted employment between 2007 and 2008, and 13 million francs for Senegalese agricultural development (Bouilly 2008a: 29). Although 4,000 Senegalese migrants were repatriated in 2006 (BBC 2006c), the target number of visas was not reached and legal options diminished whilst controls expanded.

Locally, however, connections made with President Wade and his son Karim, through the 'political labour' of the women, attracted international aid (Bouilly 2008a: 29). The Comisión Española de Ayuda al Refugiado (CEAR – Spanish Commission for Assistance to Refugees) was one donor to the Collective, illustrating the blurring between humanitarian crisis and labour migration in this community. Their actions encourage local development as a solution to the loss of young people. Both here and in Rufisque, there was the common sentiment that 'young people should have the materials and the means to do their trade' (interview no. 41, Thiaroye-sur-Mer, 6 June 2008). One failed clandestine migrant gained a horse and carriage so that he could access markets for fish at a distance from the beach (interview No. 39, Thiaroye-sur-Mer, 3 June 2008).

## Conclusion

This analysis of the dynamics of emigration and the conditions under which remittances are sent exposes the limitations of viewing this phenomenon as a poverty-alleviation mechanism. The reasons for this are twofold. Firstly, the evidence from Senegal shows that migrants have put the remittances to productive use where possible. The new developmentalist approach prioritises measurement and detection of the macroeconomic role of remittances to the detriment of recognising the diversity of migrants' strategies and their high levels of success. The issue that reproduces migration and poverty is not a lack of financial knowledge nor an inability to overcome processes of underdevelopment, but is instead the pervasive power of capital accumulation.

The activities of the Collective of Women for the Fight Against Clandestine Emigration are based on meeting subsistence needs, on equipping workers with the tools for their trade and on finding a marketplace for producers and traders. For this community endowed with marine resources and artisanal skills, the significance of accumulation by dispossession is clear. This is not a single act, but instead it is supported by an infrastructure of institutionalised exclusion that erodes the entire process of migration.

Secondly, remittances have been approached as an expanding market, which opens up a new path for financial dispossession that would be disruptive to well-organised channels for remitting. If profit for the banking sector is created out of remittances, this diminishes the funds' capacity to compensate households *directly* for the costs of renewal that have rested with them while the migrant is away, creating the need for longer migration or for another household member to migrate and 'earn a living like the other emigrants do'.

# 9 Conclusion

## Unfree labour mobility between west Africa and Europe

This book has identified how sites of political and economic power regulate patterns of migration and mobility in contemporary global capitalism. It has approached the phenomenon panoramically and, in so doing, it has delinked mobility from an empowering globalism. It has, instead, placed the concept of unfree labour mobility at its core, a theory that shows how expansively labour is cheapened in the global era. Consequentially, we are asked to reconsider which trajectories truly challenge west Africa's established role in global capitalism, and which ones further entrench its underdevelopment. State political economies, global security and labour regimes have thereby been examined in a dynamic relationship to the actions of migrants, households and middlemen (Papastergiadis 2000: 35).

This final chapter summarises these dynamics and attempts to locate them in the historical development of global capitalism. It highlights some of the key similarities and differences found in colonial and contemporary labour regimes, notably that there has been less association between sender and receiver since the mid-1970s. The expansion of possibilities that this indicates lends itself not to a borderless world but, instead, to one with an unprecedented number of check-points and frontiers. These restrictions keep the underdeveloped regions contained and enforce the 'global life-chance divide' (Duffield 2010: 63). This divide does not end when border controls are crossed or circumvented. It demands resourcefulness and adaptability at all stages. The linkages between capitalist economies, frontiers and sending communities continue to constrain migrants' trajectories in their various combinations of abjection, partial incorporation, and locally constructed alternatives.

The institutional form of the global labour market resides in the creation of a mobile labour force by processes of global capitalism, which is constrained by states' use of selective citizenship and partial sovereignty. This contradiction between mobility and borders is not always a tension between the economic and the political, as geostrategic interests such as those of AFRICOM set free markets and the control of natural resources within militarised boundaries. Broadly speaking, however, the OECD, the IMF, the World Bank and European state development agencies often promote the mobility of labour. In the case of the first two, this is generally for the purpose of capital accumulation, while the latter link labour mobility more with the alleviation of poverty. European interior ministers, AFRICOM and client states in north Africa determine the undesirability and, ultimately, the illegality of sub-Saharan migrancy. These contradictory discourses and policies regulate an unstable experience for migrants.

This book's discussion of unfree labour has presented a critique of global capitalism that sits on its unfulfilled promise of free circulation. However, this institutional character of regional labour mobility does not predetermine individual migrants' trajectories. When artisanal fishermen are freed from any means of production of their own, this does not transform them necessarily into free or unfree labourers. They are securitised, illegalised, and may enter destitution. They may recover the means of production as a result of incorporation or by finding local alternatives to proletarianisation, whether this is by benefiting from community development initiatives or by trafficking labourers towards Europe. Similarly, we can see that on the grand level, the EU's border controls fail to prevent unauthorised movement because their concentration in one area detracts from another. However, on the local level, they bring thousands of migrants' plans to an abrupt and often shocking end, or change them dramatically (see box 5.1). There are certainly more possibilities for migrants in the contemporary era, and this complexity cannot be captured with ethnography or structural analysis in isolation. This is the significance of a multi-scalar approach, with which we now identify more precisely how patterns of migration and mobility are created and constrained.

## Summary of the contemporary migration regime

The demand for migrant labour has persistently played a central role in global capitalism. Imperialism established the relations between capitalist and sending economies, which would keep the latter outside capitalism's 'sphere of production' but within its 'sphere of circulation' (Meillassoux 1975). These relations were the outcome of primitive accumulation, by which land, labour and natural resources were commodified and privatised during the eras of the slave trade, colonialism and neo-colonialism. Beyond these historical eras, an ongoing process of accumulation by dispossession persists, by which the displacement of labour energises capital accumulation in a process of 'creative destruction' (Harvey 2003; Bauman [Schumpeter] 2004). This is the effect of reproducing the separation of labourers from the means of production, on a continually expanding scale (Marx 1867/1970: 714). It is why contemporary patterns of west African migration diverge from Samir Amin's (1972a/b) regionalisation, in which labour moved from the interior to the coast. This departure from colonial patterns is not for favourable reasons, but because processes of underdevelopment and dependence were not 'completed' in Africa. Instead they continue in aggressive forms.

The book has examined the argument that, just as peasantries were created by imperialism and dissolved by global trade networks (Bryceson 2000), 'modern' labour reserves have also undergone a number of similar processes. This is indicated by the lack of connection between sender and receiver. In west Africa, colonial economies altered patterns of production and established labour reserves to develop commodities including cocoa, coffee and groundnuts. Labour reserves in west Africa were not constructed in the same sense as those in South Africa, but there were geographical areas of production and dispossessed populations outside those areas that were compelled to seek wage labour. Labour was therefore manipulated from one place to another, sometimes explicitly (Riddell 1981; Arthur 1991; Plange 1979).

With changes to these patterns of production, the export of labour did not, however, 'collapse', but instead is closely managed at every level by the intertwined logics of competition and territory. Mobile labour continues to run alongside, and also underpin, capital accumulation. Displacement from one place to another by 'predation, fraud and violence' continues to be the overriding factor in migrants' entry to Europe. Clandestine migration from the west African coasts to the Canary Islands by *pirogue* evolved from a number of factors. They include the repression of other routes to Europe, the seafaring ability of fishermen, the non-profitability of fishing, and high under-employment. Rather than comprising a cohesive network, this migration often occurs within a transport infrastructure that is similar to the bush taxi system. This has challenged the adage that locates migrants in relative wealth. Instead, the fishing communities were dispossessed by the privatisation of land; the mortgaging of property; fishing agreements between the Senegalese and other states; and food and oil price hikes in the imported goods on which they were dependent.

While Senegalese migration is well-researched and mapped up to recent times, stepwise migration from Ghana, Nigeria and Cameroon is more difficult to gauge. Migrants from these latter countries revealed significant variation in the circumstances of leaving; socioeconomic background; conditions, length of time and cost of the journey; countries transited; and, notably, the reason for successful entry to Europe, which could be attributed to luck rather than wealth or power in most cases. However, migrants would usually link their departures with structural economic factors, which amounted to dispossession. There were common attributions to unfavourable global markets, which undermined household economies, and to the elites' extraction of minerals and other natural resources. Converging with historical and empirical understandings of west African migration, it was generally a strategy of household survival and this had diverse meanings among migrants. For many migrants, staying represents an inability to meet all but the existential needs of the household, broadly defined. A homeless and destitute Nigerian migrant in Spain had migrated because he would otherwise be unable to send his children to university, as his parents had done for he and his siblings (interview no. 25, Barcelona, 28 February 2008). Another migrant claimed that 'life is not only about food and drink' (interview no. 76, Barcelona, 18 August 2008). However, in some migrants' circumstances, it is; and we have particularly seen this in the women who seasonally enter Mauritania from underdeveloped and famished areas of the Sahel, and in migrants who trekked through the Sahara. This book has clarified how the broader phenomena of inequality and poverty lead particular people to migrate while others do not, and this is not only explained by personal motivations and aspirations, but also owes to the structural processes of capital accumulation and their local articulations. It is a 'hopping' phenomenon (Ferguson 2006: 38) but in the global south, it is also particularly intense on the national and regional scales, acutely revealed in relations of food production (see Bush 2010). It has been a long and continuous historical process that is seemingly without bounds.

The EU, at the same time, prevents a free flow of labour and, instead, manages a labour reserve. European policy has followed a process of securitisation after 9/11, by which migrants are categorised as a threat. This leads to a 'state of exception' in which migrants' rights are submerged by constructed security imperatives (Bigo 2005b). In travelling to Mauritania, sub-Saharan migrants are entering a key frontier in the US's territorial incursions and are also integrated in its strategy. The EU and US have militarised the borders and have installed a system of border management, which brings formality and 'legality' to the movement of people; yet this rests on the foundation of legal exclusion and a lack of citizenship rights for southern Mauritanians and foreign workers. At the time of fieldwork, rapid measures to irregularise this movement across African borders, with Spanish and French assistance, resulted in arrests, detentions and extortion of migrants at border posts. This added tension to established patterns of migration from Sahelian communities.

Patterns of labour migration from the south into Mauritania have been essential to the latter's development and it is likely that they will continue while efforts to separate the Sahara from 'Africa' are renewed. In many cases, better returns could be found on emigration here compared to Europe, owing to the ease in frequent crossing, currency exchange and access to the informal market. Groups from the Senegal River Valley enter Mauritania as a means of household diversification and although they are less likely to be troubled by border guards, the danger of expulsion lingers as a result of political instability. Displaced west African workers from further afield are extremely constrained, especially since the destabilisation of Libya, which had been an alternative option. At the time of fieldwork in 2008, extortion at Mauritania's border with Senegal had increased for migrants who might be suspected of transiting to Europe and some reported losing all of their cash upon entry, as they do in other Maghreb countries. The EU has externalised many of the repressive and arbitrary elements of its migration regime and this might in turn drive more migrants to take the risk of going towards Europe instead of remaining in the Sahara.

EU 'partnerships' such as the Union for the Mediterranean and those in the Global Approach to Migration and Mobility are determined to prevent migrants from entering. Mechanisms that formalise and reinforce this policy include the deployment of FRONTEX patrols, restrictive visa and asylum policies, and agreements with sending countries for repatriation and the prevention of emigration. The EU is uncompromising in its aims to determine who can and cannot legally enter according to the needs of member states. It incorporates labour mobility selectively, not as a 'concession' but to meet the labour shortages of EU member states. It limits all types of migration into unfree forms. The case study in Spain showed that migrants who have entered by aeroplane with a visa have lost their legal status and faced destitution. Senegalese households, moreover, had sent both legal and illegal migrants to Europe with little distinction between the two. Even the 'skilled' migrants who meet the labour demands of EU member states may lose their legality if their skills are no longer required or if they demand too much from the state. Labour mobility is clearly unstable. In the middle of these interconnected security and mobility policies there is a moving population of exploited labourers who are excluded from an obtuse framework, which, unlike many NGOs, civil society organisations, unions and protest movements, does not institutionally recognise the role of illegal labourers in competitive European economies.

The regime creates a means of distinguishing between free and unfree labour and ensures that the migrants who bypass the controls do not circulate freely . It provides the opportunity for European states to systematically determine the place of 'illegal' labour in their territory (Cohen 1987; Miles 1987; Sassen 1988). States have 'messages' that encourage or repel migrants (Sassen 1999: 136–7). Fishermen, sending families, transit migrants or those in Spain frequently mentioned immigration policy under different state regimes in Europe, particularly discussing the differences in policy between Spain, France and Italy over periods of time. The tension between the mobility of labour and border enforcement is at its most evident and most finely balanced when migrants enter the country and are employed whilst carrying an expulsion order. This category of worker is incorporated in Spain's economic development. Racial discrimination is repeatedly reconstructed in this order of labour, and is often propagated by the same politicians who create the security elements of EU policy. Partial or complete illegality is likely to constrain absorption in the labour market into low-paid and productive positions, representing the capitalist logic of power. If unbalanced, the scales tip towards the territorial logic of power, leading to migrants' detention and return. The fluctuations between legality and illegality, enforced and unenforced, provide states with a mechanism for controlling the circulation of labour. It is a form of adverse incorporation, with its pervasive insecurity undermining the credibility of migrant labour as a development strategy. Furthermore, while migrants are coerced into a lower-cost workforce having been 'freed', their sending communities continue to bear the cost of reproducing the labour-power (Miles 1987; Cohen 1987; Bush 2007; Burawoy 1980).

Migrants are not merely satisfying the appetite of capitalism for cheap labour, but they are also using wage labour to maintain and support sending household economies. Migrants remit often in order to set up their families and to 'help Africa', but these transformations cannot be achieved without migrating. In many cases only essential needs can be met and sending is sporadic. This has a bearing on migrants' comparisons of living conditions and access to resources between home and destination. Among migrants in Barcelona, conditions of life in Europe were found to be unimportant compared to changes to the family home in Africa; for example spending on water, electricity and other basic needs is money wasted, while cash and goods sent to Africa are an investment. It is not the commonly assumed search for a better life in Europe that usually guides migrants there, nor is it 'traditional' values of collectivity; instead it is a strategy to overcome the destruction to communities that is caused by waves of capital accumulation.

The case studies in Thiaroye-sur-Mer and Rufisque showed that successful migration has spurred further attempts to migrate. Returning migrants have successfully overturned the struggle to maintain houses, send family members to school and meet the needs of the family, leading others to attempt to earn a living in this way. Contracts for work that Spain developed in partnership with Senegal fell short of this outcome, leading workers into illegality. Furthermore, the visas benefited people with political connections and were fewer than the number of repatriations. The success of some of the pioneers of the 1,500-kilometre Atlantic stretch makes *pirogue* migration a reasonable aim, but deaths at sea and the more recent development of instant repatriation make the risks of this route considerable. In Rufisque, young people protested because the promised support of young people in their trades, and legal means to migrate, did not materialise. In Thiaroye-sur-Mer, the Collective of Women for the Fight Against Clandestine Emigration, established by mothers of disappeared youth, emphasised the importance of local development as well as the improvement of legal options to migrate. By managing a *tontine*, a 'kitty' that all members pay in to and which can then provide communal goods and emergency funds, work opportunities for would-be *clandestins* were created.

This may lead to a realist approach to migration and development that posits that since the process of migration is unstable, perhaps remittances can be channelled in such a way that the conditions creating emigration are alleviated. The financial approach of development banks, however, does not acknowledge the historical role of remittances in development, which in Senegal have frequently been channelled towards community projects and investment in situations where the funds are greater than the needs of the household. Instead, the agenda that is driven by the World Bank has suggested that the financial sector should compete with established channels of remittances and bring knowledge of finance to migrants and their families who currently remit informally. The deregulation of money-transfer operators, who charge proportionally higher fees for smaller amounts, is in one report linked with the competitive costs and efficiency of 'traditional' channels (DMA and DfID 2011).

The global capitalist economy has a greater part to play in the migrant's journey than the promise of enhanced mobility in the global era. Borders and boundaries have stood their ground in the age of global interconnectedness. More than the compression of time and space, global institutional agendas of labour mobility and migration as a development strategy and the contradictory determination of border enforcement shape trajectories and are closely linked, especially within EU policy. More than altering human mobility, globalisation has refashioned the lens through which it is examined and this obscures migrants' relationships with sending communities, states and the international political economy. This broader approach was common practice in the 1970s and 1980s and has been renewed here to show how capital accumulation creates and dominates patterns of migration and mobility in the contemporary era.

# Appendices
# Interviews and life histories

Core questions in the interviews examined generational changes, including occupations and education of grandparents, parents and siblings; household resources over time, including land and livestock; and family and village migration history. In total, there were 134 interviews in 12 towns, and some in transit, with respondents from Senegal, Mali, Mauritania, Ghana, Nigeria, Gambia, Cameroon and Ivory Coast. Table A.1 lists the locations and respondents for interviews.

*Table A.1* Fieldwork locations

| *Date* | *Location* | *No. of interviews* | *Respondents' country of origin* | *Language used* | *Who was interviewed?* |
|---|---|---|---|---|---|
| 07.05.07 | Nouakchott (female and male recruitment points; beach; market) | 16 | Mauritania, Senegal, Mali, Cameroon, Gambia | Pulaar, Wolof, French, English | Combination of transit, circular and longer-term migrants |
| 15.05.07 | Saint-Louis port, Senegal | 1 | Senegal | Wolof | Fisherman |
| 20.05.07 | Gouraye frontier, Mauritania | 1 | Mauritania | French, Hassaniya | Customs officer |
| 23.02.08 | Salt (telecentres and shop), Girona, Spain | 3 | Nigeria, Gambia | English | West African labour migrants |
| 26.02.08–28.02.08 | Barcelona (ACCEM centre for migrants; Raval café) | 8 | Gambia, Nigeria, Ghana, Cameroon, Senegal, Ivory Coast | English, French | Recent (last 2 years) immigrants seeking work |
| 08.04.08 | Thiaroye-sur-Mer beach, Senegal | 1 | Senegal | Wolof | Fisherman repatriated from Tenerife |

*Table A.1* continued

| *Date* | *Location* | *No. of interviews* | *Respondents' country of origin* | *Language used* | *Who was interviewed?* |
|---|---|---|---|---|---|
| 08.04.08 | Colobane, Dakar (large industrial area on outskirts) | 1 | Senegal | French/ Wolof | Attempted clandestine journey, head of youth association |
| 14.05.08–20.05.08 | Nouakchott (female recruitment point; barber; house; church) | 4 | Senegal; Nigeria; Ghana | Pulaar, English | Follow-up from earlier interview; transit (and repatriated) migrants |
| 17.05.08–18.05.08 | Nouadhibou (church, restaurant in progress, barber) | 5 | Ghana, Nigeria | English | Long-term transit migrants; immigrants |
| 03.06.08–16.06.08 | Thiaroye-sur-Mer (households, association HQ, shops), Senegal | 43 | Senegal, Mali | Wolof, French | Repatriated migrants; family of deceased or overseas migrants; association members; local delegates; youth |
| 18.06.08–08.07.08 | Rufisque (households, shops, carpenter), Senegal | 46 | Senegal | Wolof, French | Repatriated migrants; migrants' parents and spouses; youth; delegates; imam; fishermen |
| 28.07.08 | Elinkine café, Casamance, Senegal | 1 | Senegal | French | Head of fishermen's association |
| 17.08.08–20.08.08 | Barcelona (Parc de la Ciutadella) | 3 | Senegal, Gambia | French, English | Immigrants there for several years |
| 21.08.08 | Lleida (apartment), Spain | 1 | Cameroon | English | Follow-up interview to investigate conditions of living and work |

The first round of interviews in Nouakchott were located in zones where migrants seek employment in separate groups of men and women, most of whom are Senegalese (interviews nos 1–9). The links between these migrants and Europe are sometimes indirect, but these interviews offered some essential perspective on the connections between regional and intercontinental migration, and for perceptions of European migration to be explored. Remittances could also be examined in these groups. The interviews extended to the market and the fishing port, where links with clandestine migration were articulated (interviews nos 10–13). A year later, there was a return to the recruiting zone and the next group of respondents in Mauritania was accessed through a Ghanaian church in Nouakchott. This led to more interviews in Nouadhibou, where I had previously been unable to meet respondents without such connections (interviews nos 30–8).

Migrants who are supposedly in transit to Europe have travelled from different regions in Ghana and Nigeria as well as other west African countries, also inclusive of those who have left Ivory Coast, Sierra Leone and Liberia as a result of conflict. The way that interviews snowballed revealed a cohesive community that included Anglophone and Francophone west Africans, Muslims and Christians, refugees and labour migrants. It is this cohesion that justifies discussion of 'west African' migration. Nouadhibou is a peninsula that borders western Sahara and is around five hours from Nouakchott by road. Settled migrants in both towns may have failed an attempt to go to the Canary Islands by boat or could have decided against the journey upon seeing the dangers. Successful entry to Europe may also result in deportation back to Mauritania as a 'third country'. As dispersed as towns and villages of origin are, destinations in Europe also vary greatly, despite the popularity of Barcelona as the target. For example, if undocumented west Africans arrive in the Canary Islands and are not repatriated after detention, they might be flown to different regions of the Spanish mainland and subsequently will move towards promising locations of recruitment. It would be misleading to link labour migrants in Mauritania with a particular network in Africa or Europe.

The fieldwork in Spain was based in Catalonia, beginning with homeless arrivals in Barcelona who had passed through several countries including Mauritania, Libya, Algeria or Morocco from west Africa. It expanded to the predominantly African municipality of Salt to interview longer-established migrants about their livelihood trajectories. Migrants who had flown to Europe with a visa and subsequently lost their legal status were also interviewed. In a similar light to the Lebu communities, some migrants' stories connected with Nouakchott and Nouadhibou, but they also enabled the exploration of other channels and consideration of the success of some journeys over others. The interviews mainly focused on Ghanaian, Nigerian, Gambian and Senegalese migrants, introduced by key informants. Migrants were accessed on the first stay via the Red Cross and were located in the ACCEM (Spanish Catholic Commission on Migration) centre in Barcelona (interviews nos 19–22, 24–7), subsequently moving on to personal contacts (interviews nos 23, 76–8). In Salt, it was possible to interview migrants with the assistance of a key informant from Cameroon (interviews nos 16–18). Compared to Senegal, there were fewer but more detailed interviews both here and in Mauritania, extending in some to life histories and livelihood trajectories (interviews nos 16, 22, 25, 33, 38, 76). Informants for the life-history interviews were selected strategically, based on their relations with others in the community and their migration experiences. During the second stay in Barcelona, for example, there was a life-history interview with the head of a diaspora association who organised informal work for undocumented migrants (interview no. 76). He discussed strategies for working and lodging. Other migrants had already discussed forms of resistance against instability and illegality, but this series of in-depth interviews gave more insight into the dynamics of resistance. Furthermore, an extensive personal history of intra-African and European migration enabled the past and present comparison of labour migration.

The ideal in fieldwork is to attain suitable language skills for the community. Otherwise, complications arise because translation represents 'a social relationship involving power, status and the imperfect mediation of cultures' (Bujra 2006: 172). However, in Mauritania and Spain there were several languages among respondents. Although most spoke English or French, this was never the mother tongue. In Barcelona, no interpreters were employed, and instead, other migrants acted as intermediaries when necessary. In Mauritania, interpreters interviewed respondents in Hassaniya, Pulaar, Wolof and French. These interviews were recorded and then translated by Khady Gueye, a different interpreter in Senegal who was a social researcher and also became an ethnographic informant.

Despite spending the most time in Senegal, the expansive quantity of existing migration research in the country posed a challenge for a new researcher with little prior connection. Khady Gueye helped to access the community in Thiaroye-sur-Mer and had strong links with the district in Rufisque (interviews nos 39–75). Her extended family provided a base for fieldwork over some months. During the initial months in Dakar, Khady's deskwork of transcribing the Mauritanian interviews in French and mine of examining existing Senegalese studies prepared us for the fieldwork. Once in the field, Khady interpreted constantly while I participated in households' social life. During interviews, however, our groundwork allowed me to minimise interference. We surveyed all households and community figures in the district, who provided information that could be systematised. The interview schedule (see below) required adaptability to the broad range of respondents' situations and they would ultimately determine the order of questioning. The interviews were still semi-structured because the determined areas of enquiry were consistently explored. After the interview and transcription period in Senegal, Khady submitted comparative reports of the findings in Thiaroye-sur-Mer and Rufisque. This contributed to 'bottom-up' content analysis, by which data was thematically organised according to responses rather than by predetermined themes. The content was analysed during transcription and translation on return to Leeds.

## Participant observation

The fieldwork incorporated participant observation methods during two selected west African journeys that passed through significant transit towns and border crossings: the first in the Soninké regions of Mauritania, Senegal and Mali; and the second from Burkina Faso, through Mali, to the Senegalese coast. They both included the transit towns of Kayes and Tambacounda. The first journey was a round trip from Nouakchott to Dakar and then east to Mali before re-entering Mauritania (see Figure A.1). An officer from the International Organisation for Migration (IOM) in Nouakchott assisted with the journey planning. Most of the route covered Soninké towns along the Senegal River, including Bakel and Kayes, and passed four border crossings. A Mauritanian research assistant, Mariam Kane, chatted with passengers in the bush taxis about their routes, plans and motivations. These encounters led to conceptions of migration that would underpin the development of questionnaires. Mariam successfully arranged candid and useful interviews with a border guard and a fisherman. Much of the fortnight was occupied with long desert journeys, totalling 71 hours. We often encountered young men who intended to migrate to Europe and witnessed discrimination against them at the border checkpoints. Key observations on the journey also related to the movement of goods along the routes, linking migration with livelihoods and trade in the region.

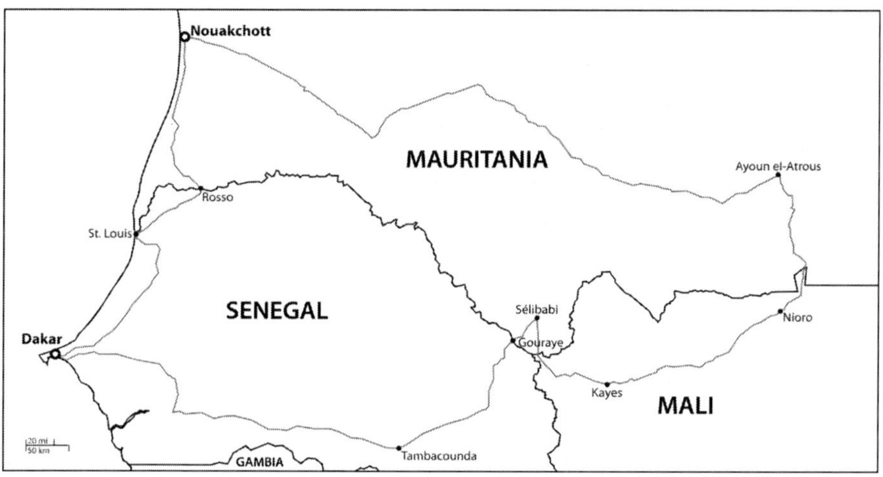


*Figure A.1* Journey from Nouakchott to Senegal River border crossings
Illustrator: Alex van Zomerplaag

The second journey to be examined was from Ouagadougou, Burkina Faso, through Mali, to Elinkine in the Casamance region of Senegal, for which I was accompanied by a political analyst, Núria Tomàs (see Figure A.2). The route was devised with the help of a Ghanaian NGO worker who I had previously spoken to in Barcelona and subsequently interviewed (interview no. 79, Barcelona 26 July 2009). During the fortnight, unprovoked discussions of Europe, which emerged frequently, were undoubtedly triggered by our presence. The length and content of these discussions, however, indicated the importance of migration to

Europe in the region. People that we encountered on journeys described associates who had left in secret, talked of people lost at sea, or expressed anger that young men of the family had to stay in the house doing nothing when their fathers and grandfathers had worked in Europe or served in the French army; these situations arose frequently. It was possible on this journey, also, to observe the difficulties that people encounter when deciding on clandestine migration.

Figure A.2 Journey from Ouagadougou to Elinkine
Illustrator: Alex van Zomerplaag

Interpretations of the data collected in west Africa were shared in Barcelona. This led to a photo exhibition and seminar, which depicted the journey from Ouagadougou to Elinkine (Cross and Tomàs 2009a). The seminar necessitated a fast appraisal of key research findings. Some of the interviewed migrants attended. This helped to validate that the research was grounded in observation and information from migrants as well as the theoretical foundation. Polzer points out that dissemination can test the interpretations of the researcher against the experiences and opinions of the researched, and that an 'interactive feedback method' avoids a closed and authoritative account of the research findings (Polzer 2007: 7). By feeding back interpretations to study participants, it is more likely that 'theory fits the reality(ies) of the respondents' lives' (Bailey *et al.*, cited in Baxter and Eyles 1999: 180). It was not possible to undertake this process of dissemination and feedback in Senegal or Mauritania except on a very loose, ongoing level through frequent casual debate and discussion with the people I encountered professionally and personally. Showing photographs of migrants' journeys taken in Burkina Faso, Mali, Senegal and Mauritania, and informally discussing experiences and observations of these journeys, however, developed trust with respondents and paved the way for further observation. The documentary that my travel companion had been filming during this second journey similarly opened conversation (Cross and Tomàs 2009b). Film footage included bustling activity in the *gares routières* (bush taxi stations); Sahel landscape passing by; crates of chickens, bags of textiles and buckets of food being passed to the roofs of buses and bush taxis; shots of people waiting on wooden benches in the sand; and the major international bus company logos in Burkina Faso. Visits in Barcelona to a building that had been occupied by migrants, and to lodgings in towns in the region, followed these exchanges. Furthermore, respondents discussed their livelihoods in Spain, including clandestine activity and assistance from compatriots or kin. Initially gaining access to the community through NGOs and academic contacts, acceptance was later found among key individuals as a result of sharing experiences and discussing interpretations.

This examination of migration dynamics has much in common with the work of Ellis and MacGaffey (1996) on sub-Saharan Africa's unrecorded international trade. This is because at least some stages of migration, from conception of the journey to remitting funds, involve clandestine, unrecorded activity. This book considers migration as an economic phenomenon, for which Ellis and MacGaffey emphasise holistic study. For data collection, they discuss the use of snowball sampling among networks based on kinship, friendship and other ties. Furthermore, active participation of someone from the milieu is required and an assistant who can speak the local language. Patterns emerge and data can be systematised from detailed information on motivations, organisation, decisions, and strategies for coping with economic and political change (ibid.: 25–7). Similarly to inform this book, in each location, participants from the community assisted with finding new respondents, hence snowball sampling was the main technique. It was usual practice to be accompanied to informants' homes, businesses and to public areas by a key informant, who would remain for interviews. Therefore, the fieldwork adopted a personal nature and depended on establishing mutual trust. Because the range of interviewed people was broad, the focus was on the detail, but there were salient consistencies between the various groups, between migrants at different stages of the journey, and between migrants and sending communities.

# Interview schedules

The interview schedules are displayed for Mauritania, Spain and Senegal, where interviews started in May 2007, February 2008 and April 2008 respectively.

All interviews were preceded by an introduction to the research, a request for recording, and a statement of confidentiality.

## Mauritania: migrants, both Mauritanian and cross-border

### *Introductory questions*

What is your home country? Where and when did you cross the border (if so)? How long do you intend to stay? Is it a length of time or goal that determines this? What length of time/goal?

### *Life before migrating*

Where were you living before (town/village/region)? Did/do you have land? Livestock? Did you and/or siblings go to school?
What were you doing before you moved, and where were you doing this? Was it the same activity that your grandparents, parents and siblings did?
Would you say that your household has influence?
What alternatives are there to migrating? Did you try other options? If so, why did they not work out?
Whose idea was it for you to migrate? Have people always gone from your area? If so, where do they go to?

### *Early migration experiences*

Did you migrate to anywhere before here? Where and for how long?
What work did you do? Was this migration successful? Why/why not?
Did it change your expectations or way of migrating?

### *Travel and arrival*

Are there recruiters in your village?
Was the journey easy? How long did it take to get from home to here? Did many people from your village move too? Did you travel alone or with help? What kind of help did you get to come here? Where were the transit points? Did anyone help you to cross borders?
Were you stopped at any checkpoints between the border and Nouakchott/Nouadhibou? Were there any problems with controls? Did you have a residence permit?
How was your arrival? If you migrated before, was it easier or harder this time to cross borders? What was your best experience? What was the worst experience?

### *Current situation*

Why did you choose Mauritania? Did you know or have links with people here? Has there been a lot of movement between your village and here in the past?
How easy was it to find work and accommodation? What type of work? How is it different from work at home? Do you have a contract? Do you have wages and the resources that you expected? Do employers pay you what they promise to pay?
How can you get medical help? Are you treated as a Mauritanian is, or differently?
Do you have family here, or do you think you may bring family here?

### *Effects on community*

How is/are trade/agriculture/herding etc. being taken care of in your village?
If you are here, who looks after the income-generating activities in your home in your absence?
What is your household living on/doing at the moment? What will be the impact of your migration on your household?
Has your migration led to your family moving house, or will it? To where?
Do you send remittances? How, with which method, and how often? Do you have difficulties with remitting? Has this always been the same?
Who decides how the remittances are used? How are/will they be used?

### *Plans and perspectives*

Have you ever tried or considered migrating to Europe?
*If no:* Why do you think people migrate to Europe? What puts you off this option when others are determined?
*If yes:* For how long have you tried/considered this? Do you have a preferred European country? If so, why? Do you have family in Europe or are there people from your village who are living/working there? What links are there with migrants in Europe?
Do you have plans for work and accommodation? What kind of work do you

expect to do there? How do you plan to get to Europe? How do you find help? Will you go alone or with others? Who can help and how can they help? What do you need to do to benefit from this help?
What information do you have about the journey from here to Europe? Have you ever spoken to someone who was sent back from Europe? If so, what happened to them?
If you are sent back, how will you return the help you received?
Why do you think people go to Europe? Why some and not others?
What influences who goes or who stays? Are they more likely to be female or male? Are they likely to be the oldest or youngest child?

## Senegal: household members (sending and non-sending), returned and repatriated migrants, aspiring migrants, stayers

### *Introductory questions*

How long have you lived here? Where were you living before? Why did you move (if so)?
Do you have land? Livestock? Fishing boats and tools?
Would you say that your household has influence?
What activities do you do? Are these the same kinds of activities that your grandparents, parents and siblings do/did?
Did you go to school? To which level? How about siblings and parents?
Are you married?

### *Migration background*

Who has migrated? Where to? Why him/her? Has anyone else migrated from this household? Was it successful? Why/why not?
Who made the decisions? Did many people from your district move as well?
Were other options tried? If yes, why did they not work out?
Have people always migrated from here? If so, where do they go to? What influences who goes or stays? Are they more likely to be female or male? Are they likely to be the oldest or youngest?

### *About the migrant*

Are there recruiters here?
Did (s)he/you travel alone or with help? What kind of help was available? Was the journey easy? How long did it take?
Did anyone help her/him/you to cross the border? Were there any problems with controls? How was the arrival?
How easy was it to find work and accommodation? What type of work? How different was it from work at home. How was the return? What happened when you came back?

### *Effects on community*

Has there been a lot of movement between here and other places in the past? Where to and how has it changed?
Do you receive remittances? How are they sent? Where do they go to and how often? Who decides how they are used? How important are they compared to other incomes?
What do you think should be done about clandestine migration?

## Spain: West African migrants in Catalonia

### *Introductory questions*

What is your home country and region? Why did you come here? How did you get here?

### *Life before migrating*

Where were you living (town/village etc.)? Did you have land? Livestock? What were you doing before you moved and where was this? Was it the same as what your grandparents/parents/siblings were doing? Why different/the same?
Does your household have influence?
What alternatives were there to migrating? Did you try other options? If so, why did they not work out? If applicable; can you explain the main problems in your village and why they were seen by many to be a problem?
Have people always migrated from your village? Did they migrate in the time of your parents/grandparents? If so, where have they gone to and why?
What influences who goes or who stays? Are they more likely to be female or male? Are they likely to be the oldest or youngest child?
More generally; why do people go to Europe? Why some and not others?

### *Early migration experiences*

Did you migrate to anywhere before here? Where and for how long?
What work did you do? Is this what you wanted to do? Why/why not?
Did it change your expectations or way of migrating?

### *Travel and arrival*

How and why did you decide to migrate? Whose idea was it for you to migrate?
What did others think of you leaving?
Were there recruiters in your town/village?
Did many people from your village move too? Did you travel alone? Did you receive any help?
Was the journey easy? How long did it take to get from home to here? Where were the transit points?

Did anyone help you to cross borders or to get here? If you encountered any checkpoints, what happened? Were there any problems with controls? Did you have paperwork?
How was your arrival? If you migrated before, was it easier or harder to cross borders? What was your best experience? What was the worst experience?

### *Current situation*

Why did you choose Spain? Did you know or have links with people here?
How easy was it to find work and accommodation? What type of work? How is it different from work at home? Do you have a contract? Do you have wages and the resources that you expected? Do employers pay you what they promise to pay?
How can you get medical help? Do you know what your legal rights are to health, education and housing? How are you treated in comparison to Spanish people?
Do you have family here, or do you think you may bring family here?

### *Effects on community*

How is trade/agriculture/herding etc. being taken care of in your village?
Who looks after the income-generating activities while you are here?
What is your household living on/doing at the moment?
Has your migration led to your family moving house, or will it? From where to where?
Do you send remittances? How, with which method, and how often? Do you have difficulties with remitting? Has this always been the same? What would make it easier to send money?
Who decides how the remittances are used? How are/will they be used?
Are you remitting what you expected to remit? If not, why not?

### *Plans and outlook*

If you are sent back, how will you return the help you received?
How long do you expect to stay here? How long do you want to or need to stay?
What determines the length of your stay?
Is this different to your initial plans?

# Referenced interviews

| *Interview no.* | *Date* | *Location of interview* | *Male/ female* | *Country of birth (hometown/region)* | *Occupation/position of respondent* | *Remittances/household* | *Migration notes* |
|---|---|---|---|---|---|---|---|
| 1 | 07.05.07 | Mauritania (Nouakchott) | F | Gambia (Serekunda) | Housemaid, seeking work | Sends 20,000 UM to mother every 3 months via ambassador – used for food and other expenses. | In Mauritania for 1 year 9 months and plans to return to Gambia by the end of the year; has work permit. |
| 2 | 07.05.07 | Mauritania (Nouakchott) | M | Mauritania (Kaedi) | Farmer, seeking work as housemaid | Sends to parents, depending on income, via acquaintances.<br>Does not know how the money is used; more important income to parents than farming. Parents also dye textiles. | In Nouakchott for 6 years. Has attempted clandestine migration to Spain twice – was stopped both times by patrols (Nouadhibou and Morocco). |
| 3 | 07.05.07 | Mauritania (Nouakchott) | F | Senegal (near Richard Toll) | Housemaid, seeking work | No remittances (parents deceased). | Has migrated more than once to Nouakchott. |
| 4 | 07.05.07 | Mauritania (Nouakchott) | F | Senegal (Podor) | Housemaid, seeking work | Occasionally sends remittances to mother via acquaintances. Used for food and rent; farming does not bring enough income. | Migrates to Nouakchott for periods of 3–9 months. |
| 5 | 07.05.07 | Mauritania (Nouakchott) | F | Senegal (Louga) | Housemaid, seeking work. | Sends remittances to parents via people who are going through Rosso. Does not know how they are spent. Father: retired local government worker. | Has migrated to Mauritania a few times. |

| *Interview no.* | *Date* | *Location of interview* | *Male/ female* | *Country of birth (hometown/region)* | *Occupation/position of respondent* | *Remittances/household* | *Migration notes* |
|---|---|---|---|---|---|---|---|
| 6 | 07.05.07 | Mauritania (Nouakchott) | M | Mauritania (Nouakchott) | Fisherman | No remittances – most family in Nouakchott. | Has friends who have migrated clandestinely; plans to attempt this from Nouadhibou. |
| 7 | 07.05.07 | Mauritania (Nouakchott) | F | Mauritania (Maghama) | Housemaid, seeking work (plans to be trader) | Sends 5,000 – 10,000 UM to mother whenever possible via taxi drivers. Household grows rice but relies on her income to buy rice. | Moved to Nouakchott when young and is the only family member to be working and remitting. |
| 8 | 07.05.07 | Mauritania (Nouakchott) | M | Senegal (Rosso) | Fisherman | Carries remittance money or sends children to carry it. Meets basic consumption needs. Household has market gardens but no tools. | Staying in Nouakchott with his wife. |
| 9 | 07.05.07 | Mauritania (Nouakchott) | M | Mauritania (Bogué) | Trader (shoes) | Sends remittances every 1 or 2 months via acquaintances, or if need arises. | Has family in Nouakchott. |
| 10 | 07.05.07 | Mauritania (Nouakchott) | M | Mauritania (Bogué) | Fish trader | Sometimes sends money to family through relatives; used for food. Parents are in Nouakchott. | Has attempted clandestine migration once. |
| 11 | 07.05.07 | Mauritania (Nouakchott) | M | Mauritania (Bogué) | Fisherman | Sends 8,000–15,000 UM to family every 2 months via relatives. Has family members in business and government. | Has lived in Nouakchott for almost 25 years. Tried to go to Europe through Libya. Is considering trafficking people to the Canary Islands. |

| *Interview no.* | *Date* | *Location of interview* | *Male/ female* | *Country of birth (hometown/region)* | *Occupation/position of respondent* | *Remittances/household* | *Migration notes* |
|---|---|---|---|---|---|---|---|
| 12 | 07.05.07 | Mauritania (Nouakchott) | M | Senegal (Saint-Louis) | Fisherman, formerly traded fish | Was sending 5000 – 6000 UM per month but now is making less profit. Parents both work in fishing. Wages are used for school fees for children. | Has lived in Mauritania for 27 years. Has family who migrated clandestinely to Europe but he is not interested. |
| 13 | 07.05.07 | Mauritania (Nouakchott) | F | Senegal (Saint-Louis) | Fish trader | Sends oil and rice to parents. | Has lived in Nouakchott for 6 years with husband. Sends oil and food to family. |
| 14 | 15.05.07 | Senegal (Saint-Louis) | M | Senegal (Saint-Louis) | Fisherman | | Occasionally goes to fish in Mauritania. |
| 15 | 20.05.07 | Mauritania (border post, Senegal River) | M | Mauritania | Customs officer | | Observes movement of people and goods between Mauritania and Senegal. |
| 16 | 23.02.08 | Spain (Salt) | F | Nigeria (Owele) | As a migrant, has worked as housemaid, care assistant, dishwasher and in abattoir | Sends money to parents via Western Union. It is used for food and also for animal feed/fertiliser. Father worked in brewery; now farms. | Has been in Spain for 7 years. Arrived by boat from Morocco; had passed through Libya and Algeria. This took 1 year, then crossed to Spain by pirogue. |

| *Interview no.* | *Date* | *Location of interview* | *Male/ female* | *Country of birth (hometown/region)* | *Occupation/position of respondent* | *Remittances/household* | *Migration notes* |
|---|---|---|---|---|---|---|---|
| 17 | 23.02.08 | Spain (Salt) | M | Gambia (Serekunda) | Does not work; former teacher | | Left Gambia as a result of government surveillance. Arrived in Spain by pirogue four months prior from Morocco; passed through Senegal and Mali; travelled for a year overland. |
| 18 | 23.02.08 | Spain (Salt) | M | Nigeria (Edo state) | Works on a farm | Sends between €120 and €200 to mother and father every month. They use it for food, fridge, farm equipment. Father works in university; mother is businesswoman. | Left Nigeria with a visa over 2 years ago, has residence permit. |
| 19 | 25.02.08 | Spain (Barcelona) | M | Gambia | Unemployed, homeless | Household: groundnut farming. Cannot sell crops. Education: senior secondary. | Migrated to Guinea, Mali, Mauritania, Morocco, Senegal. Travelled from Casamance to Canary Islands by pirogue. |
| 20 | 25.02.08 | Spain (Barcelona) | M | Ivory Coast (Abidjan) | Unemployed, shares a room with 25 people | Household: formerly cocoa production but stopped after war. | Has been in Barcelona for 2 months. Flew to Italy then train through France. Has brother in Libya. |
| 21 | 26.02.08 | Spain (Barcelona) | M | Ghana (northern) | Unemployed. Car washing in Libya. Short-term manual labour in Italy | Household: subsistence farming, cannot pay for fertiliser. | Left Ghana in 2002, travelled through Burkina Faso, Mali, Niger, Libya (27 days); Libya for 3 years. Italy by boat, stayed for 2 years. |

| *Interview no.* | *Date* | *Location of interview* | *Male/ female* | *Country of birth (hometown/region)* | *Occupation/position of respondent* | *Remittances/household* | *Migration notes* |
|---|---|---|---|---|---|---|---|
| 22 | 26.02.08 21.08.08 | Spain (Barcelona and Lleida) | M | Cameroon (Nkambe) | Agricultural work. Construction work in North Africa | Sends remittances – last time was €400. Household: farming – corn and beans. Cannot sell for profit. | Travelled through Chad, Libya, Algeria, Morocco, by bush taxis and trekking, for roughly 5 years. Boat from Morocco to Spain. Grandparents moved back and forth to Nigeria. |
| 23 | 26.02.08 | Spain (Barcelona) | M | Ivory Coast (Tingréla) | Factory work | Unable to send remittances. | In Barcelona for 1 month. Was targeted by military for supporting former Ivorian prime minister (Rassemblement de Républicains). Travelled through Mali and Mauritania; pirogue journey to Spain. |
| 24 | 27.02.08 | Spain (Barcelona) | M | Ghana (Tafo) | Formerly mechanic in Ghana and Libya. No work, sleeping in airport | No contact with family – fled after causing electrical fire. | Passed through Burkina Faso, Niger, worked in Libya, boat to Italy, train to Spain. |
| 25 | 28.02.08 | Spain (Barcelona) | M | Nigeria (Eastern) | Not working, formerly imported motorcycles; steel factory worker in South Korea. | Two houses in Nigeria, built using remittances from previous migration. Siblings: diplomat, doctor, college lecturer. University education. | Flew to Germany then train to Barcelona. Previous migration to South Korea after Malaysia visit was unsuccessful. |

| *Interview no.* | *Date* | *Location of interview* | *Male/ female* | *Country of birth (hometown/region)* | *Occupation/position of respondent* | *Remittances/household* | *Migration notes* |
|---|---|---|---|---|---|---|---|
| 26 | 28.02.08 | Spain (Barcelona) | M | Nigeria (East) | Not working | Household: farming cassava, yam; traders. | Three years to reach Spain – 2 years in Morocco. Boat to Spain 6 months ago. |
| 27 | 28.02.08 | Spain (Barcelona) | M | Nigeria | Not working | Household: farming cassava, yam; all siblings farming. | Travelled to Spain in fishing boat from Sierra Leone. |
| 28 | 08.04.08 | Senegal (Thiaroye-sur-Mer) | M | Senegal (Thiaroye-sur-Mer) | Fisherman | Parents fish/trade fish. | Has been repatriated from Tenerife after 45 days in camp. |
| 29 | 08.04.08 | Senegal (Colobane) | M | Senegal (Fatick) | Mechanic, head of repatriate association | | Attempted journey to Spain; turned around in storm. Will not try again. |
| 30 | 14.05.08 | Mauritania (Nouakchott) | F | Senegal | Is seeking kitchen work. Profession on passport: trader | Sends money to mother. | Has been in Mauritania for 9 years. Is trying to go to Europe to find work in trade or open a restaurant but will not go by pirogue. |
| 31 | 17.05.08 | Mauritania (Nouadhibou) | M | Nigeria (South) | Preacher | Parents are farmers; grandfather has land; no machinery. | In Nouadhibou for 12 years – abandoned attempt to go to Europe.Travelled to Niger, Algeria and Mali before Mauritania. |

| *Interview no.* | *Date* | *Location of interview* | *Male/ female* | *Country of birth (hometown/region)* | *Occupation/position of respondent* | *Remittances/household* | *Migration notes* |
|---|---|---|---|---|---|---|---|
| 32 | 17.05.08 | Mauritania (Nouadhibou) | M | Ghana (Cape Coast) | Disability worker; opening restaurant; humanitarian worker | Grandparents: farmers; father: seaman. Family still has land; brothers at university. | Has been in Mauritania for 7 years. Went through Burkina Faso, Mali and Senegal. Aimed to go to Europe. |
| 33 | 17.05.08 | Mauritania (Nouadhibou) | M | Nigeria (West) | Barber – wants to work in fish transporting | Sends money every month, between $60 and $100, via Western Union and sometimes through acquaintances. Brings fish and rice when he returns to household. Mother had bars and restaurants; family has land. Household relies on income from him and brother. | Does not plan to go to Europe because cost of living/phonecalls is high. Has brother in the UK. |
| 34 | 18.05.08 | Mauritania (Nouadhibou) | M | Nigeria (Imo state) | Barber/factory work | Unable to send remittances. | In Mauritania for 2 years. May attempt a clandestine journey to Europe – needs to gather passengers and then can go without paying. |
| 35 | 20.05.08 | Mauritania (Nouakchott) | M | Ghana | Formerly worked for shipping company | Unable to send remittances. Mother has land; has siblings who teach/manage hotel. | Entered Mauritania 6 years ago after being repatriated to Senegal from Spain. |
| 36 | 20.05.08 | Mauritania (Nouakchott) | M | Ghana | Preacher | | Has no intention to go to Europe. |

| *Interview no.* | *Date* | *Location of interview* | *Male/ female* | *Country of birth (hometown/region)* | *Occupation/position of respondent* | *Remittances/household* | *Migration notes* |
|---|---|---|---|---|---|---|---|
| 37 | 20.05.08 | Mauritania (Nouakchott) | M | Nigeria (Delta) | Businessman | Sends money to daughter – \$200–\$500 every 1–2 months via Western Union. Household – engineering/ business. Family has land and some tools for farming. They need income from remittances. | Has been in Mauritania for 2 years – flew from Benin. Will go to Europe if he has the opportunity. |
| 38 | 20.05.08 | Mauritania (Nouakchott) | F | Nigeria (Rivers) | Works in nursery school; formerly worked in restaurant | No remittances – wants to finish studies. Family grows yam/cassava; house was built when parents were young; water is collected from village. | In Mauritania for 5 years; formerly in Senegal for 3 years. Will go on to other countries if she has the opportunity. |
| 39 | 03.06.08 | Senegal (Thiaroye-sur-Mer) | M | Mali (Guélémou) | Transports fish | Sends money to parents for food. Siblings in Koranic school. Household has goats and cows. | Has been in Senegal for 7 years. Two failed attempts to go to Spain – shipwrecked in Nouadhibou on first attempt. |
| 40 | 03.06.08 | Senegal (Thiaroye-sur-Mer) | M | Senegal (Thiaroye-sur-Mer) | Fisherman | All family are cultivators or work in fishing industry. Has 2 brothers in Europe who send remittances via Western Union or through someone returning; money is used for food. | Failed attempt to go to Spain – broke down at coast. Lots of family/friends in Spain, Italy, US, formerly to France – babysitting, trade, road sweeping. Percussionists in Germany and Netherlands. |

| *Interview no.* | *Date* | *Location of interview* | *Male/ female* | *Country of birth (hometown/region)* | *Occupation/position of respondent* | *Remittances/household* | *Migration notes* |
|---|---|---|---|---|---|---|---|
| 41 | 06.06.08 | Senegal (Thiaroye-sur-Mer) | F | Senegal (Thiaroye-sur-Mer) | Association member | Household: fishing, gardener, son is tailor. Does not receive remittances. | Son is in Spain but no longer working. Other people in district have migrated to France and Italy. |
| 42 | 06.06.08 | Senegal (Thiaroye-sur-Mer) | F | Senegal (Thiaroye-sur-Mer) | Association member | Rents house. One son is fisherman. Son in Spain sends 200,000 F CFA per month, of which she receives half; his brother and father receive the rest. | Son in Spain. Other son was rescued on first attempt; repatriated on second attempt. Has other sons in Touba and Kaolack. Nephews are lost at sea (have had funerals). |
| 43 | 06.06.08 | Senegal (Thiaroye-sur-Mer) | F | Senegal (Thiaroye-sur-Mer) | Association member | Household: fishing and trade. Son sends 60,000 F CFA per month from Spain. Also receives remittances from son in Italy, both builders. | France was targeted before Italy and Spain. |
| 44 | 06.06.08 | Senegal (Thiaroye-sur-Mer) | F | Senegal (Thiès) | Association member, formerly food vendor | Household: fishing; work for Senelec. | Has son in Spain who is not working/remitting. |
| 45 | 06.08.08 | Senegal (Thiaroye-sur-Mer) | F | Senegal (Thiaroye-sur-Mer) | Association member | Household: grandfather's land. Sons – carpentry, building and welding. | Son was returned from Morocco by a Senegalese delegation. Has other family who are lost at sea. |

| *Interview no.* | *Date* | *Location of interview* | *Male/ female* | *Country of birth (hometown/region)* | *Occupation/position of respondent* | *Remittances/household* | *Migration notes* |
|---|---|---|---|---|---|---|---|
| 46 | 07.06.08 | Senegal (Thiaroye-sur-Mer) | F | France | Association member, doughnut vendor | Household: fish trading. Son worked as joiner. Not working in Spain. | Son and his half-brothers in Spain – were among the first to leave, before patrols. |
| 47 | 07.06.08 | Senegal (Thiaroye-sur-Mer) | M | Senegal (Thiaroye-sur-Mer) | Fisherman | – | Repatriated from Morocco. Over 100 young people from district are lost at sea (families not always comfortable to mention this in interviews). |
| 48 | 18.06.08 | Senegal (Rufisque) | M | Senegal (Rufisque) | Tiler | Household: fishing; siblings builder/welder. | Has relatives in France. Was repatriated from Spain. |
| 49 | 18.06.08 | Senegal (Rufisque) | M | Senegal (Rufisque) | Fisherman and fish trader | Household: father worked in factory (closed down). | Has formerly migrated to Rosso and Mauritania to trade.<br>Five clandestine attempts to go to Spain; reached Spain twice and was repatriated. Friends who he travelled with are still there. |
| 50 | 18.06.08 | Senegal (Rufisque) | M | Senegal (Rufisque) | Fishing, factory work | Household: plumbers, fishermen, traders. | Was repatriated on first attempt to reach Spain; encountered a storm the second time.<br>Knows people in Italy who have residence and return sometimes. |

| Interview no. | Date | Location of interview | Male/ female | Country of birth (hometown/region) | Occupation/position of respondent | Remittances/household | Migration notes |
|---|---|---|---|---|---|---|---|
| 51 | 18.06.08 | Senegal (Rufisque) | M | Senegal (Rufisque) | Builder | Father: Sonatel agent; mother: fishmonger. | Failed attempt to reach Spain: problem with pirogue.<br>There are as many legal as illegal emigrants in district. |
| 52 | 20.06.08 | Senegal (Rufisque) | F | Senegal (Rufisque) | Civil servant | Has son in the army; other children in school. Receives remittances but respondent and sister do not rely on extra income. | Has sons in Italy who work with short-term contracts; they do not yet have papers. |
| 53 | 20.06.08 | Senegal (Rufisque) | M | Senegal (Rufisque) | Trader (mobile phones, phone cards) and has opened a telecentre | Receives remittances from daughters via Western Union. Meets basic expenses and has funded the construction of a house. | Three daughters in France. |
| 54 | 20.06.08 | Senegal (Rufisque) | M | Senegal (Rufisque) | Formerly a plumber; now unemployed | Mother: vegetable vendor in Dakar. Father: retired mechanic. Siblings: plumbing/unemployed. | Was repatriated from Spain. Has half brothers in Spain who are legalised. |
| 55 | 20.06.08 | Senegal (Rufisque) | M | Senegal (Rufisque) | Welding, building | Mother: fishmonger | Does not intend to migrate. Has friends in Spain who send money back to their households, though do not have papers. |

| *Interview no.* | *Date* | *Location of interview* | *Male/ female* | *Country of birth (hometown/region)* | *Occupation/position of respondent* | *Remittances/household* | *Migration notes* |
|---|---|---|---|---|---|---|---|
| 56 | 24.06.08 | Senegal (Rufisque) | M | Senegal (Rufisque) | Trained in building | Younger son worked as teacher, no longer sending money from US; older child worked as translator for NGO and now sends money from Italy occasionally but is unemployed. | Younger son is in US; had a teaching contract. Older son went to Italy to work as trader.<br>Earlier clandestine migrants in district are now sending money and have built houses. |
| 57 | 24.06.08 | Senegal (Rufisque) | F | Senegal (Rufisque) | Textile worker | Husband does construction work for an oil company and sends money, which met household needs but since price hikes, income put aside for sewing materials is also used for the essentials. | Husband in Equatorial Guinea (previously had a contract but now undocumented).<br>No other emigrants in family. |
| 58 | 24.06.08 | Senegal (Rufisque) | F | Senegal (Rufisque) | Trader. Member of women's association | Daughter worked in factory but left to work as trader.<br>Husband gained contract for Spain, 2–3 years agricultural work. Has generously contributed to household but now out of work and learning Spanish. | Goes to Mauritania for trade. Daughter in Spain.<br>No other emigrants. |

| *Interview no.* | *Date* | *Location of interview* | *Male/ female* | *Country of birth (hometown/region)* | *Occupation/position of respondent* | *Remittances/household* | *Migration notes* |
|---|---|---|---|---|---|---|---|
| 59 | 24.06.08 | Senegal (Rufisque) | M | Senegal (Rufisque) | Tiler | Household: building, carpentry. Occasional remittances. One brother was formerly in the army and then taxi driver. | Has sister who has lived in Italy, France and Spain as trader. Two brothers in Spain who left clandestinely with cousins; one is working for a small company; the other has little work. |
| 60 | 24.06.08 | Senegal (Rufisque) | F | Senegal (Rufisque) | Textile worker, trades fruit in Casamance | | Wants to travel to Europe. Husband worked in Portugal on fishing trawler, moved on to Spain when contract finished. Uncle worked in Italy and Spain. |
| 61 | 24.06.08 | Senegal (Rufisque) | M | Senegal (Rufisque) | Electrician | Household has been supported by his remittances; wife is trader. Children at school; daughter is hairdresser. | First travelled to Italy, then on to Spain. Now has documentation and returns to Senegal regularly. Has relatives and acquaintances in Italy and Spain. |
| 62 | 24.06.08 | Senegal (Rufisque) | M | Senegal (Rufisque) | Fisherman | Household: mechanics and fishermen. Not yet receiving remittances. | Has brother who went to Spain clandestinely, first working as fisherman in Mauritania. Has a friend who reached Spain by pirogue days before interview. |

| *Interview no.* | *Date* | *Location of interview* | *Male/ female* | *Country of birth (hometown/region)* | *Occupation/position of respondent* | *Remittances/household* | *Migration notes* |
|---|---|---|---|---|---|---|---|
| 63 | 24.06.08 | Senegal (Rufisque) | M | Senegal (Rufisque) | Trained as architect; now is recruiter on building site | | Attempted a clandestine journey to Spain. Would try again.<br>Arrested by Senegalese navy near Morocco.<br>Has one brother in USA and another in Saudi Arabia. |
| 64 | 02.07.08 | Senegal (Rufisque) | F | Senegal (Rufisque) | Fishmonger | Husband was gendarme then policeman. Sons were fishermen before travelling. Formerly received remittances through Western Union from the 'legal' son, who now seeks fishing work; 'illegal' son sends money from Italy. | Both sons attempted clandestine journey to Spain and were intercepted in Morocco. Following this, one son gained an 8-month contract for agricultural work (expired); the other went to Spain by pirogue then joined uncle in Italy. |
| 65 | 02.07.08 | Senegal (Rufisque) | M | Senegal (Rufisque) | Mechanic | House was built with remittances from Saudi Arabia: he works there and contributes 50,000–100,000 F CFA at a time. | Had a contract in Saudi Arabia, gained from Nigerian contacts. Brother is also in Saudi Arabia without contract but returns to Senegal for holidays. |
| 66 | 02.07.08 | Senegal (Rufisque) | M | Senegal (Rufisque) | Sells phonecards and aloe vera products | Studied electro-tech but had to abandon course when father died. Father was timber merchant. | Was repatriated from Spain. Would try again. Has cousin who went to Spain clandestinely and sends remittances. |

| *Interview no.* | *Date* | *Location of interview* | *Male/ female* | *Country of birth (hometown/region)* | *Occupation/position of respondent* | *Remittances/household* | *Migration notes* |
|---|---|---|---|---|---|---|---|
| 67 | 02.07.08 | Senegal (Rufisque) | M | Senegal (Rufisque) | Fisherman, builder | Father and whole family are fishermen, fishmongers. 20 youths living in household. | Journey to Spain was aborted in a storm; has friends who were also unsuccessful. |
| 68 | 02.07.08 | Senegal (Rufisque) | M | Senegal (Rufisque) | Sells radios, clothes; building ('all except theft!') | Household: fishing or unemployed. | Will go to Spain if aunt can arrange contract. |
| 69 | 02.07.08 | Senegal (Rufisque) | M | Senegal (Rufisque) | Joiner, market trader | Household: fishing, trading. Some remittances from Italy. | Would risk life to go to Spain by pirogue. Household member is trader in Italy and returns for holidays. |
| 70 | 02.07.08 | Senegal (Rufisque) | F | Ivory Coast | | Son worked as carpenter. Sent remittances from Spain when recruited on farms; now sends less regularly but younger son has been able to go college. | Son went to Spain by pirogue. |
| 71 | 02.07.08 | Senegal (Rufisque) | F | Senegal (Rufisque) | Retired trader | One son worked as security guard at university before going to Spain. Worked as trader in Spain and remitted but recently his merchandise was confiscated by police. Other son worked as joiner and then gained contract for agricultural work but this has expired. | Two sons in Spain: 1 left clandestinely and the other with a contract. |

| *Interview no.* | *Date* | *Location of interview* | *Male/ female* | *Country of birth (hometown/region)* | *Occupation/position of respondent* | *Remittances/household* | *Migration notes* |
|---|---|---|---|---|---|---|---|
| 72 | 02.07.08 | Senegal (Rufisque) | F | Senegal (Rufisque) | Trader | Husband worked as builder. Son in Mauritania is trader and sends remittances or merchandise for his wife to sell; son in France is rarely able to send money. | Has travelled to Gambia and Mauritania to buy stock. Has son who was repatriated from Spain on first migration attempt and is now in France. Other son is in Mauritania. |
| 73 | 02.07.08 | Senegal (Rufisque) | M | Senegal (Rufisque) | Carpenter | | Was repatriated from Spain. Brother formerly migrated to Ivory Coast. 2 uncles are in Spain, who left clandestinely. |
| 74 | 02.07.08 | Senegal (Rufisque) | M | Senegal (Rufisque) | Teacher | Brother works for oil company in Kaolack; sends 40,000 F CFA per month (€60.98). Father is a retired teacher. | Has not migrated. |
| 75 | 08.07.08 | Senegal (Rufisque) | M | Senegal (Rufisque) | Imam | | People from different horizons go towards Spain from Rufisque; because people do not have work, clandestine migration continues. |

| *Interview no.* | *Date* | *Location of interview* | *Male/ female* | *Country of birth (hometown/region)* | *Occupation/position of respondent* | *Remittances/household* | *Migration notes* |
|---|---|---|---|---|---|---|---|
| 76 | 17.08.08<br>18.08.08<br>20.08.08<br>21.02.09 | Spain (Barcelona) | M | Senegal (Ziguinchor) | Trader | Sends money to siblings in Ziguinchor and Dakar through Islamic bank. Sent €600 in June 08. Household: traders. Have completed further education. | Family formerly migrated to and from Guinea, trading tobacco. He has worked in Guinea and Gambia. Flew to Portugal with brother and they traded arts and crafts, took the train to Barcelona and living there for 10 years. Has sisters in France. |
| 77 | 18.08.08 | Spain (Barcelona) | M | Gambia (Serekunda) | Unemployed, formerly mechanic | Family has rice crops. Formerly sent €10–€100 at a time. Brothers occasionally send remittances. | Formerly migrated to London then Dakar. In Spain for 18 years; no work for a year and unable to return to Gambia. |
| 78 | 19.08.08 | Spain (Barcelona) | M | Senegal | Tailor, translator (voluntary) | Large household with some land. Sends €200–300 each month via Western Union. | In Spain for 15 years – flew and had visa; intends to return but unable to at present. |
| 79 | 26.07.09 | Spain (Barcelona) | M | Ghana (Sawla) | Worker for a migrant NGO | Returns annually to Ghana and works in a development NGO. | Travelled from Ghana through Burkina Faso, Niger, Algeria and Libya for 2.5 years; intercepted en route to Italy and sent to Tunisia, eventually went to Morocco and then Canary Islands. |

# Glossary

| | |
|---|---|
| acquis (EU) | legal rights and obligations |
| bush taxi | public transport system for travel between villages, towns and countries, usually in cars or minibuses, with set routes and *gares routières* designated for those routes |
| bassin arachidier | groundnut basin |
| Bidan | 'white Moor' tribes of mixed Arab and Berber descent |
| boutiquier | shopkeeper |
| cayuco | canoe |
| Communauté | community (commonwealth) |
| corvée | duty, chore; -labour: a type of forced labour |
| clandestin (Fr.); clandestine (En.) | (n) clandestine; a person who emigrates clandestinely |
| corruption ambiante | pervading corruption |
| deuxiéme portion militaire | second military portion; military labour service |
| l'économie de traite | French term to describe the colonial economy |
| emir | leader (Arabic) |
| evolué | educated African (term of French colonial administration) |
| Françafrique | relationship between France and former African colonies; network of politicians and businessmen in France and Africa |
| gare routière | station (buses, coaches, bush taxis) |
| Generalitat | Government of Catalonia |
| grands commerçants | big traders |
| Guardia Civil | civil guard (Spanish gendarmerie) |
| Halpulaar; Haalpulaar'en (pl.) | Speaker(s) of Pulaar (Peul, Fulani; Tukolor) |
| haratin | Arab-speaking 'black Moors'; freedmen |
| imam | prayer leader in a mosque |
| l'aventure | adventure (common term used to describe the *pirogue* voyage from the west African coast to the Canary Islands) |
| lutte | fight; wrestling match |
| marabout | Muslim holy man (north and west Africa) |

| | |
|---|---|
| métier | trade, job, occupation |
| Mouride | Islamic brotherhood |
| navétane | temporary migrant (colonial) |
| patera | small boat |
| Padrón | municipal register (Spain) |
| pirogue | small wooden boat |
| piroguier | *pirogue* driver |
| quartier traditionnel | traditional district (Senegal) |
| refoulement | repression; holding back |
| taximen | taxi drivers |
| tontine | common fund |

# Bibliography


Abrahamsen, R. (2004) 'A breeding ground for terrorists? Africa and Britain's 'war on terrorism', *Review of African Political Economy*, 31 (102): 677–84.

Adamou, A. *et al.* (2010) 'Prisoners of the desert: investigation into the consequences of European migration policies at the Mali-Mauritanian border', *La Cimade*, December.

Addy, D. Nii, Wijkström, B. and Thouez, C. (2003) 'Migrant remittances – country of origin experiences'. International Conference on Migrant Remittances: Developmental Impact and Future Prospects. London: DFID and World Bank.

Adepoju, A. (2006) 'Leading issues in international migration in sub-Saharan Africa'. In D. Gelderblom, C. Cross, N. Roux and J. Mafukidze (eds) *Views on Migration in Sub-Saharan Africa: Proceedings of an African Migration Alliance Workshop.* Cape Town: HSRC Press.

Adepoju, A., Boulton, A. and Levin, M. (2007) 'Promoting integration through mobility: free movement and the ECOWAS Protocol'. UNHCR Research Paper No. 150, Geneva.

*Africa Confidential* (2003) 'Warriors and marabouts: Nouakchott cracks down on Islamists and Arab nationalists ahead of November's elections', 44 (20), October.

Africa Trade Policy Centre (2011) 'Africa Trade Forum 2011. Can Africa Trade Itself out of Poverty? Accelerating Intra-African Trade and Enhancing Africa's Participation in Global Trade', September.

African Development Bank (AfDB) (2009a) 'Migrant remittances: a development challenge', 3 February. Available at: http://www.afdb.org/en/documents/publications/migrant-remittances-a-development-challenge/ [accessed 25 June 2009].

African Development Bank (2009b) 'AfDB approves US$ 175 million loan for mining operation in Mauritania', 17 September. Available at: http://www.afdb.org/en/news-events/article/afdb-approves-us-175-million-loan-for-mining-operation-in-mauritania-5094/ [accessed 17 October 2009].

*African Terrorism Bulletin* (2005) 'Africa: the breeding ground for terrorism?', Issue 2, March, Institute for Security Studies.

Afrol News (2009) 'Mauritania election compromise reached'. 3 June. Available at: http://www.afrol.com/articles/33441 [accessed 2 July 2009].

Agence France-Presse (2006) 'Ils étaient partis du Sénégal: Au moins 14 clandestins morts et 179 rescapés en Mauritanie', 27 August. Available at: http://www.lesoleil.sn/imprimer.php3?id_article=15915 [accessed 25 June 2009].

Agence Nouakchott d'Information (2008) 'Mauritanie: 116 immigrés clandestins repatriés dans leurs pays d'origine', 3 November. Available at: http://fr.allafrica.com/stories/printable/200811040189 [accessed 25 June 2009].

Agence de Presse Africaine (2008) 'Arrestation à Nouadhibou de 78 jeunes clandestins pour la plupart des Maliens', 18 November. Available at: http://193.149.120.213/pays/mauritanie/article_depeche.asp?art_cle=APA53858arressneila0 [accessed 25 June 2009].

Agencia Española de Cooperación Internacional para el Desarrollo (AECID) (2012) 'AECID and the Economic Community of West African States hold the meeting of the 4th Steering Committee of the Spain/ECOWAS Migration and Development Fund', 24 May.

Ahmed-Salem, Z. Ould (2005) 'Mauritania: a Saharan frontier-state', *The Journal of North African Studies*, 10 (3–4): 491–506.

Ahmed-Salem, Z. Ould (2010) 'Genèse des frontières et enjeux migratoires en Mauritanie', *CARIM Notes d'analyse et de synthèse,* 2010/53.

Albert, I. O. (2008) 'Historicizing migration: convenor's report on the 2008 extended workshop on social history', CODESRIA and SEPHIS. Saint-Louis, Senegal, 3–21 March.

Alliot-Marie, M. (2008) 'Colloque: service de cooperation technique de police', 1 September. Available at: http://www.interieur.gouv.fr/misill/sections/a_1_interieur/le_ministre/interventions/archives-mam/colloque-sctip/view [accessed 1 July 2009].

Alscher, S. (2005) 'Knocking at the doors of 'Fortress Europe': migration and border control in southern Spain and eastern Poland'. Working Paper No. 126, Center for Comparative Immigration Studies, University of California, San Diego.

Amin, S. (1972a) 'Underdevelopment and dependence in Black Africa: historical origin', *Journal of Peace Research*, 9: 105–19.

Amin, S. (1972b) 'Underdevelopment and Dependence in Black Africa: origins and contemporary forms', *The Journal of Modern African Studies*, 10 (4): 503–24.

Amin, S. (1974) 'Introduction'. In S. Amin (ed.) *Modern Migrations in Western Africa*. London: Oxford University Press.

Amin, S. (1995) 'Migrations in contemporary Africa: a retrospective view'. In J. Baker and T. A. Aina (eds) *The Migration Experience in Africa*. Uppsala: Nordiska Afrikainstitutet.

Amin, S. (2010) 'Managing the euro: mission impossible!', *Monthly Review*, 17 June.

Amin, S. and El-Kenz, A. (2005) *Europe and the Arab World: Patterns and Prospects for the New Relationship.* London: Zed Books.

Ammassari, S. (2006) 'Migration management and development policies: maximising the benefits of international migration in West Africa'. No. 72E. International Labour Office: Geneva.

Ammassari, S. and Black, R. (2001) 'Harnessing the potential of migration and return to promote development: applying concepts to West Africa'. Sussex Centre for Migration Research.

Amnesty International (2008) 'Mauritania: torture at the heart of the state'. 3 December. Available at: http://www.amnesty.org/en/library/asset/AFR38/009/2008/en/da7e84ca-bfa0-11dd-9f1c-69adff6d2171/afr380092008en.pdf [accessed 22 June 2009].

Amuedo-Dorantes, C. and de la Rica, S. (2005) 'Immigrants' responsiveness to labour market conditions and its implications on regional disparities: evidence from Spain'. IZA Discussion Paper No. 1557. Available at: http://papers.ssrn.com/sol3/papers.cfm?abstract_id=702887 [accessed on 15 September 2009].

Anderson, J. and Shuttleworth, I. (2004) 'Theorising state borders in capitalism: spatial fixes old and new'. CIBR/WP04-2. Centre for International Borders Research, Queens University Belfast.

Andreas, P. (2001) *Border Games: Policing the US–Mexico Divide*. Ithaca: Cornell University Press.

Angel de Lucas, M. (2006) 'Las asociaciones canarias unen esfuerzos en apoyo a la inmigración', *Periódico Diagonal*, 37, 7 October.

Anyanwu, J.C. (2011) 'International remittances and income inequality in Africa', *Working Paper Series*, No. 135, August: African Development Bank Group.

Arendt, H. (1958/1998) *The Human Condition*. Chicago, IL: University of Chicago Press.

Arthur, J.A. (1991) 'International labour migration patterns in West Africa', *African Studies Review*, 34 (3): 65–87.

Ashman, S. and Callinicos, A. (2006) 'Capital accumulation and the state system: assessing David Harvey's *The New Imperialism*', *Historical Materialism*, 14 (4): 107–31.

Asociación Comisión Católica Española de Migraciónes (ACCEM) (2006) 'Aproximació a les condicions de vida de la població subsahariana sense sostre a Barcelona'. October–December, Barcelona.

Austin, G. (2005) *Labour, Land and Capital in Ghana: From Slavery to Free Labour in Asante*. Rochester, NY: University of Rochester Press.

Austin, G. (2007) 'Reciprocal comparison and African history: tackling conceptual Eurocentrism in the study of Africa's economic past', *African Studies Review*, 50 (3): 1–28.

Austin, G. (2009) 'Poverty and development in sub-Saharan Africa, c1450–c1900: reflections on the development of economic historiography'. Position paper for 'The State of Economic History in the World. EHES Conference, Geneva, 4 September.

Auty, R. and Pontara, N. (2008) 'A dual-track strategy for managing Mauritania's projected oil rent', *Development Policy Review*, 26 (1): 59–77.

Azam, J.-P. and Gubert, F. (2006) 'Migrants' remittances and the household in Africa: a review of evidence', *Journal of African Economies*, 15 (2): 426–62.

Ba, C.O. and Choplin, A. (2005) 'Tenter l'aventure par la Mauritanie', *Autrepart*, 36: 1–21.

Ba, C.O. and Ndiaye, A.I. (2008) 'L'émigration clandestine sénégalaise', *Terra-Infos*, March. Available: http://terra.rezo.net/article717.html [accessed 16 June 2008].

Baduel, P.R. (1994) 'La Mauritanie dans l'ordre international', *Politique africaine*, 55: 11–19.

Baldwin-Edwards, M. (1999) 'Where free markets reign: aliens in the twilight zone'. In M. Baldwin-Edwards and J. Arango (eds), *Immigrants and the Informal Economy in Southern Europe*. London and Portland, OR.: Frank Cass.

Baldwin-Edwards, M. (2004) 'Mediterranean migration: regionalism versus globalisation', *Finisterra*, XXXIX, 77: 9–20.

Baldwin-Edwards, M. (2005a) 'Migration in the Middle East and Mediterranean: a regional study', prepared for the Global Commission on International Migration, January. Mediterranean Migration Observatory.

Baldwin-Edwards, M. (2005b) Migration into southern Europe: non-legality and labour markets in the region. Mediterranean Migration Observatory Working Paper, No. 6, December.

Baldwin-Edwards, M. (2006) ''Between and rock and a hard place': north Africa as a region of emigration, immigration and transit migration', *Review of African Political Economy*, 33 (108): 311–24.

Balfour, S. (2005) 'The reinvention of Spanish conservatism: the popular party since 1989'. In S. Balfour (ed.) *The Politics of Contemporary Spain*. London and New York: Routledge.

Balzacq, T. (2005) 'The three faces of securitization: political agency, audience and context', *European Journal of International Relations*, 11 (2): 171–201.

Balzacq, T. (2008) 'The external dimension of EU justice and home affairs: tools, processes, outcomes', CEPS Working Document, No. 303, September.

Balzacq, T. and Carrera, S. (2005) 'Migration, borders and asylum: trends and vulnerabilities in EU policy'. Brussels: Centre for European Studies.

Barajas, A. *et al.* (2010) 'The global financial crisis and workers' remittances to Africa: What's the Damage?', IMF Working Paper, WP/10/24.

Barro, I. (2008) 'Emigrés, transferts financiers et creation de PME dans l'habitat'. In M.-C. Diop (ed.) *Le Sénégal des migrations: Mobilités, identités et societés.* Dakar-Paris-Nairobi: CREPOS-Karthala-ONU Habitat.

Barry, B. (1998) *Senegambia and the Atlantic Slave Trade.* Cambridge: Cambridge University Press.

Bauman, Z. (2004) *Wasted Lives: Modernity and its Outcasts.* Cambridge: Polity Press.

Baxter, J. and Eyles, J. (1999) 'Prescription for research practice? Grounded theory in qualitative evaluation', *Area*, 31 (2): 179–81.

Beblawi, H. and Luciani, G. (1987) 'Introduction'. In H. Beblawi and G. Luciani (eds) *The Rentier State, Vol. II.* London, New York and Sydney: Croom Helm Ltd.

Beck, U. (2004) 'Cosmopolitical realism: on the distinction between cosmopolitanism in philosophy and the social sciences', *Global Networks*, 4 (2): 131–56.

Benabid, Ô. (2008) 'Girona's permanent immigration observatory (territorial views and partnership dynamisation)'. Girona: ACCEM.

Bennoune, M. (1978) 'The political economy of Mauritania: imperialism and class struggle', *Review of African Political Economy*, 5 (12): 31–52.

Bensaâd, A. (2008) 'L'irrégularité de l'immigration en Mauritanie: une appréhension nouvelle, conséquence d'enjeux migratoires externes', Série sur la migration irrégulière, CARIM AS, 2008/76, Robert Schuman Centre for Advanced Studies, San Domenico di Fiesole (FI): Institut universitaire européen.

Bernstein, H. (1977) 'Notes on capital and peasantry', *Review of African Political Economy*, 4 (10): 60–73.

Bernstein, H. (2005) 'Development studies and the Marxists'. In U. Kothari (ed.) *A Radical History of Development Studies: Individuals, Institutions and Ideas.* London and New York: Zed Books.

Bertozzi, S. (2008) 'European pact on migration and asylum: a stepping stone towards common European migration policies'. *Programa Migraciones*, CIDOB. 28 November.

Besteman, C. (2008) 'Beware of those bearing gifts', *Anthropology Today,* 24 (5): 20–1.

Beuving, M. (2008) 'FRONTEX: its role and organisation', The SECURINT Collection. Working Paper No. 8. Université Robert Schuman.

Bigo, D. (2005a) 'Consequences of September 11th on the immigration and foreign policies in Europe'. Institut d'Etudes Politiques de Paris. Available at: http://64.207.171.242/PDFs/Bigo.pdf [accessed 24 November 2005].

Bigo, D. (2005b) 'Frontier controls in the European Union: Who is in Control?'. In D. Bigo and E. Guild (eds) *Controlling Frontiers: Free Movement into and within Europe.* Aldershot: Ashgate.

Bigo, D. and Guild, E. (2005) 'Policing at a distance: Schengen Visa Policies'. In D. Bigo and E. Guild (eds) *Controlling Frontiers: Free Movement into and Within Europe.* Aldershot: Ashgate.

Blanchet, K. and Keith, R. (2006) 'Africa's medical deficit', *Le Monde Diplomatique*, 12 December. Available: http://mondediplo.com/2006/12/12africa [accessed 28 April 2009].

Bond, P. (2006) *Looting Africa: The Economics of Exploitation.* London, New York and Pietermaritzburg: Zed Books and University of Kwazulu-Natal Press.

Bonté, P. (1975) 'Multinational companies and national development: MIFERMA and Mauretania', *Review of African Political Economy*, 2 (2): 89–109.

Bonté, P. (1981) 'Kinship and politics: The formation of the state among the pastoralists of the Sahara and the Sahel'. In H. J. M. Claessen and P. Skalník (eds) *The Study of the State*, The Hague and New York: Mouton.

Bonté, P. and Guillaume, H. (1994) 'Mauritanie: questions pour l'avenir'. *Politique africaine*, 55: 2–10.

Bouhga-Hagbe, J. (2004) 'A theory of workers' remittances with an application to Morocco', WP/04/194. International Monetary Fund.

Bouilly, E. (2008a) 'Les enjeux féminins de la migration masculine', *Politique africaine*, 109: 16–31.

Bouilly, E. (2008b) 'La couverture médiatique du collectif pour la lutte contre l'immigration clandestine de Thiaroye-sur-Mer (Dakar–Sénégal). Un mise en abîme du discours produit au 'Nord' sur le 'Sud'', *Terra-Infos*, March. Available: http://terra.rezo.net/article721.html [accessed 16 June 2008].

Bourdieu, P. (2000) 'Making the economic habitus', *Ethnography*, 1 (1): 17–41.

Bourdieu, P. and Wacquant, L. (2000) 'The organic ethnologist of Algerian migration', *Ethnography*, 1 (2): 173–82.

Bracking, S. (2003) 'Sending money home: are remittances always beneficial to those who stay behind?' *Journal of International Development*, 15 (5): 633–44.

Bracking, S. (2009) Money and power: great predators in the political economy of development. London: Pluto Press.

Brandariz García, J.A. and Fernández Bessa, C. (2009) 'The construction of migrants as a risk category in Spain'. In S. Palidda (ed.) *Criminalisation and Victimisation of Migrants in Europe*. Sixth Framework Programme and Dipartimento di Scienze Antropologiche Università degli Studi di Genova.

Brewer, J.D. (2000) *Ethnography*. Maidenhead: Open University Press.

BBC (1999) 'Mauritania to quit Ecowas'. 26 December. Available at: http://news.bbc.co.uk/1/hi/world/africa/578966.stm [accessed 11 June 2009].

BBC (2000) 'Spain struggles with race riots', 8 February. Available at: http://news.bbc.co.uk/1/hi/world/europe/635092.stm [accessed 10 August 2010].

BBC (2006a) 'Canaries migrant death toll soars'. 28 September. Available at: http://news.bbc.co.uk/2/hi/europe/6213495.stm [accessed 9 January 2009].

BBC (2006b) 'Gambia – new front in migrant trade'. 10 October. Available at: http:news.bbc.co.uk/2/hi/africa/5383080.stm [accessed 13 February 2009].

BBC (2006c) 'Spain and Senegal in migrant deal'. 5 December. Available at: http://news.bbc.co.uk/2/hi/africa/6208744.stm [accessed 13 February 2009].

BBC (2009) 'Mali resists aiding French deportations'. 19 May. Available at: http://news.bbc.co.uk/2/hi/africa/8055749.stm [accessed 20 May 2009].

Brothers, C. (2007) 'Criminal gangs profit from smuggling of illegal immigrants from Africa into Europe'. *International Herald Tribune*, 20 March.

Bryceson, D.F. (1999) 'African rural labour, income diversification and livelihood approaches: a long-term development perspective', *Review of African Political Economy*, 26 (80): 171–89.

Bryceson, D. (2000) 'Disappearing peasantries? rural labour redundancy in the neo-liberal era and beyond'. In D. Bryceson, C. Kay and J. Mooij (eds) *Disappearing Peasantries? Rural Labour in Africa, Asia and Latin America*, London: Intermediate Technology Publications.

Bujra, J. (2006) 'Lost in translation? The use of interpreters in fieldwork'. In V. Desai and R. B. Potter (eds) *Doing Development Research*. London: Sage.

Burawoy, M. (1980) 'Migrant labour in South Africa and the United States'. In T. Nichols (ed.) *Capital and Labour: A Marxist Primer*. London: Fontana.

Bush, R. (2007) *Poverty and Neoliberalism: Persistence and Reproduction in the Global South*. London: Pluto Press.

Bush, R. (2010) 'Food riots: poverty, power and protest', *Journal of Agrarian Change*, 10 (1): 119–29.

Bush, R., Cliffe, L. and Jansen, V. (1984) 'The crisis in the reproduction of the cheap labour economics of southern Africa', paper presented to the 1984 Review of African Political Economy conference on the world recession and the crisis in Africa, 29–30 September, University of Keele.

Bush, R. and Keenan, J. (2006) 'North Africa: power, politics and promise', *Review of African Political Economy*, 33 (108): 175–84.

Cameron, J. (2005) 'Journeying in radical development studies: a reflection on thirty years of researching pro-poor development'. In U. Kothari (ed.) *A Radical History of Development Studies: Individuals, Institutions and Ideologies*. London and New York: Zed Books.

Cammack, P. (2008) 'Universal convergence on competitiveness'. Papers in the Politics of Global Competitiveness, No. 10, Institute for Global Studies: University of Manchester.

Carrera, S. (2007a) 'Frontex and the EU's Integrated border management strategy'. In J. Lodge (ed.) *Are You Who You Say You Are? The EU and Biometric Borders*. Nijmegen, The Netherlands: Wolf Legal Publishers.

Carrera, S. (2007b) 'The EU border management strategy: FRONTEX and the challenges of irregular immigration in the Canary Islands'. CEPS Working Document, No. 261, March.

Carrera, S. and Guild, E. (2008) The French presidency's European pact on immigration and asylum: intergovernmentalism vs. Europeanisation? Security vs. rights? *CEPS Policy Brief*, No. 170, September.

Cassarino, J.-P. (2006) *The EU Return Policy: Premises and Implications*. MIREM Project, European University Institute. Available at: www.mirem.eu/research/reports/mechanisms-eu_return_policies.pdf [accessed 25 June 2009].

Castells, M. (1998) *End of Millennium*, 2nd edn. *The Information Age: Economy, Society and Culture.* Volume III. Oxford: Blackwell Publishers Ltd.

Castles, S. (2003) 'Why migration policies fail', *Ethnic and Racial Studies*, 27 (2): 205–27.

Castles, S. and G. Kosack (1973) *Immigrant Workers and Class Structure in Western Europe*. London: Oxford University Press.

Castles, S. and Miller, M.J. (2003) *The Age of Migration: International Population Movements in the Modern World*, 3rd edn. Basingstoke and New York: Palgrave Macmillan.

Charmes, J. (1994) 'L'économie mauritanienne au risque de l'informalisation', *Politique africaine*, 55: 74–7.

Chauzy, J.-P. (2006) 'Mother courage fights irregular migration in Senegal', *Migration*, December, IOM.

Cheru, F. (2002) *African Renaissance: Roadmap to the Challenge of Globalization*. London: Zed Books.

Choplin, A. (2008) 'L'immigré, le migrant, l'allochtone: circulations migratoires et figures de l'étranger en Mauritanie', *Politique africaine*, 109: 73–89.

Chou, M.-H. and Gibert, M. (2010) From Cotonou to circular migration: the EU, Senegal and the 'agreement duplicity'. Paper for 'Migration: a world in motion', Maastricht, 18–20 February.

Cilliers, J. (2003) 'Terrorism and Africa', *African Security Review*, 12 (4): 91–103.

Cillo, R. and Perocco, F. (2008) 'Migrant labour in the underground economy: between processes of irregularization and informalization'. Undocumented Worker Transitions: EU Sixth Framework Programme, December.

Cohen, M. and Garrett, J.L. (2009) 'The food price crisis and urban food (in)security'. Human Settlements Working Paper Series. IIED and UNFPA. Available at: http://pubs.iied.org/pdfs/10574IIED.pdf [accessed 13 July 2012].

Cohen, R. (1987) *The New Helots: Migrants in the International Division of Labour.* Aldershot: Avebury.

Cohen, R., Copans, J. and Gutkind, P.C.W. (1978) 'Introduction'. In P.C.W. Gutkind, R. Cohen and J. Copans (eds) *African Labor History*. Beverley Hills, CA and London: Sage Publications.

Collinson, S. (2009) 'The political economy of migration processes: an agenda for migration research and analysis'. International Migration Institute Working Papers: University of Oxford.

Comisión Española de Ayuda al Refugiado (CEAR) (2007) *La situación de los refugiados en España*. Madrid: Entimema.

Commission of the European Communities (2005) 'Policy plan on legal migration'. COM, 669, 21 December.

Commission of the European Communities (2006) 'The global approach to migration one year on: towards a comprehensive European migration policy'. COM 735, 30 November.

Commission of the European Communities (2007a) 'Communication on circular migration and mobility partnerships between the European Union and third countries'. COM 248, 16 May.

Commission of the European Communities (2007b) 'Interim progress report on the global approach to migration'. SEC 1632, 5 December.

Commission of the European Communities (2007c) 'First Euro-Mediterranean ministerial meeting on migration', Algarve, 18, 19 November.

Commission of the European Communities (2009) 'Entry and residence of highly qualified workers (EU Blue Card)', 18 August.

Commission of the European Communities (2011) 'The Global Approach to Migration and Mobility'. COM(2011) 743, 18 November.

Conde Zabala, J. (2007) 'Migration and development: a necessary binominal'. Available at: http://www.fiiapp.org/index.php/contenidos/vercontenido/id_contenido/1039/n/2 [accessed 1 July 2009].

Confederación Sindical de Comisiones Obreras (CCOO) (2008) 'CCOO apuesta por una inmigración con derechos en un mercado de trabajo regulado', 11 August. Available: http://www.ccoo.es/csccoo/menu.do?Areas:Migraciones:Actualidad:34544 [accessed 18 August 2009].

Consortium for Applied Research on International Migration (CARIM) (2010) 'POP31 – emigrants by country of residence'. Available at: http://www.carim.org/index.php?callContent=59&callTable=1574 [accessed 8 August 2010].

Constantin, F.G. (1995) 'The foreign policy of francophone Africa: clientelism and after'. In A. Kirk-Greene and D. Bach (eds) *State and Society in Francophone Africa since Independence.* New York: St Martin's Press.

Conway, D. (1980) 'Step-wise migration: toward a clarification of the mechanism', *International Migration Review*, 14 (1): 3–14.

Cooper, F. (2005) *Colonialism in Question: Theory, Knowledge, History*. Berkeley and Los Angeles, CA: University of California Press.

Cooper, F. (2008) 'Possibility and constraint: African independence in historical perspective', *Journal of African History*, 49 (2): 167–96.

Coquery-Vidrovitch, C. (1991) 'Colonial history and decolonisation: the French imperial case', *The European Journal of Development Research*, 3 (2): 28–43.

Cornelius, W.A. (2004) 'Spain: the uneasy transition from labor exporter to labor importer'. In W.A. Cornelius (ed.) *Controlling Immigration: A Global Perspective.* Stanford, CA: Stanford University Press.

Council of the European Union (2005) 'The Hague programme: strengthening freedom, security and justice in the European Union' (OJ C 2005/C 53/01), 3 March.

Council of the European Union (2008) '14th ECOWAS–EU ministerial troika meeting – final communiqué'. Ref CL08-194EN, 23 October.

Coussy, J. (1995) 'The franc zone: original logic, subsequent evolution and present crisis'. In A. Kirk-Greene and D. Bach (eds) *State and Society in Francophone Africa since Independence.* New York: St Martin's Press.

Crespo Ubero, R. (2006) 'Globalización y migraciones: dos nociones interdependientes desde los orígenes', *Revista Académica de Relaciones Internacionales*, 4: 1–17.

Crisp, J. (1999) 'Policy challenges of the new diasporas: migrant networks and their impact on asylum flows and regimes'. UNHCR Working Paper No. 7, Geneva.

Cross, H. (2008/09) 'Migration, remittances and development in West Africa: the case of Senegal', *Global Development Studies*, 5 (3–4): 133–64.

Cross, H. (2009) 'Migration, mobility and borders: the EU and West African migrant communities', LUCAS Bulletin, 71: 46–50.

Cross, H. (2011) 'Rents, rights, rejections and resistance: West African migrants, the EU's migration regime and militarisation in Mauritania', *International Journal of Human Rights*, 15 (6): 827–46.

Cross, H. (forthcoming) 'Globalisation du marché du travail, frontières et migrations à partir du Sénégal'. In M.-C. Diop (ed.) *Senegal 2000–2010* [working title]. Paris: Karthala.

Cross, H. and Cliffe, L. (2012) 'A comparative political economy of regional migration and labour mobility in west and southern Africa' presented at the biennial conference of the African Studies Association UK, Leeds, 6–8 September.

Cross, H. and Tomàs, N. (2009a) Seminar and photo exhibition: 'Destinació Elinkine: following a west African migration route to the coast'. Servei Civil Internacional, Barcelona, 19 February.

Cross, H. and Tomàs, N. (2009b) Documentary: *Africans en ruta: reflections on emigration.* Previewed at Docupolis festival at Centre de Cultura Contemporanea de Barcelona (CCCB), 4 October.

Crosse, B. and Hesseling, G. (1994) 'Transformations foncières dans la vallée du Sénégal: enjeux politiques et ethniques', *Politique africaine*, 55: 89–100.

Crowder, M. (1968) *West Africa Under Colonial Rule.* London: Hutchinson and Co. Ltd.

Crowley, J. (2005) 'Where does the state actually start? The contemporary governance of work and migration'. In D. Bigo and E. Guild (eds) *Controlling Frontiers: Free Movement into and within Europe*. Aldershot: Ashgate.

Cruz Roja (2007) 'Una vivienda humanitaria'. *Canarias*, 993.

Daffé, G. (2008) 'Les transferts d'argent des migrants sénégalais: entre espoir et risques de dépendance'. In M.-C. Diop (ed.) *Le Sénégal des migrations: mobilités, identités et societés.* Dakar, Paris and Nairobi: CREPOS, Karthala and ONU Habitat.

Davidson, B. (1992) *The Black Man's Burden: Africa and the Curse of the Nation-State.* London: James Currey.

de Haan, A. (2000) 'Migrants, livelihoods, and rights: the relevance of migration in development policies'. Social Development Working Paper, No. 4. London: DFID.

de Haas, H. (2007) 'Remittances, migration and social development: a conceptual review of the literature'. Social Policy and Development Programme Paper, No. 34. UNRISD.

de Haas, H. (2008a) 'Migration and development: a theoretical perspective'. Working Paper No. 9, International Migration Institute, University of Oxford.

de Haas, H. (2008b) 'Irregular migration from west Africa to the Maghreb and the European Union: an overview of recent trends'. Geneva: IOM.

de Jonge, K. (1979) 'Peasant fishermen and capitalists: development in Senegal', *Review of African Political Economy*, 6 (15, 16): 105–23.

Den Boer, M. (2001) 'The incorporation of Schengen into the TEU: a bridge too far?'. In J. Monar and W. Wessels (eds), *The European Union after the Treaty of Amsterdam*. London and New York: Continuum.

Denzin, N.K. (1997) *Interpretive Ethnography: Ethnographic Practices for the 21st Century*. Thousand Oaks, CA: Sage.

UK DFID (Department for International Development) (2005) 'Fighting poverty to build a safer world: a strategy for security and development'. London: DFID.

Developing Markets Associates Ltd (DMA) and Dept for International Development (DfID) (2011) 'Constraints in the UK to Ghana remittances market'. Available at: http://www.dfid.gov.uk/Documents/publications1/Constraints-UK-Ghana.pdf [accessed 14 September 2012].

Diagne, Y.S. and Diané, F. (2008) 'Impact des transferts des migrants sur la pauvrété au Sénégal'. Document d'Etude No. 7, Direction de la Prévision et des Etudes Economiques. Dakar.

Di Bartolomeo, A. *et al.* (2010) 'CARIM – migration profile: Senegal'. Robert Schumann Centre for Advanced Studies, European University Institute: CARIM.

Diop, C.A. (1960) *L'Afrique noire pre-coloniale: Etude comparée des systèmes politiques et sociaux de l'Europe et de l'Afrique Noire, de l'antiquité à la formation des états modernes*. Paris: Présence Africaine.

Diouf, M. (2000) 'The Senegalese Murid trade diaspora and the making of vernacular cosmopolitanism' (trans. S. Rendall), *Public Culture*, 12 (3): 679–702.

Direction de la Prévision de la Statistique (DPS) (2004) 'Enquête Senegalaise auprès des ménages: rapport de synthèse'. Dakar.

Duffield, M. (2001) *Global Governance and the New Wars: The Merging of Development and Security*. London and New York: Zed Books.

Duffield, M. (2010) 'The liberal way of development and the development–security impasse: exploring the global life-chance divide', *Security Dialogue*, 41: 53–76.

Dussauze-Ingrand, E. (1974) 'L'emigration sarakollaise du Guidimakha vers la France'. In S. Amin (ed.) *Modern Migrations in West Africa*. London: Oxford University Press.

Ebnou, Moussa Ould (2009).'Mauritanie: L'Amérique et le Général Aziz', Agence Nouakchott d'Information, 23 June. Available at: http://fr.allafrica.com/stories/printable/200906240115.html [accessed 25 June 2009].

Economic Community of West African States (ECOWAS) (2008) 'ECOWAS, Spain sign document on management of 10 million euro fund on migration and development'. No. 065/2008, Abuja, 4 July.

*Economist* (2007) 'No more murk'. 23 May. Available at: http://www.economist.com/agenda/PrinterFriendly.cfm?story_id=9216999 [accessed 26 November 2008].

*Economist* (2008) 'Another president booted out'. 7 August.

*Economist* (2012) 'Labour reform in Spain: Spanish practices', 18 February. Available at: http://www.economist.com/node/21547831 [accessed 13 July 2012].

EIU (Economist Intelligence Unit) (2009a) Country Report: Spain, February. London: EIU.

EIU (2009b) Country Report: Spain, October. London: EIU.

EIU (2009c) Country Report: Mauritania, October. London: EIU.

El Mundo (2012) 'No atender a los inmigrantes es una especie de asesinato', 13 September.

*El País* (2009) '46.426 "sin papeles" de 29 países, repatriados en 2008', 13 January.

*El País* (2012) 'Unos 60 subsaharianos de Isla de Tierra han regresado ya a Marruecos'. 5 September.

*El Periódico* (2012) 'La orden de desalojo tensa los ánimos en una fábrica ocupada por 300 personas en Sant Martí', 13 July.

*El Periôdico de Catalunya* (2008) 'Solo se ejectuan el 20% de las expulsiones', 16 December.

Ellis, S. and MacGaffey, J. (1996) 'Research on sub-Saharan Africa's unrecorded international trade: some methodological and conceptual problems', *African Studies Review,* 39 (2): 19–41.

Eurostat (2009) Data Navigation Tree. Available at: http://epp.eurostat.ec.europa.eu/portal/ [accessed 11 January 2009].

Fage, J.D. (1989) 'African societies and the Atlantic slave trade', *Past and Present*, 125: 97–115.

Faist, T. (2000) *The Volume and Dynamics of International Migration and Transnational Social Spaces.* Oxford: Clarendon Press.

Fall, A.S. (2002) 'Enjeux et défis de la migration internationale de travail ouest-Africaine'. chaire de recherche du Canada en développement des collectivités. Série rapport de recherche No. 3. Université de Quebec en Outaoais.

Fall, A.S. and Cissé, R. (2007) 'Migrations internationales et pauvreté en Afrique de l'ouest'. Working Paper No. 5. Manchester: Chronic Poverty Research Centre.

Fall, B. and Mbodj, M. (1989) 'Forced labour and migration in Senegal'. In A. Zegeye and S. Ishemo (eds) *Forced Labour and Migration: Patterns of Movement within Africa*. London, Munich and New York: Hans Zell.

Fall, P.D. (2008) 'Migration internationale et développement local dans le Nguènar sénégalaise'. In M.-C. Diop (ed.) *Le Sénégal des migrations: Mobilités, identités et societés*. Dakar, Paris and Nairobi: CREPOS, Karthala and ONU Habitat.

Fargues, P. (2009) 'Irregularity as normality among immigrants south and east of the Mediterranean'. Irregular Migration Series: CARIM AS, 2009/02, Robert Schumann Centre for Advanced Studies.

Ferguson, J. (2006) *Global Shadows: Africa in the Neoliberal World Order*. Durham and London: Duke University Press.

Fernández, C. and Ortega, C. (2006) 'Labour market assimilation of immigrants in Spain: employment at the expense of bad job-matches?' Working Paper No. 644, IESE Business School, University of Navarra.

Fidler, S. (2002) 'Sense of crisis as migrants keep moving'. *Financial Times*, 24 July.

Findley, S. *et al.* (1995) 'Emigration from the Sahel', *International Migration*, 33 (3&4): 469–507.

Fine, B. and Saad-Filho, A. (2004) *Marx's Capital,* Fourth Edition. London: Pluto Press.

Flynn, D. (2007) 'US Navy to fight crime, terror along African coast', *Reuters*. Available at: http://www.alertnet.org/thenews/newsdesk/L19151194.htm [accessed 29 September 2007].

Frattini, F. (2006) 'Migration and development: time for creative and courageous appproaches'. EU–AFRICA ministerial conference on migration and development, Tripoli, 22 November.

Gano, S. (2012) 'Senegal: agricultural activity to slow clandestine emigration from Senegal', Inter Press Service. Available at: http://allafrica.com/stories/201209101166.html [accessed 10 September 2012].

Geddes, A. (2001) 'International migration and state sovereignty in an integrating Europe', *International Migration*, 39 (6): 21–42.

Geddes, A. (2005) 'Europe's border relationships and international migration relations', *Journal of Common Market Studies*, 43 (4): 787–806.

Gille, Z. and Ó Riain, S. (2002) 'Global ethnography', *Annual Review of Sociology*, 28: 271–95.

Gillespie, R. (2005) 'Between ambition and insecurity: Spanish politics and the Mediterranean'. In S. Balfour (ed.) *The Politics of Contemporary Spain*. London and New York: Routledge.

Gobernio de Canarias (2009) *Padrón municipal de Canarias*. Instituto Canario de Estadística.

Godenau, D. and Zapata Hernandez, V.M. (2008) 'The case of the Canary Islands (Spain): a region of transit between Africa and Europe'. In D. Godenau *et al.* (eds) *Migraciones*, 17, CIDOB, December.

Gomez, M.A. (2006) 'Diasporic Africa: a view from history'. In M.A. Gomez (ed.) *Diasporic Africa: A Reader.* New York and London: New York University Press.

González-Enriquez, C. (2005) 'Active civic participation of immigrants in Spain'. Project POLITIS, Oldenburg.

González-Enriquez, C. (2009) 'Irregular migration in Spain: counting the uncountable: data and trends across Europe'. Clandestino Research Project, European Commission, July. Available at: http://clandestino.eliamep.gr/wp-content/uploads/2009/08/spain-research-brief_july-09.pdf [accessed 9 September 2009].

Graham, D.T. (2000) 'The people paradox: human movements and human security in a globalising world'. In D. T. Graham and Nana K. Poku (eds) *Migration, Globalisation and Human Security*. London: Routledge.

Grégoire, E. and Labazée, P. (1993) 'Introduction: approche comparative des réseaux marchands ouest-africains contemporains'. In E. Grégoire and P. Labazée (eds) *Grands commerçants d'Afrique de l'Ouest: logiques et practiques d'un groupe d'hommes d'affaires contemporains*. Paris: Karthala-Orstrom.

Grillo, R. (2007) 'Betwixt and between: trajectories and projects of transmigration', *Journal of Ethnic and Migration Studies*, 33 (2): 199–217.

*Guardian* (2010) 'Al-Qaida group hints at ransom payment for freed Spanish hostages', 24 August. Available at: http://www.guardian.co.uk/world/2010/aug/24/al-qaida-spanish-aid-workers [accessed 28 August 2010].

Gubert, F. (2008) '(In)cohérence des politiques migratoires et de codéveloppement françaises: illustrations maliens', *Politique africaine,* 109, March: 42–55.

Guild, E. (2005) 'Who is entitled to work and who is in charge? Understanding the legal framework of European labour migration'. In D. Bigo and E. Guild (eds) *Controlling Frontiers: Free Movement into and within Europe*. Aldershot: Ashgate.

Guild, E. (2007) EU policy on labour migration: a first look at the commission's blue card initiative. CEPS Policy Brief, No. 145, November.

Guild, E., Carrera, S. and Balzacq, T. (2008) 'The changing dynamics of security in an enlarged European Union'. *Challenge Research Paper,* No. 12, October.

Gyimah-Brempong, K. and Asiedu, E. (2009) 'Remittances and poverty in Ghana', African Economic Conference 2009: Fostering Development in an Era of Financial and Economic Crises. Addis Ababa: 11–13 November.

Hahn, H.P. (2008) 'The phenomenon of migration: threat or chance for the world society?' Paper presented at convention on international law and politics, University of St Gallen, 24 November.

Hammar, T. and Tamas, K. (1997) 'Why do people go or stay?' In T. Hammar, G. Brochmann, K. Tamas and T. Faist (eds) *International Migration, Immobility and Development: Multidisciplinary Perspectives*. Oxford: Berg.

Harrison, J. and Corkhill, D. (2004) *Spain: A Modern European Economy*. Aldershot: Ashgate.

Harvey, D. (2003) *The New Imperialism*. Oxford: Oxford University Press.

Harvey, D. (2005) *A Brief History of Neoliberalism*. Oxford: Oxford University Press.

Hayter, T. (2000) *Open Borders: The Case against Immigration Controls*. London: Pluto Press.

Held, D., McGrew, A., Goldblatt, D. and Perraton, J. (1999) *Global Transformations: Politics, Economics and Culture*. Cambridge: Polity Press.

Hill, P. (1963) *The Migrant Cocoa-Farmers of Southern Ghana: A Study in Rural Capitalism*. Cambridge: Cambridge University Press.

Hills, A. (2006) 'Trojan horses? USAID, counter-terrorism and Africa's police', *Third World Quarterly*, 27 (4), 629–43.

Hobsbawm, E. (1994) *Age of Extremes: The Short Twentieth Century 1914–1991*. London: Michael Joseph.

Hogart, K. and Mendoza, C. (2000) *African Immigrant Workers in Spanish Agriculture*. Working Paper No. 2, Centre for Comparative Immigration Studies. University of California, San Diego, CA.

Home Office, Border and Immigration Agency (UK) (2007) *Frontex Inquiry Written Evidence*. E/06-07/F140 FRO. 14 September.

Hopkins, A. (1973) *An Economic History of West Africa*. London: Longman.

Human Rights Watch (2008) 'Returns at any cost: Spain's push to repatriate unaccompanied children in the absence of safeguards', 17 October. 1-56432-388-9. UNHCR Refworld. Available at: http://www.unhcr.org/refworld/docid/48f844642.html [accessed 6 March 2009].

Huysmans, J. (2000) 'The European Union and the securitization of migration', *Journal of Common Market Studies*, 38 (5): 751–77.

INE (Instituto Nacional de Estadistica) (2007a) 'Inmigrantes, llegados a España después de 1990, por medio de transporte utilizado, según año de llegada'. Available at: http://www.ine.es/jaxi/tabla.do?path=/t20/p319/a2007/p01/l0/&file=06017.px&type=pcaxis&L=0 [accessed 11 January 2009].

INE (2007b) 'Inmigrantes, llegados a España después de 1990, por lugar geográfico de partida y medio de transporte'. Available at: http://www.ine.es/jaxi/tabla.do?type=pcaxis&path=/t20/p319/a2007/p01/l0/&file=04015.px [accessed 11 January 2009].

INE (2008) 'Cifras de población referidas al 01/01/2008'. Available at: http://www.ine.es/jaxi/tabla.do [accessed 17 September 2009].

Integrated Regional News Networks (IRIN) (2006) 'Mauritania–Senegal: new cattle migration accord cools long-standing flashpoint', 5 May. Available at: http://www.irinnews.org/report.aspx?reportid=58931 [accessed 13 October 2007].

IRIN (2007) 'MAURITANIA: Who will help the next stranded ship?', 9 March. Available at: http://irinnewsorg/PrintReport.aspx?ReportId=70616 [accessed 10 April 2007].

IRIN (2008a) 'Mauritania: more would-be migrants fleeing post-coup', 14 August. Available at: http://www.irinnews.org/Report/79831/MAURITANIA-More-would-be-migrants-fleeing-post-coup [accessed 10 September 2012].

IRIN (2008b) 'West Africa: policy overhaul needed to halt illegal migration', 10 September. Available at: http://www.irinnews.org/Report.aspx?ReportId=80286 [accessed 10 September 2008].

IRIN (2009) 'BURKINA FASO: would-be migrants stuck on border', 4 February. Available at: http://www.irinnews.org/Report.aspx?ReportId=82732 [accessed 18 May 2009].

International Crisis Group (2005) 'Islamist terrorism in the Sahel: fact or fiction?' *Africa Report* No. 92, 31 March. Available at: http://www.crisisgroup.org/home/index.cfm?l=1&id=3349 [accessed 9 March 2006].

International Labour Office (ILO) (2009) 'Global employment trends: update'. Geneva: ILO.

*International Labour Review* (1936) 'Labour conditions in French West Africa', 34 (4): 506–9.

IMF (International Monetary Fund) (2009) 'Economic health check: hard landing for Spain'. 24 April. Available at: http://www.imf.org/external/pubs/ft/survey/so/2009/car042409b.htm [accessed 14 September 2009].

IMF (2010) 'World economic outlook database'. Available at: http://www.imf.org/external/pubs/ft/weo/2010/01/weodata/weoselser.aspx?c=184&t=1 [accessed 15 August 2010].

IOM (International Organisation for Migration) (2005) 'World migration report 2005: costs and benefits of international migration'. IOM World Migration Report Series.

IOM (2007) *Global Estimates and Trends*. Available at: http://www.iom.int/jahia/Jahia/cache/offonce/pid/254 [accessed 10 July 2010].

IOM (2008) 'World migration 2008: managing labour mobility in the evolving global economy', Vol. 4, IOM World Migration Report Series.

IOM (2009) 'Migration au Sénégal: profil national 2009'. Available at: http://publications.iom.int/bookstore/free/Senegal_Profile_2009.pdf [accessed 5 August 2010].

IOM (2012) 'Global estimates and trends'. Available at: http://www.iom.int/jahia/Jahia/about-migration/facts-and-figures/lang/en [accessed 29 August 2012].

Jahn, A. and Straubhaar, T. (1999) 'A survey of the Economics of illegal migration'. In M. Baldwin-Edwards and J. Arango (eds), *Immigrants and the Informal Economy in Southern Europe*. London: Frank Cass.

Jane's Information Group (2009) 'Navy (Senegal), navy, sentinel security assessment, West Africa', 3 February. Available at: http://www.janes.com/articles/Janes-Sentinel-Security-Assessment-West-Africa/Navy-Senegal.html [accessed 5 July 2009].

Jeandesboz, J. (2008) 'Reinforcing the surveillance of EU borders: the future development of FRONTEX and EUROSUR'. Challenge Research Paper, No. 11, August.

Jean-Matthew, T. (2012) 'Senegal hits back over visa rule on citizens', The Nation (Kenya), 5 December. Available at: http://www.nation.co.ke/News/africa/Senegal-hits-back-over-visa-rule-on-citizens-/-/1066/1637616/-/nsbyyyz/-/index.html [accessed 14 January 2013].

Jonsson, G. (2007) 'Migration, immobility and youth in a Malian Soninké village'. Paper presented at the AEGIS European Conference on African Studies, 11–14 July. African Studies Centre, Leiden, the Netherlands.

Jourde, C. (2007) 'Constructing representations of the 'Global War on Terror' in the

Islamic Republic of Mauritania', *Journal of Contemporary African Studies*, 25 (1): 77–100.

Kea, R.A. (1982) *Settlements, Trade, and Polities in the Seventeenth-Century Gold Coast.* Baltimore, MD and London: Johns Hopkins University Press.

Keenan, J. (2004) 'Terror in the Sahara: The implications of US imperialism for north and west Africa', *Review of African Political Economy*, 101: 475–96.

Keenan, J. (2007) 'The banana theory of terrorism: alternative truths and the collapse of the "second" (Saharan) front in the war on terror', *Journal of Contemporary African Studies*, 25 (1): 31–58.

Keenan, J. (2008) 'US militarization in Africa: what anthropologists should know about AFRICOM', *Anthropology Today*, 24 (5): 16–20.

Keenan, J. (2009) *The Dark Sahara*. London: Pluto Press.

King, R., Fielding, A. and Black, R. (1997) 'The international migration turnaround in southern Europe'. In R. King and R. Black (eds) *Southern Europe and the New Immigrations*. Brighton: Sussex Academic Press.

Klare, M. and Volman, D. (2006) 'America, China and the scramble for Africa's oil', *Review of African Political Economy*, 33 (108): 311–24.

Koch, A. (2005) 'Briefing: the US in Africa', Jane's, 12 January.

Koita, T. (1994) 'Migrations, pouvoirs locaux et enjeux sur l'espace urbain', *Politique africaine*, 55: 101–9.

Kothari, U. (2002) 'Migration and chronic poverty'. Working Paper No. 16. Institute for Development, Policy and Management, University of Manchester.

Kothari, U. (2005) 'From colonial administration to development studies: a post-colonial critique of the history of development studies. In U. Kothari (ed.), *A Radical History of Development Studies: Individuals, Institutions and Ideas*. London and New York: Zed Books.

Kothari, U. (2008) 'Global peddlers and local networks: migrant cosmopolitanisms', *Environment and Planning D: Society and Space*, 26: 500–16.

Kyle, D. and Koslowski, R. (eds) (2001) *Global Human Smuggling*. Baltimore, MD and London: Johns Hopkins University Press.

Lamazou, Z. (2008) 'Un 'Guantánamo' en Mauritanie', *Le Monde Diplomatique*, October.

Le Billon, P. (2000) *The Political Economy of War: What Relief Agencies Need to Know*. London: Overseas Development Institute.

L'Humanité (2008) 'Entretien avec Ibrahima Thioub. Esclavage', 24 June. Available at: http://www.humanite.fr/Entretien-avec-Ibrahima-Thioub-Esclavage [accessed 20 April 2009].

Lemarchand, R. (1992) 'Uncivil states and civil societies: how illusion became reality', *The Journal of Modern African Studies*, 30 (2), 177–91.

Levinson, A. (2005) 'Regularisation programmes in Spain'. In *The Regularisation of Unauthorised Migrants: Literature Survey and Country Case Studies*. University of Oxford: Centre on Migration, Policy and Society.

Löwy, M. (1981) *The Politics of Combined and Uneven Development: The Theory of Permanent Revolution*. London: NLB.

Lydon, G. (2005) 'Writing trans-Saharan history: methods, sources and interpretations across the African divide', *The Journal of North African Studies*, 10 (3–4): 293–324

Mabogunje, A. (1972) *Regional Mobility and Resource Development in West Africa*. Montreal and London: McGill-Queen's University Press.

Mafukidze, J. (2006) 'A discussion of migration and migration patterns and flows in Africa'. In D. Gelderblom, C. Cross, N. Roux and J. Mafukidze (eds), *Views on*

*Migration in Sub-Saharan Africa: Proceedings of an African Migration Alliance Workshop.* Cape Town: HSRC Press.

Magharebia (2010) 'Migration, counter-terrorism top '5+5' ministerial summit', 20 April. Available at: http://www.magharebia.com/cocoon/awi/xhtml1/en_GB/features/awi/features/2010/04/20/feature-01 [accessed 10 August 2010].

Mamdani, M. (1996) *Citizen and Subject: Contemporary Africa and the Legacy of Late Colonialism*. Princeton, NJ: Princeton University Press.

Mandraud, I. (2010) 'Mauritania tries to close its borders', *Guardian Weekly*, 8 June. Available at http://www.guardian.co.uk/world/2010/jun/08/mauritania-closing-borders-al-qaida [accessed 5 July 2011].

Marcuse, P. (2004) 'Said's orientalism: a vital contribution today', *Antipode*, 36: 809–17.

Marsh, D. (2002) 'Marxism'. In D. Marsh and G. Stoker (eds) *Theory and Methods in Political Science.* Basingstoke: Palgrave Macmillan.

Martin, P., Martin, S. and Weil, P. (2002) 'Best practice options: Mali', *International Migration,* 40 (3): 87–101.

Martínez-Veiga, U. (1999) 'Immigrants in the Spanish labour market'. In M. Baldwin-Edwards and J. Arango (eds) *Immigrants and the Informal Economy in Southern Europe*. London and Portland, OR: Frank Cass.

Martín Urriza, C. (2007) 'Los salarios en España: Las consecuencias sobre los salarios de un modelo de crecimiento poco productivo'. Confederación Sindical de Comisiones Obreras, September. Available at: http://www.ccoo.es/comunes/temp/recursos/1/48589.pdf [accessed 30 August 2009].

Marx, K. (1867/1970) *Capital*, Vol. 1. London: Lawrence and Wishart.

Mayoux, L. (2006) 'Quantitative, qualitative or participatory? Which method, for what and when?' In V. Desai and R. B. Potter (eds) *Doing Development Research*. London: Sage.

Mazzucato, V. (2005) 'Ghanaian migrants' double engagement: a transnational view of development and integration policies', *Global Migration Perspectives*, 48. Geneva: Global Commission on International Migration.

Mazzucato, V. (2006) 'Informal insurance arrangements in Ghanaian migrants' transnational networks: the role of reverse remittances and geographic proximity'. Paper presented at the conference: 'Reducing poverty and inequality: How can Africa be included?' Centre for the Study of African Economies, University of Oxford, 19–21 March.

Mbodji, M. (2008) 'Imaginaires et migrations: le cas de Sénégal' in M.-C. Diop (ed.) *Le Sénégal des migrations: mobilités, identités et societés*. Dakar-Paris-Nairobi: CREPOS-Karthala-ONU Habitat.

Mbow, P. and Tamba, M. (2007) *L'emigration clandestine, le profil des candidats: étude réalisée par le bureau des jeunes du mouvement citoyen.* Dakar: Mouvement Citoyen.

McCaskie, T.C. (1995) *State and Society in Pre-Colonial Asante.* Cambridge: Cambridge University Press.

McDougall, E.A. (2007) 'Constructing emptiness: Islam, violence and terror in the historical making of the Sahara', *Journal of Contemporary African Studies*, 25 (1): 17–30.

Mechlinski, T. (2007) '"This is between us blacks": analytic reflections on ethnographic fieldwork and analysis', *Migration Methods and Field Notes*, No. 5. University of the Witwatersrand.

Meillassoux, C. (1975) *Maidens, Meal and Money: Capitalism and the Domestic Community*. Cambridge: Cambridge University Press.

Mendoza, C. (1997) 'Foreign labour immigration in high-unemployment Spain: the role of African-Born workers in the Girona labour market'. In R. King and R. Black (eds) *Southern Europe and the New Immigrations*. Brighton: Sussex Academic Press.

Mendoza, C. (2000) 'The role of the state in influencing African labour outcomes in Spain and Portugal'. Working Paper 3. Centre for Comparative Immigration Studies, University of California, San Diego, CA.

Miguélez, F. and Carrasquer, P. (1995) 'The repercussions of the Olympic Games on labour'. WP 043, Centre d'Estudis Olimpics, Universitat Autònoma de Barcelona.

Miles, R. (1987) *Capitalism and Unfree Labour: Anomaly or Necessity?* London and New York: Tavistock Publications.

Ministère de l'Emploi, de l'Insertion et de la Formation Professionelle (2008) 'Ceremonie de lancement de la session de formation de 50 promoteurs dans le cadre du programme auto emploi 2008'. Ministerial meeting in Nouadhibou, Mauritania, 18 May.

Ministère de l'Immigration, de l'Integration, de l'Identité Nationale et du Développement Solidaire – France (2008) 'The European pact on immigration and asylum'. October.

Ministère des Affaires Etrangères – Senegal (2006) 'Me. Wade à la fête de l'excellence à sorano: "Le plan Reva, gage d'une immigration clandestine zéro"'. Dakar, 12 September.

Ministry of Interior (2009) 'Spain: asylum and migration data'. General Directorate of Police.

Mitsilegas, V., Monar, J. and Rees, W. (2003) *The European Union and Internal Security: Guardian of the People?* Basingstoke: Palgrave Macmillan.

Mohan, G. and Zack-Williams, A.B. (2002) 'Globalisation from below: conceptualising the role of the African diasporas in Africa's development', *Review of African Political Economy*, 29 (92): 211–36.

Monar, J. (2008) 'Justice and home affairs', *Journal of Common Market Studies*, 46: 109–26.

Moya, J.C. (1998) *Cousins and Strangers: Spanish Immigrants in Buenos Aires, 1850–1930*. Berkeley, CA and London: University of California Press.

Naudé, W. and Bezuidenhout, H. (2012) 'Remittances to sub-Saharan Africa in the wake of a financial crisis: source of resilience or vulnerability?'. In I. Sirkeci, J. Cohen and D. Ratha (eds) *Migration and Remittances during the Global Financial Crisis and Beyond*. Washington, DC: The World Bank.

Ndah Mohammed-Saleh, S. (2008) 'Le migration irrégulière en Mauritanie', Série sur la migration irrégulière: CARIM AS, 2008/52, Robert Schuman Centre for Advanced Studies, San Domenico di Fiesole (FI): Institut Universitaire Européen.

N'Doye, E. (1974) 'Migration des pionniers Mourid wolof vers les terres neuves: role de l'économique et du religieux'. In S. Amin (ed.) *Modern Migrations in West Africa*. London: Oxford University Press.

Neal, A.W. (2009) 'Securitization and risk at the EU border: the origins of FRONTEX', *Journal of Common Market Studies,* 47 (2): 333–56.

Niessen, J. and Kate, M.-A. (2008) 'Guide to locating migration policies in the European Commission, 2nd edn. European Programme for Integration and Migration and Migration Policy Group.

Noguer, M. and Costa-Pau, M. (2001) 'El Ayuntamiento expulsa a los inmigrantes de la plaza de Catalunya sin ofrecerles alternativas', *El Pais*, 7 August.

Nzula, A.T., Potekhin, I. I. and Zusmanovich, A. Z. (1979) 'The economic oppression of the peasantry'. In R. Cohen (ed.) *Forced Labour in Colonial Africa*. London: Zed Books.

Office Nationale de la Statistique (ONS) (1995) 'Etude sur la migration et l'urbanisation en Mauritanie'. Projet Mau/92/P01, July.

Organisation for Economic Co-operation and Development (OECD) (2009a) 'Economic policy reforms: going for growth'. Available at: http://www.oecd.org/dataoecd/23/17/42224632.pdf [accessed on 26 August 2009].

OECD (2009b) 'Promoting entrepreneurship, employment and business competitiveness: the experience of Barcelona'. Available at: http://www.oecd.org/dataoecd/2/33/43505170.pdf [accessed 26 August 2009].

Ortega Pérez, N. (2003) 'Spain: forging an immigration policy'. Migration Policy Institute. Available at: http://www.migrationinformation.org/Profiles/display.cfm?ID=97 [accessed 13 August 2010].

Oulalou, F. and Jaidi, L. (1987) 'Fiscal resources and budget financing in the countries of the Maghreb (Algeria, Morocco, Tunisia, Libya and Mauritania)'. In H. Beblawi and G. Luciani (eds) *The Rentier State*, Vol. II. London, New York and Sydney: Croom Helm Ltd.

Ould-Mey, M. (2006a) *Global Restructuring and Peripheral States: The Carrot and the Stick in Mauritania*. Lanham, MD and London: Littlefield Adams Books.

Ould-Mey, M. (2006b) 'Currency devaluation and poverty in Mauritania'. In K. Konadu-Agyemang and K. Pandford, *Africa's Development in the Twenty-first Century*. Aldershot and Burlington, VT: Ashgate.

Pajares, M. (2009a) *La inserció laboral de la població immigrada*. Barcelona: Fundació Jaume Bofill.

Pajares, M. (2009b) 'Inmigración y mercado de trabajo'. Ministerio de Trabajo e Inmigración.

Pambazuka News (2009) 'Mauritanie: les réfugiés de retour reçoivent leurs pièces d'état civil', 21 January. Available at: http://www.pambazuka.org/fr/category/refugees/53410 [accessed 5 July 2009].

Panitch, L. and Gindin, S. (2004) 'Global capitalism and American empire'. In L. Panitch and C. Leys (eds) *Socialist Register 2004*. London: Merlin Press.

Pana (2008) '172 clandestins repatriés de Mauritanie vers leurs pays d'origine', 4 February. Available at: http://www.lesoleil.sn/imprimer.php3?id_article=33232 [accessed 26 June 2009].

Pana (2009) 'Wade accuses Europe of cutting off North Africa', 27 July. Available at: http://www.afriquejet.com/news/africa-news/wade-accuses-europe-of-cutting-off-north-africa-2009072832477.html [accessed 10 August 2010].

Papadopoulou, A. (2005) 'Exploring the asylum–migration nexus: a case study of transit migrants in Europe'. *Global Migration Perspectives*, 23, January.

Papastergiadis, N. (2000) *The Turbulence of Migration: Globalization, Deterritorialization and Hybridity*. Cambridge: Polity Press.

Parris, M. (2003) 'Only the Tories can cut the state down to size', *The Spectator*, 30 April.

Patterson, T.R. and Kelly, R.D.G.(2000) 'Unfinished migrations: reflections on the African diaspora and the making of the modern world', *African Studies Review,* 43 (1): 11–45.

Perelman, M. (1983) *Classical Political Economy, Primitive Accumulation and Social Division of Labor*. Totowa, NJ: Allanheid and Rowman.

Perkowski, N. (2012) 'A normative assessment of the aims and practices of the European border management agency Frontex'. Working Paper Series, No. 81, Refugee Studies Centre, University of Oxford.

Pieke, F., Van Hear, N. and Lindley, A. (2007) 'Beyond control? The mechanisms and dynamics of 'in-formal' remittances between Europe and Africa', *Global Networks*, 7 (3): 348–66.

Pinyol, G. (2008) 'Protecting borders? Managing irregular migration on the EU's southern flank'. In D. Godenau *et al.* (eds) *Migraciones*, 17, CIDOB, December.

Plange, Nii-K. (1979) 'Underdevelopment in northern Ghana: natural causes or colonial capitalism?' *Review of African Political Economy*, 6 (15–16): 4–14.

Polzer, T. (2007) 'Disseminating research findings in migration studies: methodological considerations', *Migration Methods and Field Notes,* 6. University of the Witwatersrand.

Pophiwa, N. (2007) 'Exploring borderlands and clandestine activities: some methodological and fieldwork experiences', *Migration Methods and Field Notes*, 3. University of the Witwatersrand.

Potts, D. (2011) *Circular Migration in Zimbabwe and Contemporary Sub-Saharan Africa*. Oxford: James Currey.

Quirk, J. (2006) 'The Anti-slavery project: linking the historical and contemporary', *Human Rights Quarterly*, 28: 565–98.

Ratha, D. (2007) 'Policy brief: leveraging remittances for development'. Washington, DC: Migration Policy Institute.

Ratha, D. and Silwal, A. (2012) 'Remittances flows in 2011 – an update', *Migration and Development Brief*, 18, 23 April.

Ratha, D. and Xu, Z. (2006) 'Migration and remittances factbook'. Development Prospects Group. World Bank.

Reporters Without Borders (2009) 'Leading journalist escapes murder attempt', 14 May. Available at: http://www.unhcr.org/refworld/country,,,,MRT,456d621e2,4a110b871a,0.html [accessed 2 July 2009].

Reyneri, E. (2003) 'Immigration and the underground economy in new receiving south European countries: manifold negative effects, manifold deep-rooted causes', *International Review of Sociology*, 13 (1): 117–43.

Riddell, J.B. (1981) 'Beyond the description of spatial pattern: the process of proletarianization as a factor in population migration in west Africa', *Progress in Human Geography*, 5: 370–92.

Rius Sant, X. (2006a) 'Centros de expulsión', *El Pais*, 26 June.

Rius Sant, X. (2006b) *El libro de la inmigración en España: historia, legislación, política y debate social desde el franquismo hasta nuestros dias*. Córdoba: Almuzara.

Rius Sant, X. (2008) 'España: claroscuros en inmigración', *El País*, 15 January.

Robert, R. (2004) 'The social dimension of regional integration in ecowas'. Geneva: Policy Integration Dept., International Labour Office.

Rodney, W. (1966) 'African slavery and other forms of social oppression on the upper Guinea coast in the context of the Atlantic slave trade', *Journal of African History*, 7 (3): 431–43.

Sabater, A. and Domingo, A. (2012) 'A new immigration regularization policy: the settlement program in Spain'. *International Migration Review*, 46 (1): 191–220.

Said, E. (1978) *Orientalism*. London: Penguin.

Sakho, P. (2007) 'Les migrations internationales senegalaises: potential financier et changement social. Actes du Dîner-Débat. Institut de Formation et de Recherche en Population, Développement et Santé de la Population'. Dakar: Université Cheikh Anta Diop.

Sall, A. and Morand, P. (2008) 'Pêche artisanale et emigration des jeunes Africains par voie piroguière', *Politique africaine*, 109, March, 32–41.

Samers, M. (1999) '"Globalization", the geopolitical economy of migration and the "spacial vent"', *Review of International Political Economy*, 6 (2): 166–99.

Samy, S. (2008) 'Irregular migration in the south eastern Mediterranean: socio-political perspectives'. Irregular Migration Series: CARIM AS, 2008/69, Robert Schumann Centre for Advanced Studies. San Domenico di Fiesole (FI): Institut universitaire européen.

Sassen, S. (1988) *The Mobility of Labor and Capital*. Cambridge: Cambridge University Press.

Sassen, S. (1999) *Guests and Aliens*. New York: The New Press.

Sayad, A. (2004) *The Suffering of the Immigrant*. Cambridge: Polity Press.

Schmitz, J. (2008) 'Migrants ouest-Africains vers l'Europe: historicité et espace moraux', *Politique africaine*, 109: 5–15.

Scott, J.C. (1998) *Seeing like a State: How Certain Schemes to Improve the Human Condition have Failed*. New Haven, CT: Yale University Press.

Searing, J.F. (1988) 'Aristocrats, slaves, and peasants: power and dependency in the wolof states, 1700–1850', *International Journal of African Historical Studies*, 21 (3): 475–503.

Seddon, D. (1996) 'The political economy of mauritania: an introduction', *Review of African Political Economy*, 23(68): 197–214.

Seddon, D. (2000) 'Unfinished business: slavery in Saharan Africa', *Slavery and Abolition*, 21 (2): 208–36.

Skeldon, R. (1997) *Migration and Development: A Global Perspective*. Harlow: Longman.

Sow, B. (2012) 'Inondations: un collectif de femmes évalue ses pertes à 25 millions de francs CFA', *Le Soleil*, 20 August. Available at: http://www.lesoleil.sn/index.php?option=com_content&view=article&id=18876:inondations-un-collectif-de-femmes-evalue-ses-pertes-a-25-millions-de-francs-cfa&catid=140:actualites [accessed 23 August 2012].

Sow, P. (1999) 'Mobilité sociale urbaine et politique de décentralisation dans l'agglomeration de Dakar' in C. Stein (ed.) *Development and Urban Africa: Report on an International Seminar held in Barcelona, Spain*. Barcelona: Centre d'Estudis Africans.

Sow, P. (2007) 'Epargne populaire des africains en Catalogne: types et formes souterraines de practiques financières des immigrants'. Grup d'Estudis i de Reflexió sobre Africa, September. Barcelona: Fondació Jaume Bofill.

Stalker, P. (2000) *Workers without Frontiers: The Impact of Globalization on International Migration*. Boulder, CO: Lynne Reinner Publishers, Inc.

Stone, D. (1994) 'Aspects du paysage religieux: marabouts et confréries', *Politique africaine*, 55: 52–6.

Sutcliffe, B. (2004) 'Crossing borders in the new imperialism'. In L. Panitch and C. Leys (eds) *The New Imperial Challenge: Socialist Register 2004*. London: Monthly Review Press.

Swindell, K. (1995) 'People on the move in West Africa: from pre-colonial polities to post-independence states'. In R. Cohen (ed.) *The Cambridge Survey of World Migration*. Cambridge: Cambridge University Press.

Tall, S.M. (2008) 'La migration internationale sénégalaise: des recrutements de main-d'œuvre aux pirogues'. In M.-C. Diop (ed.) *Le Sénégal des migrations: Mobilités, identités et societés*. Dakar, Paris and Nairobi: CREPOS, Karthala and ONU Habitat.

Tandia, D. (1994) 'Les ajustements économiques et financiers', *Politique africaine*, 55: 66–73, October.

Thiaw, C. (2012) 'Afrique: Dr. Cherif Salif Sy "En vérité, le continent est bien dans la crise"' *Le Soleil* [Senegal], 26 January. Available at: http://fr.allafrica.com/stories/201201270251.html [accessed 1 July 2012].

Traoré, A. (2007a) *L'Afrique Humiliée*. Paris: Fayard.

Traoré, A. (2007b) 'L'Afrique devient une prison'. *L'Humanité*. Available at: http://www.humanite.fr/2007-08-31_Medias_Aminata-Traore-L-Afrique-devient-une-prison [accessed 24 February 2009].

Tremlett, G. (2009) 'Satellite system to track illegal immigrants', *The Guardian*, 8 January.

Uyanga, J. (1981) 'African mobility: a source paper', *International Migration Review*, 15 (4): 707–36.

United Nations, Department of Economic and Social Affairs Population Division (UN DESA) (2009a) 'International migration 2009 wallchart'. New York: United Nations Publications.

UN DESA (2009b) 'Trends in international migrant stock: the 2008 revision'. United Nations Database (POP/DB/MIG/Stock/Rev.2008).

UN DESA (2009c) 'World population prospects: the 2008 revision'. Population Database. Available at: http://esa.un.org/unpp/index.asp?panel=2 [accessed 12 August 2010].

United Nations Development Program (UNDP) (2009) 'Human development report: overcoming barriers: human mobility and development'. New York: UNDP.

United Nations High Commissioner for Refugees (UNHCR) (2004) 'UNHCR hails Mauritania's new national refugee law', 31 August. Available at: http://www.unhcr.org/4134a9934.html [accessed 3 December 2006].

UNHCR (2007a) Interview in Nouakchott, Mauritania, 17 May.

UNHCR (2007b) 'Mauritania: appeal for US$7 million for Mauritanian refugee return', 31 August. Available at: http://www.unhcr.org/46d7f3042.html [accessed 10 October 2007].

UNHCR (2008) 'UNHCR recommendations for the ministerial conference of the Euro-African process on migration and development'. Paris, 20–21 October. Available at: http://www.unhcr.org/refworld/pdfid/4891db212.pdf [accessed 2 March 2009].

UNHCR (2012a) 'UNHCR country operations profile – Côte d'Ivoire'. Available at: http://www.unhcr.org/pages/49e484016.html [accessed 10 September 2012].

UNHCR (2012b) 'Sharp increase in Malian refugee arrivals in Mauritania, critical low funding levels', *Briefing Notes*, 10 July. Available at: http://www.unhcr.org/4ffc06c19.html [accessed 30 August 2012].

UN News Service (2012) 'International response to Malian refugee crisis severely underfunded – UN top official', 2 August. Available at: http://www.unhcr.org/refworld/docid/5020eeb22.html [accessed 15 September 2012].

US AFRICOM (United States Africa Command) (n.d.) 'Operation Enduring Freedom trans Sahara – program overview'. Available at: http://www.africom.mil/oef-ts.asp [accessed 2 July 2009].

United States Agency for International Development (USAID) (1980) 'Projet Rams. Mission d'etudes et d'evaluation du secteur rural et des ressources humaines'. Ministère de l'Economie et des Finances, Mauritanie.

US Committee for Refugees and Immigrants (2009) 'World refugee survey 2009 – Mauritania', 17 June. Available at: http://www.unhcr.org/refworld/docid/4a40d2ad99.html [accessed 24 June 2009].

US Department of State (2009) 'Country reports on terrorism 2008 – Mauritania', 30 April. Available at: http://www.unhcr.org/refworld/docid/49fac6c21e.html [accessed 22 June 2009].

US Department of State (2011) 'Mauritania: 2011 US terrorism report: Mauritania'. Available at: http://allafrica.com/stories/201208011109.html [accessed 9 September 2012].

US Department of State (2012) 'US terrorism report: Mauritania'. Available at: http://allafrica.com/stories/201208011109.html [accessed 7 September 2011].

Van Dalen, H.P., Groenewold, G. and Schoorl, J. (2004) 'Out of Africa: What drives the pressure to emigrate?' Tinbergen Institute Discussion Paper, Netherlands Interdisciplinary Demographic Institute.

van Dijk, T.A. (2005) *Racism and Discourse in Spain and Latin America*. Amsterdam and Philadelphia, PA: John Benjamins B.V.

Van Hear, N. (2007) 'Diaspora dynamics in transition: regrouping and realignment among migrant communities in the UK and Europe'. Presented at postgraduate conference on racism, University of Leeds, 22 March.

Vargas-Lundius, R. *et al.* (2008) 'International migration, remittances and rural development', FAO and IFAD. Available at: http://web.ifad.org/pub/remittances/migration.pdf [accessed 6 March 2009].

Volman, D. (2010) 'Obama's national security policy towards Africa: the first year', *Pambazuka News*, Issue 466, 20 January. Available at: http://pambazuka.org/en/category/features/61614 [accessed 30 March 2010].

Volman, D. and Mintner, W. (2009) 'Making peace or fuelling war in Africa', *Foreign Policy in Focus*, 13 March.

Wilks, I. (1975) *Asante in the Nineteenth Century: The Structure and Evolution of a Political Order.* London: Cambridge University Press.

Willems, R. (2008) 'Les 'fous de la mer': Les migrants clandestins du Sénégal aux Îles Canaries en 2006'. In M.-C. Diop (ed.) *Le Sénégal des Migrations: Mobilités, Identités et Societés.* Dakar, Paris and Nairobi: CREPOS, Karthala and ONU Habitat.

Williams, G. (2004) 'Political economies and the study of Africa: critical considerations', *Review of African Political Economy*, 31 (102), 571–83.

Wolcott, H.F. (1999) *Ethnography: A Way of Seeing*. Oxford: AltaMira.

Wolff, S. (2008) 'Border management in the Mediterranean: internal, external and ethical challenges', *Cambridge Review of International Affairs*, 21 (1): 253–71.

World Bank (2004) 'Unlocking the employment potential in middle and north Africa: toward a new social contract'. MENA Development Report. Washington, DC.

World Bank (2008a) 'Providing for the people: policy note on utility service reform in Mauritania's mining corridor'. Report No. 40019-MR, September.

World Bank (2008b) 'Senegal at a glance'. 24 September. Available at: http://devdata.worldbank.org/AAG/sen_aag.pdf [accessed 2 July 2009].

World Bank (2008c) 'Mauritania at a glance', 24 September. Available at: http://devdata.worldbank.org/AAG/mrt_aag.pdf [accessed 2 July 2009].

World Bank (2009a) 'Remittances expected to fall by 5 to 8 per cent in 2009'. *People Move,* 23 March. Available at: http://peoplemove.worldbank.org/en/content/remittances-expected-to-fall-by-5-to-8-percent-in-2009 [accessed 28 April 2009].

World Bank (2009b) 'Mauritania: country brief', March. Available at: http://web.worldbank.org/WBSITE/EXTERNAL/COUNTRIES/AFRICAEXT/MAURITANIAEXTN/0,,menuPK:362350~pagePK:141132~piPK:141107~theSitePK:362340,00.html [accessed 2 July 2009].

World Bank (2009c) 'World development report 2009: reshaping economic geography'. Washington, DC: World Bank.

World Bank (2010) 'World development indicators'. Available at: http://data.worldbank.org/indicator/NY.GDP.MKTP.KD.ZG [accessed 20 August 2010].

Yates, D. (1996) *The Rentier State in Africa: Oil Rent Dependency and Neocolonialism in the Republic of Gabon.* Trenton, NJ and Asmara: African World Press, Inc.

Yessa, El-., A. (2008) 'Le droit à l'épreuve de la migration irrégulière en Mauritanie'. Série sur la migration irrégulière: CARIM AS, 2008/48, Robert Schuman Centre for Advanced Studies, San Domenico di Fiesole (FI): Institut universitaire européen.

Zohry, A. (2005) 'Migration without borders: north Africa as a reserve of cheap labour for Europe'. Paris: UNESCO.

Zoubir, Y.H. (2006) 'American policy in the Maghreb: the conquest of a new region?', Working Paper 13/2006. Real Instituto El Cano.

# Index

Taylor & Francis

# eBooks

FOR LIBRARIES

ORDER YOUR **FREE 30 DAY** INSTITUTIONAL TRIAL TODAY!

Over 23,000 eBook titles in the Humanities, Social Sciences, STM and Law from some of the world's leading imprints.

**Choose from a range of subject packages or create your own!**

Benefits for **you**

- Free MARC records
- COUNTER-compliant usage statistics
- Flexible purchase and pricing options

Benefits for your **user**

- Off-site, anytime access via Athens or referring URL
- Print or copy pages or chapters
- Full content search
- Bookmark, highlight and annotate text
- Access to thousands of pages of quality research at the click of a button

For more information, pricing enquiries or to order a free trial, contact your local online sales team.

UK and Rest of World: **online.sales@tandf.co.uk**

US, Canada and Latin America:
**e-reference@taylorandfrancis.com**

**www.ebooksubscriptions.com**

ALPSP Award for BEST eBOOK PUBLISHER 2009 Finalist

Taylor & Francis eBooks
Taylor & Francis Group

A flexible and dynamic resource for teaching, learning and research.